Planning, Development, and Change:
A Bibliography on Development Administration

PLANNING, DEVELOPMENT, AND CHANGE

A Bibliography on Development Administration

Compiled by

Garth N. Jones
Shaukat Ali
Richard Barber
James F. Chambers

EAST-WEST CENTER PRESS   Honolulu

Copyright © 1970 by East-West Center Press
University of Hawaii
All rights reserved
International Standard Book Number: 0-8248-0099-0
Library of Congress Catalog Card Number: 77-138823
Printed in the United States of America
First edition

CONTENTS

Preface, vii

Editors' Note, xi

A. Planning

    1.   Research Methodology, 3

    2.   Planning, 7

        a.   Comprehensive Planning, 7
        b.   Program Budgeting, 14
        c.   Systems, 18

B. Development

    1.   Economic and Social Development, 27

    2.   Political and Administrative Development, 44

        a.   General, 44
        b.   Bureaucracy, 67

C. Change

    1.   Organizational Theory and Behavior, 75

    2.   Social Change, 102

    3.   Planned Change, 116

        a.   General, 116
        b.   Institution Building and Development, 137
        c.   Technical Assistance/Cooperation, 139
        d.   Diffusion, 149
        e.   Innovation, 151

D. Bibliographies and Supplementary Items

    1. Bibliographies, 157

    2. Supplementary Items, 161

Index, 165

PREFACE

This bibliography is a specific research tool, prepared primarily to facilitate my own research and writing on planned organizational change, a concept carefully defined and delineated.[1] As a specialist bibliography on planned change within the field of organizational theory, the frame of reference is narrowly perceived. Bibliographical entries have been selected on the grounds either of: (1) research approaches which are useful in studying the processes and the results of planned organizational change, or (2) studies which contribute to an overall understanding of the subject of planned organizational change.

This bibliography has a relatively long history and is a product of my own research projects and of several times the number of persons who are noted as the compilers. Its antecedent is one which I prepared with Robert Giordano, assisted by students in my experimental graduate seminar in development administration, held at the University of Southern California School of Public Administration, Spring semester 1964.[2]

---

[1] Garth N. Jones, <u>Planned Organizational Change, A Study in Change Dynamics</u> (New York: Frederick A. Praeger, 1969). Also published in London by Routledge, and Kegan Paul.

[2] Garth N. Jones and Robert Giordano, "Planned Organizational Change: A Working Bibliography," Washington, D. C.: Comparative Administrative Group of the American Society for Public Administration, 1964 (mimeographed).

The students in the experimental seminar who assisted in the preparation of this bibliography were Robert P. Biller, Disabong Dhipayamontri, James C. Gerdes, Robert N. Giordano, Edward J. Hess, Nasir Islam, M. Anwar Khan, Mujib Skeikh, and Anwar H. Siddiqui.

In the Fall of 1964 I went to Pakistan as Chief of Party of the University of Southern California Public Administration project. To facilitate the development of research activities in Pakistan, Dr. Shaukat Ali of the Department of Administrative Science of the University of the Panjab, and I prepared a bibliography on the field of development administration.[3] It included nearly all of the references contained in the earlier Jones-Giordano bibliography.

The frame of reference of this latest revision has been expanded to include my current research interests in: (1) applying socio-economic exchange theory to the analysis of planned organizational change and (2) developing criteria against which to measure and evaluate the consequences of planned change endeavors.[4]

References to case studies have been kept to a minimum since an earlier publication provides an analysis of 190 cases on planned organizational change.[5] Likewise only a few references on national development of specific countries or regions have been included since such bibliographies are already available, among them those for Pakistan and India[6] which I have either prepared or co-authored in the course of my own work.

As I stated earlier, this bibliography is a product of a larger number of

---

[3] Shaukat Ali and Garth N. Jones, <u>Planning, Development and Change, An Annotated Bibliography on Development Administration</u> (Lahore: University of the Panjab Press, 1966).

[4] Garth N. Jones, "Change Behavior in the Planned Organizational Change Process: Application of Socio-economic Exchange Theory," <u>Philippine Journal of Public Administration</u> (forthcoming) and <u>Monastery Model of Development: Towards a Strategy of Large Scale Planned Change</u>, Honolulu: East-West Center, 1970 (processed).

[5] Garth N. Jones, <u>Planned Organizational Change: A Set of Working Documents</u>, Los Angeles: Center for the Study of Public Organization, School of Public Administration, University of Southern California, 1964 (mimeographed).

A fellow Senior Specialist at the East-West Center, Toshio Yatsushiro, is preparing a supplementary or updated list of case studies which should soon be available.

persons than Jones and Ali. I would like to acknowledge a few of them. Richard Barber and James F. Chambers, who were my graduate assistants at the East-West Center, worked so diligently in the revision of the original Ali-Jones bibliography that Dr. Shaukat Ali and I were pleased to place their names along with ours as the compilers. We must thank the typists of the East-West Center who struggled with the manuscript in several forms and in particular Kathleen Matsumoto and Jill Chinen. Then there are Mrs. Hazel Tatsuno, Senior Administrative Assistant, and Mrs. Arline Uyeunten, Stenographer, of the Institute of Advanced Projects, who carefully scheduled the use of the typing pool and the related facilities which bring the work of the Senior Specialists to the printed page. We owe them a particular debt of gratitude.

Special thanks should be given to Miss Joyce Wright, Director, East-West Center Library, and the three readers, Shiro Saito, Raymond Nunn and Stanley West, who offered a number of constructive comments and recommended that this bibliography be published.

To my fellow Senior Specialist, Toshio Yatsushiro, I wish to extend my thanks for his help and stimulating suggestions for improvement of this bibliography and also of my other studies completed during my stay at the East-West Center.

Last of all is a word of appreciation to Minoru Shinoda, Director of the Institute of Advanced Projects, East-West Center, whose kind and able leadership makes it an exciting and pleasant place for scholarly work.

Garth N. Jones
June 1970

---

[6]Garth N. Jones and Shaukat Ali, <u>Pakistan Government and Administration: A Comprehensive Bibliography</u> (Islamabad, Pakistan: Research Centre on Public Administration, 1970) and Garth N. Jones, <u>Bibliography--Publications in English: Indonesian Social-Political-Economic Life and Institutions</u>, Jogjakarta: Public Administration Center, University of Gadjah Mada, 1960 (mimeographed). I am now updating the Indonesian bibliography with the assistance of James F. Chambers. /Possibly it will appear in print in 1971./

EDITORS' NOTE

This bibliography has been organized under four general headings: (A) Planning, (B) Development, (C) Change, and (D) Bibliographies and Supplementary Items. These in turn are subdivided. All items have been numbered consecutively. A few items, added after the bibliography had nearly been completed, have been included in their proper order by the use of decimal numbers to expand the system (e.g. 55.1 is placed between 55 and 56). Some numbers are skipped (e.g. 117) because the items were deleted or shifted to another section.

Section D2 (Supplementary Items) encompasses a number of works which were added too late in the compilation to be included in the main body of the manuscript. These items have been coded as to the section in which they would normally have been placed.

The entire bibliography has been indexed by author, or by the institution which issued the work. The index notes both the sections and the numbers under which an author's entries may be found. Stars (*) indicate joint authorship.

A. PLANNING

(A1)

1. RESEARCH METHODOLOGY

1. Ackoff, Russell L., and others, <u>Scientific Methods: Optimizing Applied Research Decisions</u>, New York: John Wiley and Sons, 1962.

2. Adams, Richard N., and Jack J. Preiss, <u>Human Organization Research: Field Relations and Techniques</u>, Homewood, Ill.: The Dorsey Press, 1960.
   The selected readings in this volume analyze research problems encountered by field research workers, and the methods used to solve such problems. Emphasis is on the process of research rather than substantive findings.

3. Backstrom, Charles H., and Gerald D. Hursh, <u>Survey Research</u>, Evanston, Ill.: Northwestern University Press, 1963.

4. Blalock, Hubert M., Jr., and Ann B., <u>Methodology in Social Science</u>, New York: McGraw-Hill Book Co., 1968.
   A treatise on the application of mathematics and statistics to the study of change as well as to the other general aspects of social science.

5. Blalock, Hubert M., Jr., <u>Social Statistics</u>, New York: McGraw-Hill Book Co., 1960.

6. Borgatta, Edgar, and Betty Crowther, <u>A Workbook for the Study of Social Interaction Processes</u>, New York, Chicago, San Francisco: Rand McNally, 1968.

7. Borko, Harold (ed.), <u>Computer Applications in the Behavioral Sciences</u>, Englewood Cliffs, N. J.: Prentice-Hall, 1962.

8. Braibanti, Ralph, "The Relevance of Political Science to the Study of Underdeveloped Areas," in Ralph Braibanti and Joseph J. Spengler (eds.), <u>Traditions, Values and Socio-Economic Development</u>, Durham, N. C.: Duke University Press, 1961, 139-180.

9. Brody, Richard A., <u>Experimentation: An Introductory Handbook for Political Scientists</u>, Evanston, Ill.: Northwestern University Press, 1965.
   This handbook provides an introduction to the logic and philosophy of experimentation as a technique for confirmation of scientific hypothesis.

10. Chance, William A., <u>Statistical Methods for Decision Making</u>, Homewood, Ill.: Irwin, 1969.

(A1)

11. Charlesworth, James C. (ed.), <u>Mathematics and the Social Sciences, A Symposium</u>, Philadelphia: The American Academy of Political and Social Science, 1963.
    This work contains six short, excellent articles on the use of mathematics in economics, political science, and sociology.

12. Christ, Carl, <u>Econometric Models and Methods</u>, New York: John Wiley and Sons, 1966.

13. Conant, James B. (ed.), <u>Harvard Case Histories in Experimental Science</u>, Cambridge, Mass.: Harvard University Press, 1957.

14. Etzioni, Amitai, "On the Need for More Analysis and the Instruments for its Advancement," <u>Behavioral Science</u>, 14(January 1969), 47-50.
    Discusses the reasons for the paucity of analysis of available information on social conditions.

15. Festinger, Leon and Daniel Katz, <u>Research Methods in the Behavioral Sciences</u>, New York: Dryden Press, 1953.
    A textbook dealing with the logic of method rather than with isolated techniques. The authors attempt an evaluation of the available research methodology as well as methodological problems encountered.

16. Gue, Ronald L., and Michael E. Thomas, <u>Mathematical Methods in Operations Research</u>, New York: Macmillan, 1968.

17. Gunnell, John G., "The Idea of the Conceptual Framework: A Philosophical Critique," <u>Journal of Comparative Administration</u>, 1(August 1969), 140-76.

18. Heaphey, James, "The Philosophical Assumptions of Inquiry in Comparative Administration: Some Introductory Comments," <u>Journal of Comparative Administration</u>, 1(August 1969), 133-39.

19. Hein, Leonard W., <u>The Quantitative Approach to Managerial Decisions</u>, Englewood Cliffs, N. J.: Prentice-Hall, 1967.

20. Janda, Kenneth, <u>Data Processing Applications to Political Research</u>, Evanston, Ill.: Northwestern University Press, 1965.
    This handbook is designed as an introduction to the use of modern data processing technology in political and related social science research. Particular attention is paid to ways in which information can be recorded in punch card form, organized and manipulated.

21. Kaplan, Abraham, <u>The Conduct of Inquiry: Methodology for Behavioral Science</u>, San Francisco: Chandler Publications, 1964.
    The author makes a significant contribution to the behavioral sciences. This book, using behavioral methodology as the major point of departure, is a critical and constructive assessment of the developing standards and strategies of contemporary social inquiry.

22. LaPorte, Robert, Jr., and James F. Petras, "Optimizing Research Opportunities: A Methodological Note on the Comparative Study of Bureaucracy," <u>Journal of Comparative Administration</u>, 1(August 1969), 234-48.

(A1)

23. Lasswell, Harold D., "The Uses of Content Analysis Data in Studying Social Change," <u>Social Sciences Information</u>, 7(February 1968), 57-70.

24. Leser, Conrad, <u>Econometric Techniques and Problems</u>, New York: Hafner, 1966.

25. Lewin, Kurt, <u>Field Theory in Social Science: Selected Theoretical Papers</u>, New York: Harper Brothers, 1951.
    A source book of the thought and methods of Kurt Lewin. All papers were originally published elsewhere, but this represents a convenient compilation.

26. Lovell, John P., <u>The Study of the Military in Developing Nations: Devising Meaningful and Manageable Research Strategies</u>, Bloomington, Ind.: Department of Government, Indiana University, 1967.

28. Massarik, Fred and Philburn Ratoosh, <u>Mathematical Explorations in Behavioral Science</u>, Homewood, Ill.: Richard D. Irwin Co., 1964.
    Reports the current theoretical and empirical inquiry in the social and behavioral sciences as proposed by a variety of mathematical models. The central feature of the book is its concern with empirical research and data gathering as it relates to making models operational.

29. Meadows, Paul, "The Metaphors of Order: Toward a Taxonomy of Organization Theory," in Llewellyn Gross (ed.), <u>Sociological Theory: Inquiries and Paradigms</u>, New York: Harper & Row, 1967, 101-10.

30. Morse, Philip M. (ed.), <u>Operations Research for Public Systems</u>, Cambridge, Mass.: M.I.T. Press, 1967.

31. Nagel, Ernest, <u>The Language of Social Research</u>, Glencoe, Ill.: The Free Press, 1955.

33. North, R. C. and others, <u>Content Analysis: A Handbook with Application for the Study of International Crisis</u>, Evanston, Ill.: Northwestern University Press, 1963.
    A valuable introduction to a useful research technique. Includes concrete illustrations plus guides for deciding whether, when, and what form of content analyses should be used. Special forms discussed include the conventional frequency count and qualitative identifications, sorts, pair-comparisons, and evaluative assertion analysis.

34. Rejai, Mostafa, "Toward the Comparative Study of Political Decision-Makers," <u>Comparative Political Studies</u>, 2(October 1969), 349-60.

34.1 Rokkan, Stein (ed.), <u>Comparative Research Across Cultures and Nations</u>, Paris and Hague: Mouton, 1968.

35. Schlaifer, Robert, <u>Probability and Statistics for Business Decisions: An Introduction to Managerial Economics under Uncertainty</u>, New York: McGraw-Hill, 1959.

36. Vickers, Geoffrey, <u>The Art of Judgement: A Study of Policy-Making</u>, New York: Basic Books, 1965.

(A1)

37. Ward, Robert E. and others, *Studying Politics Abroad: Field Research in Developing Areas*, Boston: Little-Brown, 1964.

38. Wold, Herman (ed.), *Econometric Model Building*, New York: Humanities, 1964.

39. Young, Pauline, *Scientific Social Surveys and Research*, Englewood Cliffs, N. J.: Prentice-Hall, Inc., 1956.

(A2a)

2. PLANNING

a. Comprehensive Planning

40. Agricultural Policy Institute, <u>Planning Socio-Economic Change</u>, Raleigh, N. C.: North Carolina State Print Shop, 1964.

41. Anderson, Stanford (ed.), <u>Planning for Diversity and Choice</u>, Cambridge, Mass.: The M.I.T. Press, 1968.

42. Bauer, Raymond (ed.), "Forecasting the Future," <u>Science Journal</u>, 3(October 1967), Entire issue.

43. Bell, Daniel (ed.), "Toward the Year 2000," <u>Daedalus</u>, 96(Summer 1967), Entire issue.

44. _____, "Twelve Modes of Prediction," <u>Daedalus</u>, 93(Summer 1964), 845-880.

45. Blackman, Allan, "Scientism and Planning," <u>American Behavioral Scientist</u>, 10(September 1966), 24-28.

46. Bowles, Samuel, <u>Planning Educational Systems for Economic Growth</u>, Cambridge, Mass.: Harvard University Press, 1969.
    The author builds an educational planning model and applies it to Nigeria and Greece, indicating its application to other underdeveloped areas.

47. Branch, Melville C., <u>Planning Aspects and Applications</u>, New York: John Wiley and Sons, 1966.

49. Bright, James, <u>Technological Forecasting in Industry and Government</u>, New York: Prentice-Hall, 1968.

51. Caldwell, Lynton, "Managing the Scientific Super-culture: The Task of Educational Preparation," <u>Public Administration Review</u>, 27(June 1967), 128-133.

52. Cetron, Marvin, "Forecasting Technology," <u>International Science and Technology</u>, 69(September 1967), 83-92.

53. Colm, Gerhard and Theodore Geiger, "Country Programming as a Guide to Development," <u>Development of the Emerging Countries: An Agenda for Research</u>, Washington, D. C.: The Brookings Institution, 1962.

(A2a)

54. Daland, Robert, <u>Brazilian Planning: Development, Politics, and Administration</u>, Chapel Hill, N. C.: University of North Carolina Press, 1967.
   A well-documented study illustrating the hit-and-miss nature of administrative and political aspects of planning in Brazil. Daland points out that policy formulation is generally carried on without regard to the actual situation in a society which cannot reach a consensus about what its goals should be and which has governments in power without effective control. The study indicates that comprehensive, national planning might be dispensed with in favor of regional development.

55. de Jouvenel, Bertrand, <u>The Art of Conjecture</u>, New York: Basic Books, 1967.

55.1 Donaldson, Loraine, <u>Development Planning in Ireland</u>, New York: Frederick A. Praeger, 1966.
   The case of Ireland demonstrates how a society suffering from many disadvantages can successfully mobilize its resources through sound leadership.

56. Doxiadis, Constantinas, and others, "Technology and Social Goals: The Future Environment," <u>Ekistics</u>, 27(September 1967), Entire issue.

57. Dror, Yehzkel, "Policy Analysis: A New Professional Role in Government Service," <u>Public Administration Review</u>, 27(September 1967), 197-203.

58. _____, <u>Public Policymaking Reexamined</u>, San Francisco: Chandler Publishing Co., 1968.
   The author combines the approaches of policy analysis, behavioral science, and systems analysis in his examination of public policymaking and his suggestions for its reform. Concluding chapters deal with changes needed in knowledge, personnel, structure and process patterns and in the environment to effect major improvements in public policymaking.

60. Eckous, Richard S., and K. S. Parikh, <u>Planning for Growth: Multi-Sectoral, Inter-Temporal Models Applied to India</u>, Cambridge, Mass.: The M.I.T. Press, 1968.

61. Eldredge, H. Wentworth, "Futurism in Planning for Developing Countries," <u>Journal of the American Institute of Planners</u>, 34(November 1968), 382-84.

62. Fei, John C. H., and Gustav Ranis, <u>A Study of Planning Methodology With Special Reference to Pakistan's Second Five-Year Plan</u>, Karachi: Institute of Development Economics, 1960.
   This is a technical treatise on planning methodology with illustrations extracted from Pakistan's Second Five-Year Plan. Suggestions are made to subject the planning framework to critical analysis.

64. Frieden, Bernard, "The Changing Prospects for Social Planning," <u>Journal of the American Institute of Planners</u>, 33(September 1967), 311-23.

65. Friedman, John, <u>Regional Development Policy: A Case Study of Venezuela</u>, Cambridge: The M.I.T. Press, 1966.
   Friedman shows how development must be considered essential for the

(A2a)

survival of a nation, and how planned development can be transformed from thought into action when planners concentrate on the formulation of strategy as much as they do on depicting the desired results.

65.1 _____, *Venezuela: From Doctrine to Dialogue*, Syracuse, N. Y.: Syracuse University Press, 1965.

66. Gabor, Dennis, *Inventing the Future*, New York: Knopf, 1964.

67. Grasberg, Edward, "Development Project Formats: A Design for Maximum Information," *Development Digest*, 5(July 1967), 1-30.

68. Gross, Bertram (ed.), *Action under Planning: The Guidance of Economic Development*, New York: McGraw Hill, 1967.
    This is a compendium of papers dealing with the execution of planned development. It includes a critique of excessive economic emphasis in development planning, and establishes classifications into which countries, governments, and politicians can be grouped for study.

69. _____, *The Administration of Economic Development Planning: Principles and Fallacies*, St. Louis, Mo.: Washington University, 1967.

69.1 _____ (ed.), *National Planning: The Underdeveloped Nations*, Syracuse, N. Y.: Syracuse University Press, 1965.

70. _____ (ed.), "Social Goals and Indicators for American Society," *Annals of the American Academy of Political and Social Science*, 372 and 373(June and September 1967), Entire issues.

71. Gulati, I. S., *Resource Prospects of the Third Five-Year Plan*, Bombay: Orient Longman's, 1960.
    Discusses resources available for the implementation of India's Third Five-Year Plan.

72. Henning, Dale A., and Preston P. Le Breton, *Henning-Le Breton-Planning Theory*, New York: Prentice-Hall, Inc., 1961.
    Presents a complete treatment of the planning process including both new and established theories for each major step in the planning procedure. Contents include: Setting the Foundation for a Theory of Planning; Role of Planning; Dimensions of a Plan. Theory of Need Determination. Theory of Choice. Examining the Role of Participants in Planning Process: Organizing for Planning. Role of Committees. Role of Specialists. The Role of Communication Theory in Planning. The Role of Persuasion Theory in Planning. Integrating Parts in General Theory of Planning.

72.1 Herbert, John D., and Alfred P. Van Huyck (eds.), *Urban Planning in the Developing Countries*, New York: Frederick A. Praeger Co., 1968.
    Assesses the relevance of present concepts and methods of urban planning to the needs of the developing countries. Published in cooperation with Planning and Development Collaborative International.

73. Hirschman, Albert O., *Development Projects Observed*, Washington, D. C.: The Brookings Institution, 1967.

74. Horowitz, Irving Louis (ed.), <u>The Rise and Fall of Project Camelot. Studies in the Relationship between Social Science and Practical Politics</u>, Cambridge, Mass.: The M.I.T. Press, 1967.

75. Iatridis, Demetrius, "Social Scientists in Physical Development Planning," <u>International Social Science Journal</u>, 18(4, 1966), 640-49.

76. Ivakhnenko, A. C., and V. C. Lapa, <u>Cybernetics and Forecasting Techniques</u>, New York: American Elsevier, 1967.

77. Jantsch, Erich, "Technological Forecasting for Planning and Its Institutional Implications," <u>Ekistics</u>, 26(August 1968), 150-161.

78. Kapp, W. K., <u>Hindu Culture: Economic Development and Economic Planning In India</u>, New York: Asia Publishing House, 1963.
    Examines the extent to which Hinduism, as a religion, is conducive to the development and planning of 'New India.' Concludes that certain aspects of Hindu culture, coupled with administrative defects, have retarded the economic growth of India.

79. Krauch, Helmut, "Resistance Against Analysis and Planning in Research and Development," <u>Management Science</u>, 13(December 1966), C47-58.

80. Krause, Walter, "National Planning for Economic Development," <u>Philippine Journal of Public Administration</u>, 3(July 1959), 289-97.
    This survey of the problems and issues involved in the national planning of less developed countries contends that to write a good plan is arduous, but that its implementation is even more difficult. Proper implementation depends upon the correct assessment of the environments of the country, and since environments differ from country to country, planning too must differ in all major features.

81. Lange, Oskar, <u>Essays in Economic Planning</u>, New York: Asia Publishing House, 1960.
    Summarized are Marxian planning critiques of Western concepts of indicative planning.

82. La Porte, Todd, "Politics and 'Inventing the Future,'" <u>Public Administration Review</u>, 25(June 1967), 184-96.

83. Larsson, Pieter deWolff, and Lauchlin Currie, <u>Governmental Planning and Political Economy</u>, Berkeley: Institute of Business and Economic Studies, University of California, 1957.

83.1 Lewis, W. Arthur, "Development Planning," in David L. Sills (ed.), <u>International Encyclopedia of the Social Sciences</u>, New York: Macmillan and The Free Press, 1968, v. 12, pp. 118-125.

84. _____, <u>Development Planning, The Essentials of Economic Policy</u>, London: George Allen & Unwin, 1966.

85. Loebs, C. David, "The New Comprehensiveness," <u>Journal of the American Institute of Planning</u>, 33(September 1967), 347-52.

(A2a)

86. Macesich, George, <u>Yugoslavia: The Theory and Practice of Development Planning</u>, Charlottesville, Virginia: University Press of Virginia, 1964.

87. McKinney, John C., "Structural Continuity and the Process of Planning Change," in <u>Planning Socio-Economic Change</u>, Agricultural Policy Institute Raleigh, N. C.: State Print Shop, 1964, 29-52.

87.1 Madge, Charles, Herbert J. Gans, and Richard L. Meier, "Planning, Social," in David L. Sills (ed.), <u>International Encyclopedia of the Social Sciences</u>, New York: Macmillan and The Free Press, 1968.

88. Mahalonobis, P. C., <u>Talks on Planning</u>, New York: Asia Publishing House, 1961.

89. Mahbub-ul-Haq, <u>The Strategy of Economic Planning: A Case Study of Pakistan</u>, Karachi: Oxford University Press, 1966.
    The author, one of the leading economists of Pakistan, is closely associated with planning in the country. After a theoretical explanation of the planning the author evaluates the First Five-Year Plan, gives an appraisal of the Second Five-Year Plan, and forecasts about the sum and substance of the Third Five-Year Plan.

90. Mason, Edward, <u>Economic Planning in Underdeveloped Areas: Government and Business</u>, New York: Fordham University Press, 1958.
    The author makes the suggestion that the optimal role of government in the development process varies according to time and place.

91. Meier, Richard L., <u>Developmental Planning</u>, New York: McGraw-Hill Co., 1965.

92. Meyerson, Martin, and Edward C. Banfield, <u>Politics, Planning and the Public Interest</u>, Glencoe, Ill.: The Free Press, 1955.

93. Michael, Donald, <u>The Unprepared Society: Planning for a Precarious Future</u>, New York: Basic Books, 1968.

94. Mitchell, Joan, <u>Groundwork to Economic Planning</u>, London: Secker and Warburg, 1966.

95. Mumford, Enid, and T. B. Ward, <u>Computers: Planning for People</u>, London: Batsford, 1968.

96. Myrdal, Gunnar, "The Necessity and Difficulty of Planning the Future Society," in William Ewald, Jr. (ed.), <u>Environment and Change</u>, Bloomington: Indiana University Press, 1968.

97. Narayan, Shirman, <u>Socialism in Indian Planning</u>, New York: Asia Publishing House, 1964.

97.1 National Planning Association, Center for Economic Projections, <u>State and Local Government Planning, Proceedings: ninth annual conference</u>... Washington, D. C., 1969.
    Partial contents - The next step: concerted planning, by G. Colm. Information network for concerted planning, by N. E. Terleckyj. Long term economic issues facing the United States, by A. M. Okun. Resources

for State and local government planning, by S. J. Mushkin. Data needs for State and local government planning, by R. L. Lowry. The applicability of planning, programming and budgeting systems to State and local government decision-making, by H. Hatry.

98. Papanek, Gustav F., <u>A Plan for Planning: The Need for a Better Method of Assisting Underdeveloped Countries on Their Economic Policies</u>, Cambridge: Harvard University Center for International Affairs, 1961.

99. Prehoda, Robert, <u>Designing the Future</u>, Phil., Pa.: Chilton, 1967.

100. Rahman, Habibur, <u>Growth Models and Pakistan: A Discussion of Planning Problems</u>, Karachi: The Allies Book Corporation, 1962.

101. Rahman, M. Anisur, "The Operational Logic of Planning for Industrialization," <u>The Pakistan Development Review</u>, 4(Summer 1964), 203-22.

102. Riesman, David, "Planning in Higher Education: Some Notes on Patterns and Problems," <u>Human Organization</u>, 18(Spring 1959), 12-17.

103. Rivkin, Malcolm G., <u>Area Development for National Growth</u>, New York: Frederick A. Praeger Co., 1966.

104. Robock, Stefan H., "Planning Change in the Underdeveloped Countries," in <u>Planning Socio-Economic Change</u>, Agricultural Policy Institute, Raleigh, N. C.: State Printing Office, 1964, 121-31.

105. Rome, Beatrice and Sydney, "Programming the Bureaucratic Computer," <u>Institute of Electrical Electronics Engineers Spectrum</u>, 1(December 1964), 72-92.

105.1 Rothenberg, Jerome, <u>Economic Evaluation of Urban Renewal</u>, Washington, D. C.: The Brookings Institution, 1967.

106. Schatz, Sayre P., "The Influence of Planning on Development: The Nigerian Experience," <u>Social Research</u>, 27(Winter 1960), 451-69.

107. Simmons, John L., "Agricultural Development in Iraq: Planning and Management Failures," <u>The Middle East Journal</u>, 19(Spring 1965), 129-40.
In the past Iraqi politicians, administrators and foreign observers believed that elimination of feudalism would lead to sustained development. However, many of the agricultural failures can be traced to the lack of management skills. The paper provides a brief history of the agrarian reforms since 1958 and then points out major setbacks resulting from poor planning and inefficient management.

108. Solomon, Morris J., <u>Analysis of Projects for Economic Growth. An Operational System for Their Formulation, Evaluation, and Implementation</u>, New York: Frederick A. Praeger Co., 1970.
Designed to aid project planners and administrators in developing countries, this book presents a practical system for appraising and shaping national income-producing projects. The book, which provides case studies of chemical production and orange-growing projects, incorporates principles of engineering, economics, and decision-making theory. The analysis of projects and their potential economic

contribution includes consideration of physical resource flow plans and money flows of various kinds, investments requiring imports and those not requiring imports, personnel payments, rates at which income is generated, and many other factors.

110. Steiner, George A., *Top Management Planning*, New York: The Free Press, 1969.

   The major problems associated with effective corporate planning are discussed in depth, including the critical role of the chief executive, the social responsibilities of businessmen, the importance of creativity and flexibility in planning, and the interrelationships between management scientists and managers in planning. Many charts, graphs, and illustrations are included as well as an 875-item bibliography.

111. Swee, Goh Keng, "Social, Political and Institutional Aspects of Development Planning," *The Malayan Economic Review*, 10(April 1965), 1-15.

112. Sweetman, L. T., "Prefects and Planning: France's New Regionalism," *Public Administration* (London), 43(Spring 1965), 15-30.

   In 1964 France launched a new administrative experiment to coordinate and streamline implementation of planning in the country. The country has been divided into regions, and each region has been placed under a regional prefect. His work has been divided between carrying out the government's policies with regard to economic growth and regional development, and co-ordination of the work of several government agencies in a region.

113. Tinbergen, Jan, *Central Planning*, New Haven, Conn.: Yale University Press, 1964.

114. _____, *The Design of Development*, Baltimore, Md.: Johns Hopkins Press, 1958.

115. _____, *Development Planning*, New York: McGraw-Hill, 1967.

116. Toch, Hans, "The Perception of Future Events: Case Studies in Social Prediction," *Public Opinion Quarterly*, 22(Spring 1958), 57-66.

118. U. S. Department of State, Agency for International Development, *Organization, Planning and Programming for Economic Development*, Washington, D. C.: Government Printing Office, 1963.

   This is volume VIII of United States papers prepared for the United Nations Conference on the application of science and technology for the benefit of less developed areas.

120. Walinsky, Louis J., *The Planning and Execution of Economic Development: A Non-Technical Guide for Policy Makers and Administrators*, London: McGraw-Hill Co., 1963.

121. Waterston, Albert, *Development Planning: Lessons of Experience*, Baltimore: The Johns Hopkins Press, 1969.

122. _____, *Planning in Yugoslavia: Organization and Implementation*, Baltimore, Md.: The Johns Hopkins Press, 1962.

   Since the end of the World War II there have been many studies about

(A2b)

the techniques of planning, but material about organizational and administrative aspects of planning has been very meager. To bridge this gap, the Economic Development Institute initiated studies on various developing countries in plan implementation. Planning in Morocco was the first and planning in Yugoslavia the second in this series.

123. Watson, Andrew, and Jil B. Dirlan, "The Impact of Underdevelopment on Economic Planning," <u>The Quarterly Journal of Economics</u>, 29(May 1965), 167-94.
    Various aspects are discussed including: background to planning and development in the planning period, establishing a 'Development Board,' centralization of negotiations, pressure for more planning, long-range planning vs. implementation, constraints on planning, scope of development plans, implementation, major obstacles resulting from underdevelopment, and conclusion on the orientation of planning.

125. Wilson, A. G., "Models in Urban Planning: A Synoptic Review of Recent Literature," <u>Urban Studies</u>, 5(November 1968), 249-76.

126. Winthrop, Henry, "The Sociologist and the Study of the Future," <u>American Sociologist</u>, 3(May 1968), 136-145.

127. Young, Michael, <u>Forecasting and the Social Sciences</u>, New York: Heineman Educational Books, 1968.

128. Zielinski, Janusz G., "Are There Laws of Planning? Social Planning and Its Relation to Mixed Economies," <u>Economics of Planning</u>, 5(1-2, 1965), 43-52.

b. Program Budgeting

129. Abraham, William I., "Annual Budget and Plan Implementation," <u>Annual Budgeting and Development Planning</u>, Washington, D. C.: National Planning Association, Center for Development Planning, (Planning Methods Series No. 1), 1965.

130. Chartrand, Robert, and others, <u>Information Support, Program Budgeting, and the Congress</u>, New York: Spartan, 1968.

131. Colm, Gerhard, <u>Integration of National Planning and Budgeting</u>, Washington, D. C.: National Planning Association, Center for Development Planning, (Planning Methods Series No. 5), 1968.
    Discusses improvement of "integration between national planning in developing countries...focuses on the particular issue of the type of integration that is desirable."

132. Davis, James W. (ed.), <u>Politics, Programs and Budgets: A Reader in Government Budgeting</u>, Englewood Cliffs, New Jersey: Prentice-Hall, 1969.

133. Dorfman, Robert (ed.), <u>Measuring the Benefits of Government Investments</u>, Washington, D. C.: The Brookings Institution, 1965.

(A2b)

134. Enthoven, Alain, "Economic Analysis in the Department of Defense," <u>American Economic Review</u>, 53(May 1963), 413-23.

135. George Washington University, State-Local Finances Project. <u>PPB pilot project reports from the participating 5 States, 5 counties, and 5 cities</u>, Washington, D. C.: George Washington University, 1969.
   These summary reports make clear that the strategy for implementation of PPB in each of the governments will vary, reflecting the responsiveness of that strategy to the political ecology, the power structure of its organization, the staff talent available for PPB work, and the particular demographic, economic, and social setting.

136. Goldman, Thomas (ed.), <u>Cost-Effectiveness Analysis, New Approaches in Decision Making</u>, New York: Frederick A. Praeger Co., 1967.

136.1 Golembiewski, Robert T.(ed.), <u>Public Budgeting and Finance: Readings in Theory and Practice</u>, Itasca, Ill.: F. E. Peacock Publishers, 1968.
   Forty-seven readings are used to present conceptual issues, institutional features, economic policy matters, strategies as alternatives, administration questions, behavioral issues, organizational problems, and technical features. Emphasis is placed on behavioral materials relevant to budgeting as well as on technical and institutional features.

137. Hartley, Harry J., <u>Educational Planning-Programming-Budgeting: A Systems Approach</u>, Englewood Cliffs, New Jersey: Prentice-Hall, 1968.

138. Hinrichs, Harley H., and Graeme M. Taylor (eds.), <u>Program Budgeting and Benefit-Cost Analysis; Cases, Text and Readings</u>, Pacific Palisades, California: Goodyear Publishing Co., 1969.
   Contributions have been drawn from many of the prime movers in PPB, such as Charles Schultz, Robert McNamara, Henry Rowen, Alain C. Enthoven, and John Haldi. Eleven of the fifteen cases were prepared under government contract for use by the Civil Service Commission and the Bureau of the Budget.

139. Hovey, Harold A., <u>The Planning-Programming-Budgeting Approach to Government Decision-Making</u>, New York: Frederick A. Praeger Co., 1968.
   Hovey examines the problems arising from budgetary procedures that fail to show the total impact of government action, the critical problem of tailoring PPB methods to government evaluation procedures, and the difficulties involved in establishing goals through the political process.

140. _____, <u>The Planning-Programming-Budgeting System: An Appraisal</u>, New York: Frederick A. Praeger, 1968.
   A thorough, non-mathematical explanation of the Planning-Programming-Budgeting System. To illustrate the system's use, the author presents actual examples of its application in government budgeting and political decision-making. The PPBS is then evaluated within the context of the political environment in which it must operate. Included is a comprehensive bibliography.

140.1 Jernberg, James, "Informative Change and Congressional Behavior: A Caveat for PPBS Reformers," <u>Journal of Politics</u>, 31(August 1969), 722-40.
   This article attempts to establish a framework for relating the PPBS

(A2b)

system (designed for administrators) to Congressional evaluation of government programs.

141. Johnson, A. W., "Planning and Budgeting," *Canadian Public Administration* (Toronto), 2(September 1959), 12-30.

142. Linowes, David F., "Socio-Economic Accounting," *Journal of Accountancy*, 26(November 1968), 37-42.
    Urges the collaboration of CPA's and social scientists to devise meaningful social measurements.

143. Lyden, Fremont J., and Ernest G. Miller (eds.), *Planning-Programming-Budgeting: A Systems Approach to Management*, Chicago: Markham Publishing Co., 1967.
    This book of readings is organized to give administrators and students an overview of the techniques, applications, and potential payoffs of planning-programming-budgeting. It provides valuable supplementary reading for any course in public administration.

144. Maass, Arthur, "Benefit Cost Analysis: Its Relevance to Public Expenditure Decisions," *Quarterly Journal of Economics*, 70(May 1966), 208-26.

145. Markham, Emerson, and William C. McConkey, "PPBS as an aid to Decision-Making," *Midwest Review of Public Administration*, 3(February 1969), 65-71.
    Response to an article in the August 1968 issue, "Reservations to PPBS use," by Robert I. Wessel; a reply by Mr. Wessel follows.

146. Mosher, Frederick C., *Planning-Programming-Budgeting; Program Budgeting in Foreign Affairs: Some Reflection*, (Memorandum prepared at the request of the Subcommittee on National Security and International Operations... Committee on Government Operations, United States Senate), Washington, D. C.: U. S. Government Printing Office, 1968.

147. Nasbo Institute for Budget Directors, *State Program Budgeting: Possibilities and Limitations*, Chicago: National Association of State Budget Officers, Council of State Governments, 1968.

149. Novick, D. (ed.), *Program Budgeting: Program Analysis and the Federal Budget*, Cambridge, Massachusetts: Harvard University Press, 1965.

150. "PPBS and Other Budget Applications," *Municipal Finance*, 41(May 1969), 148-76.
    Partial contents - "An approach to implementing PPB" by Larry N. Blick, "Organizing for a new approach to budgeting" by Monty C. Lish, and "Assessing the future" by Robert L. Johnson.

151. "PPBS Re-examined," A Symposium, *Public Administration Review*, 29(March-April 1969), 111-202.

153. Salazar, Rodolpho C., and Subrata K. Sen, "A Simulation Model of Capital Budgeting under Uncertainty," *Management Science (Applications Series)*, 15(December 1968), B-161-179.

154. Schick, Allen, *PPB's First Years: Premature and Maturing*, Washington, D. C.: U. S. Bureau of the Budget, 1968.

155. Schultze, Charles L., *The Politics and Economics of Public Spending*, Washington, D. C.: Brookings Institution, 1968.
   Examines the relation between the PPB analytical approach and the political bargaining approach to program and budgetary decisions, and suggests how the two can complement each other.

156. Smithies, Arthur, "A Conceptual Framework for the Program Budget," *RAND Corporation Research Memorandum 4271-RC*, (September 1964).

156.1 _____, "Government Budgeting," in David L. Sills (ed.), *International Encyclopedia of the Social Sciences*, New York: Macmillan, and The Free Press, 1968, 2, 184-192.

157. Spindler, Arthur, "PPBS Social and Rehabilitation Services," *Welfare in Review*, 7(March-April 1969), 22-28.
   Discusses HEW "experience with the PPB system in the social and rehabilitation fields."

158. U. S. Congress, Joint Economic Committee, *The Analysis and Evaluation of Public Expenditures: the PPB system* (A compendium of papers submitted to the Subcommittee on Economy in Government), Washington, D. C.: U. S. Government Printing Office, 1969. 6pts. in 3v. (91st Cong., 1st sess. Joint Committee print) Contents: v.1. pt. 1. The appropriate functions of Government in an enterprise system.- pt.2. Institutional factors affecting efficient public expenditure policy.- pt.3. Some problems of analysis in evaluating public expenditure alternatives.- v.2. pt.4. The current status of the planning-programming-budgeting system.- v.3. pt.5. The performance of program budgeting and analysis in the Federal Government.-pt.6. Analysis and evaluation in major policy areas: unresolved issues and next steps.

159. U. S. Congress, Joint Economic Committee, Subcommittee on Economy in Government, *Hearings on the Planning-Programming-Budgeting System: Progress and Potentials* (90th Congress, 1st Session, 1967).

160. U. S. Congress, Senate, Committee on Government Operations, *Planning-Programming-Budgeting; interim observations*. A study submitted by the Subcommittee on National Security and International Operations (pursuant to S.Res.212, 90th Cong.)... Washington, U. S. Government Printing Office, 1968. (90th Cong., 2nd sess. Committee print).

161. Weidenbaum, Murray L., *Planning-Programming-Budgeting Systems: Selected Case Materials*, St. Louis: Washington University, St. Louis, Dept. of Economics, (Working paper 6900), 1969.
   These materials, prepared for the author's Graduate Seminar on PPBS, include case studies of benefit-cost analysis and cost-effectiveness analysis, an exposition of the Federal Government-wide program budget, and a closing paper on the role of PPBS in business planning.

162. Wildavsky, Aaron B., "Budgeting as a Political Process," in David L. Sills (ed.), *International Encyclopedia of the Social Sciences*, New York: Macmillan, and The Free Press, 1968, 2, 192-199.

163. _____, "The Political Economy of Efficiency: Cost-Benefit Analysis, Systems Analysis, and Program Budgeting," *Public Administration*

(A2c)

Review, 26(December 1966), 292-310.

164. _____, The Politics of the Budgetary Process, Boston: Little, Brown, 1964.

165. _____, "Rescuing Policy Analysis from PPBS," American Public Administration Review, 29(March-April 1969), 189-202.
   On page 190 Wildavsky makes a comment that must be incorporated in future studies on change--"Because policy analysis is not concerned with projecting the status quo, but with tracing out the consequences of innovative action, it is a variant of planning. Complementing the agency's decision process, policy analysis is a tool of social change." Wildavsky has a number of other perceptive insights concerning depth of changes, change in a growing organization, etc.

c. Systems

166. Anthony, Robert N., Planning and Control Systems: A Framework of Analysis, Cambridge, Mass.: Harvard University Press, 1965.

167. Apter, David E., "System, Process and the Politics of Economic Development," in Bert F. Hoselitz and Wilbert E. Moore (eds.), Industrialization and Society, Paris: UNESCO-Mouton, 1966, 135-58.

168. Berrien, F. Kenneth, General and Social Systems, New Brunswick, N. J.: Rutgers University Press, 1968.

168.1 Bertalanffy, Ludwig von, "General Systems Theory: A New Approach to Unity of Science," Human Biology, 23(December 1951), 303-61.

169. Black, Guy, The Application of Systems Analysis to Government Operations, New York: Frederick A. Praeger Co., 1968.
   The principle purpose of this work is to provide non-systems analysts and administrators with some insights into the purposes which systems analysis can serve, its methods, pitfalls, and problems. A concluding chapter compares and contrasts PPBS and systems analysis.

170. Blake, Robert R., and Jane Srygley, Corporate Excellence through Good Organization Development: A System Approach, Houston, Texas: Gulf Publishing Co., 1968.

171. Buckley, Walter, Modern Systems Research for the Behavioral Scientists: A Source Book, Chicago: Aldine, 1968.

172. _____, Sociology and Modern Systems Theory, Englewood Cliffs, New Jersey: Prentice-Hall, 1967.

173. Churchman, Charles W., The Systems Approach, New York: Delacorte Press, 1968.
   Examines what the systems approach really means, not from the point of view of 'selling' the idea, but rather by examining its validity in the climate of a debate.

(A2c)

174. Cleland, David I., and William R. King, <u>Systems Analysis and Project Management</u>, New York: McGraw-Hill, 1968.
    Presents the modern ideas of systems analysis and project management in a way that demonstrates their essential unity and applicability in a wide variety of industrial and governmental management environments.

175. Cleland, David (ed.), <u>Systems, Organization, Analysis, Management: A Book of Readings</u>, New York: McGraw-Hill, 1969.

176. Cornog, Geoffrey Y., and others (eds.), <u>Electronic Data Processing Systems in Public Management</u>, Chicago: Rand McNally, 1962.

177. Easton, David, <u>Framework of a Political Analysis</u>, Englewood Cliff, N. J.: Prentice-Hall, 1965.

178. _____, <u>The Political System</u>, New York: Knopf, 1953.

179. _____, <u>A System Analysis of Political Life</u>, New York: John Wiley and Sons, 1965.
    Constructs a general theory and shows how concepts can be applied against it. Theoretical models depict life in dynamic terms, showing the way in which demands and supports flow into the system; the way in which the systems work on these, converting them into policies, decisions, and actions.

180. Emery, F. E., and E. L. Trist, "Socio-Technical Systems," <u>Management Sciences: Models and Techniques</u>, <u>Proceedings of the Sixth International Meeting of the Institute of Management Sciences</u>, Vol. 2, New York: Pergamon Press, 1960, 83-97.

181. Esman, Milton J., and John D. Montgomery, "System Approaches to Technical Cooperation: The Role of Development Administration," <u>Public Administration Review</u>, 29(September-October 1969), 507-39.

182. Goldman, A. S., and T. B. Slattery, <u>Maintainability: A Major Element of System Effectiveness</u>, New York: John Wiley and Sons, 1964.
    Using a systems-oriented approach and modern operations research, this work defines maintainability as a system characteristic. The book presents conceptual materials and principles to guide those who must make decisions regarding system development, evaluation or operation.

183. Goode, Harry H., and Robert E. Machol, <u>System Engineering</u>, New York: McGraw-Hill, 1957.

184. Gross, Bertram, <u>The State of the Nation: Social Systems Accounting</u>, New York: Barnes & Noble, 1966.

185. _____, "What are Your Organization's Objectives?--A General Systems Approach to Planning," <u>Human Relations</u>, 18(August 1965), 195-216.

186. Haas, Michael, "Types of Asymmetry in Social and Political Systems," <u>General Systems</u>, 12(1967), 69-79.

187. Hall, Arthur D., <u>A Methodology for Systems Engineering</u>, Princeton, N. J.: D. Van Nostrand Co., 1962.

(A2c)

188. Kariel, Henry S., *Open Systems: Arenas for Political Action*, Itasca, Ill.: F. E. Peacock Publishers, 1968.

189. Katz, Saul M., *A System Approach to Development Administration: A Framework for Analyzing Capability of Action for National Development*, Chicago: Comparative Administration Group of the American Society for Public Administration, 1965.
   Employing a concept of systems which was developed particularly for application to business management, Professor Katz develops an interesting and useful framework for examining the administrative development process. Within this theoretical reference, he explores its possibilities of application in manpower, finance, logistics, participation, legitimate power, and information.

190. Kolaja, Jiri, *Social System and Time and Space: An Introduction to the Theory of Recurrent Behavior*, Pittsburg, Pennsylvania: Duquesne University Press, 1969.

191. Kulp, Earl M., *Rural Development Planning, Systems Analysis and Working Method*, New York: Frederick A. Praeger, 1970.
   Mr. Kulp suggests practical planning techniques for rural development that require a minimum of capital expenditure and can readily be applied by field agents. The book provides a mathematical model of agricultural development and guidance on computerization of non-capital project planning. Its main feature, however, is the simplification of sophisticated systems analysis techniques. The book also provides a general theory of the evolution of the rural **sector,** some case studies of successful rural development, and discussion of some special problems of agricultural credit, planning with the private sector, and decentralization of planning.

192. Leondes, Cornelius, *Advances in Control Systems*, New York: Academic Press, 1964.

193. _____, *Computer Control Systems Technology*, New York: McGraw-Hill, 1961.

194. _____, *Modern Control Systems*, New York: McGraw-Hill, 1965.

195. Lerner, Daniel, "Communication Systems and Social Systems," *Behavioral Science*, 2(1957), 266-75.

196. Lyden, Fremont J., "Systems Theory in the World of Management," review of *The Social Psychology of Organizations* by Daniel Katz and Robert Kahn (New York: John Wiley and Sons, 1966), *Sociology and Modern Systems Theory* by Walter Buckley (New York: Prentice-Hall, 1967) and *Organizations in Action* by James D. Thompson (New York: McGraw-Hill, 1967) in *Public Administration Review*, 29(March-April 1969), 215-8.

197. McKean, Roland N., *Efficiency in Government through Systems Analysis*, New York: John Wiley and Sons, 1958.

198. McLaren, K. G., and E. L. Buesnel, *Network Analysis in Project Management: An Introductory Manual Based on Unilever Experience*, London: Cassell, 1969.
   This book is written for those engaged in every type of project work.

20

(A2c)

It is intended primarily for those with no previous knowledge of the subject, and can be used either as a self-instruction manual or to supplement training courses in both industry and colleges. The approach is essentially practical, comprising a set of fundamental principles which are applicable to any project situation and which are developed in a clear and logical way. Particular emphasis is laid on the value of the technique in thinking through a project in its initial stages. New ideas on procedure, such as network validation, will be of interest to the more experienced practitioner. Such factors as objectives, assumptions, risk and the use of the network to investigate alternative courses of action are discussed.

199. MacMillan, Claude, and Richard F. Gonzales, Systems Analysis: A Computer Approach to Decision Models, Homewood, Ill.: Richard D. Irwin Inc., 1968.
    First chapter on systems is particularly useful.

200. Malcolm, Donald S., and others, Management Control Systems, New York: John Wiley and Sons, 1960.

201. Manane, Joseph H., A Sociology of Human Systems, New York: Appleton-Century-Crofts, 1967.

202. Meister, David, and Gerald F. Rabideau, Human Factors in Evaluation in System Development, New York: John Wiley and Sons, 1965.
    Presents a capsule picture of how the man-machine relationship is incorporated into system design. Human factors are treated as a branch of systems engineering and analysis with particular emphasis on the working relationship between human factors, personnel and equipment engineers in an engineering-oriented environment.

203. Meshkin, Eli, and Ludwig Braum, Jr., Adaptive Control Systems, New York: McGraw-Hill, 1961.

204. Miller, R. B., "Task Description and Analysis," in R. M. Gagne (ed.), Psychological Principles in System Development, New York: Holt, Rinehart and Winston, 187-229.

205. Mockler, Robert J., "The Systems Approach to Business Organization and Decision-Making," California Management Review, 11(Winter 1968), 53-58.
    Systems theory provides a conceptual basis for establishing a more efficient system for planning, control, and operational decision-making.

206. Morse, Philip (ed.), Operations Research for Public Systems, Cambridge, Mass.: M.I.T. Press, 1967.

207. Quade, E. S., and W. I. Boucher (eds.), Systems Analysis and Policy Planning; Applications in Defense, New York: American Elsevier, 1968.
    Surveys the nature, aims, and limitations of systems analysis in current defense planning.

208. Ramo, Simon, Cure for Chaos; Fresh Solutions to Social Problems Through the Systems Approach, New York: McKay, 1969.
    In layman's terms, Dr. Ramo describes what the systems approach is, why it is useful and important, and what its limitations are, to show

(A2c)

that the systems approach can and should be used as a tool for solving our social problems.

209. Rapaport, Anatol, "Some System Approaches to Political Theory," in David Easton (ed.), <u>Varieties of Political Theory</u>, Englewood Cliffs, N. J.: Prentice-Hall, 1966, chapter six.

209.1 Talcott Parsons, William C. Mitchell, Morton A. Kaplan, and David S. Gochman, "Systems Analysis," in David L. Sills (ed.), <u>International Encyclopedia of the Social Sciences</u>, New York: Macmillan, and The Free Press, 1968, 15, p. 452-495.

210. Rima, Ingrid H. (ed.), <u>A Forum on Systems Management</u>, Philadelphia: Bureau of Economic and Business Research, School of Business Administration, Temple University, 1969.
Partial contents - "Some problems of applying a systems approach to city government" by Nachman Bench. "The potential of systems technology for the Federal Congress," by Robert L. Chartrand," and "The challenge of systems management to Government," by John Haldi.

211. Rosenhead, J. V., "Experimental Simulation of a Social System," <u>Operational Research Quarterly</u>, 19(September 1968), 242-56.

212. Sackman, Harold, <u>Computers, System Science, and Evolving Society</u>, New York: John Wiley and Sons, 1967.

213. Sanders, Ralph, "Systems Analysis and the Political Process," <u>Perspectives in Defense Management</u>, December 1968, 13-20.
Explains the way systems analysis, while maintaining its integrity as a discipline, takes on political overtones.

214. Scott, Andrew M., <u>The Functioning of the International Political System</u>, New York: MacMillan, 1967.
Applies system analysis to international politics. Principles developed generally are applicable to other organizational forms as well. Promotes analytic clarity by reducing concepts to their essentials.

215. Seiler, Karl, <u>Introduction to System Cost Effectiveness</u>, New York: Wiley-Interscience, 1969.

216. Sells, O. R., "Model for the Social System for the Multiman Extended Duration Space Ship," <u>Aerospace Medicine</u>, 37(November 1966), 1070-79.

217. Shubik, Martin, "Simulation of Socio-Economic Systems," <u>General Systems</u>, 12(1, 1967), 149-76.

218. Teitz, Michael B., "Cost Effectiveness: A Systems Approach to Analysis of Urban Services," <u>Journal of the American Institute of Planners</u>, 34 (September 1968), 303-11.

219. Wallace, Edward L., <u>Management Influence on the Design of Data Processing Systems: A Case Study</u>, Boston: Division of Research, Harvard Business School, 1961.

(A2c)

220. Weinberg, Stanley L., *Biology: An Inquiry into the Nature of Life*, Boston: Allyn and Bacon, Inc., 1966.

221. Wiseman, Herbert V., *Political Systems: Some Sociological Approaches*, New York: Frederick A. Praeger Co., 1966.

222. Young, Oran R., *Systems of Political Science*, Englewood, N. J.: Prentice-Hall, 1968.

B. DEVELOPMENT

(B1)

1. ECONOMIC AND SOCIAL DEVELOPMENT

223. Adelman, Irma, and Cynthia Morris, <u>Society, Politics, and Economic Development</u>, Baltimore: Johns Hopkins University Press, 1967.

224. Agarwala, A. N., and S. P. Singh (eds.), <u>Economics of Underdevelopment</u>, New York: Oxford University Press, 1963.

225. Anderson, Arnold C., and Mary Jean Bowmer (eds.), <u>Education and Economic Development</u>, Chicago: Aldine, 1965.

226. Ardant, G., "A Plan for Full Employment in the Developing Countries," <u>International Labour Review</u>, 87(January 1963), 15-51.
    Formulates an outline of a plan by which unemployed and underemployed masses of the developing countries could be used productively. Self-help is the principle behind the plan. The author has based his conclusions on the experiences which he had in Morocco and Tunisia.

227. Areskoug, Kaj, <u>External Public Borrowing: Its Role in Economic Development</u>, New York: Frederick A. Praeger Co., 1969.
    The findings of this study point to the need for drastic reappraisal of international development assistance policies. Following a discussion of the different ways in which external public borrowing serves as an instrument of government policy, Dr. Areskoug analyzes the conventional notions about the effects of such borrowing and illustrates why accepted theory is inadequate. By analysis of data from 22 countries, Dr. Areskoug concludes that development loans are used, to a large extent, to finance increases in consumption, and lead only in a limited way to productive investment. Since this partial failure of international lending to promote capital formation raises important questions about current lending practices, Dr. Areskoug outlines alternative approaches for policy makers.

228. Aron, Raymond, <u>World Technology and Human Destiny</u>, Ann Arbor: University of Michigan, 1963.

229. Asher, Robert E., and others, <u>Development of the Emerging Countries: An Agenda for Research</u>, Washington, D. C.: The Brookings Institution, 1962.
    This work has an excellent classification of the stages of development of nations, among other aspects.

230. Ayal, E. B., "The Meaning and Process of Development," <u>Economic Development and Cultural Change</u>, 13(April 1965), 354-57.

(B1)

231. Banani, Amin, <u>The Modernization of Iran, 1921-41</u>, Stanford: Stanford University Press, 1961.
    Professor Banani's book analyzes the reforms initiated by Raza Shah. A considerable portion of the book is devoted to the historical background which is readily available in many other books on Iran. The remainder is devoted to administration, army, public health and education.

232. Bantock, G. H., <u>Culture, Industrialization, and Education</u>, London: Routledge and Kegan Paul, 1968.

233. Baron, Paul, <u>The Political Economy of Growth</u>, New York: Monthly Review Press, 1957.

234. Baronson, J., "Development as a Scientific Discipline," <u>American Journal of Economics and Sociology</u>, 26(April 1967), 127-34.

235. Basia, K. A., "Education and Social Mobility in Economically Underdeveloped Countries," in <u>Transactions of the Third World Congress of Sociology</u>, London: International Sociological Association, 5(1956), 81-89.

236. Basu, A. K., "The Concept of Community in Developing Nations," <u>Sociology and Social Research</u>, 52(January 1968), 193-202.

237. Bauer, Peter T., and Basil S. Yamey, <u>The Economics of Underdeveloped Countries</u>, Chicago: University of Chicago Press, 1962.
    The book has been written to satisfy the needs of both the general reader and the specialist. The first part of the book is concerned with national income, capital and the labor force. The second part investigates government policy and economic development.

238. Becker, Gary S., "Investment in Human Capital: A Theoretical Analysis," <u>Journal of Political Economy</u>, 70, (October 1962), 9-49.

239. Bendix, Reinhard, "Tradition and Modernity Reconsidered," <u>Comparative Studies in Society and History</u>, 9(April 1967), 266-73.

240. Benham, Frederick, <u>Economic Aid to Underdeveloped Countries</u>, London: Oxford University Press, 1961.

241. Bereday, George Z. F. (ed.), <u>Essays on World Education: The Crisis of Supply and Demand</u>, New York: Oxford University Press, 1969.

242. Berger, Morroe (ed.), <u>The New Metropolis in the Arab World</u>, New Delhi: Allied Publishers, 1963.
    The book contains twelve articles on various aspects of urban development in the Middle East presented at an international seminar held under the Egyptian Society of Engineers and the Congress for Cultural Freedom. Except for the editor, the contributors are from countries of the Middle East, with backgrounds in city planning, engineering, and economics.

243. Beringer, Christoph, "Welfare and Production Efficiency: Two Objectives of Land Reform in Pakistan," <u>The Pakistan Development Review</u>, 2(Summer 1962), 173-88.

(B1)

       This paper treats: background material on legal, religious and customary ways of land holding; facts about the size of holdings; subdivisions and fragmentation; evaluation of land reforms and some conclusions for future direction.

244. Berrill, Kenneth, _Economic Development, With Special Reference to East Asia_, London: Macmillan, 1964.
    Proceedings of a conference held by the International Economic Association in Japan. Papers deal with problems of general development, as well as problems specifically within the Asian context.

245. Bill, J. A., "The Social and Economic Foundations of Power in Contemporary Iran," _Middle East Journal_, 17(Autumn 1963), 400-18.
    Class is used as a basic tool of analysis. The writer examines hopes and aspirations of different groups and then explores relationships between socio-political processes and social structures.

246. Blellock, David, _One Developing World: Study of Cross-Cultural Operations_, Syracuse, N. Y.: Maxwell Graduate School of Citizenship and Public Affairs, Syracuse University, 1963.
    A short essay dealing with many of the significant problems of development.

247. Blumer, Herbert, "Early Industrialization and the Laboring Class," _Sociological Quarterly_, 1(January, 1960), 5-14.

248. _____, "Idea of Social Development," _Studies in Comparative International Development_, 2(1, 1966), 1-11.

249. _____, "Industrialization and the Traditional Order," _Sociology and Social Research_, 48(January 1964), 129-38.

250. _____, and S. N. Eisenstadt, "The Sociology of Development, Plenary Session, Report on the Discussion," _Transaction of the Fifth World Congress of Sociology_, 3, 19-20.

251. Boulding, Kenneth, _The Meaning of the Twentieth Century_, New York: Harper, 1963.

252. Bowen, Howard, and Garth Mangum (eds.), _Automation and Economic Progress_, Englewood Cliffs, N. J.: Prentice-Hall, 1966.

253. Braibanti, Ralph, and Joseph Spengler (eds.), _Traditions, Values and Socio-Economic Development_, Durham, N. C.: Duke University Press, 1961.
    A book of readings devoted almost entirely to the non-economic factors in the economic development of less developed countries. Theory, ideology, values, social framework, traditions, cultural dynamics, Islamic elements in the political thought of Pakistan, and political dimensions of foreign aid are some of the major themes of the articles.

254. Bruton, Henry J., _Principles of Economic Development_, Englewood Cliffs, N. J.: Prentice-Hall, 1965.

(B1)

255. Buchanan, Norman S., and Howard S. Ellis, <u>Approaches to Economic Development</u>, New York: Twentieth Century Fund, 1955.

256. Buchanan, Robert, <u>Technology and Social Progress</u>, Elmsford, N. Y.: Pergamon, 1965.

257. Burke, John (ed.), <u>The New Technology and Human Values</u>, Belmont, Cal.: Wadsworth, 1966.

258. Cairncross, A. K., <u>Factors in Economic Development</u>, London: Allen and Unwin, 1962.
      A selection of the author's essays written over a period of several years. There is no integrated theme in the book, but the ideas on administration and planning of economic development, and comparison of various methods are useful.

259. Cowan, C. D., <u>The Economic Development of Southeast Asia</u>, New York: Frederick A. Praeger Co., 1963.

260. Cutt, James, <u>Taxation and Economic Development in India</u>, New York: Frederick A. Praeger, 1967.
      An analysis of a tax system within the context of planned economic development. The first part reviews the present Indian tax system and tax-policy objectives--growth, redistribution, and stabilization. The author investigates whether Indian federal and state taxes meet these objectives, makes recommendations for the modification of the system and for new taxes to help attain policy goals.

261. Dator, James A., "The 'Protestant Ethic' in Japan," <u>Journal of Developing Areas</u>, 1(October 1966), 23-40.

262. De Schweinitz, Karlde, <u>Industrialisation and Democracy: Economic Necessities and Political Possibilities</u>, New York: Free Press of Glencoe, 1964.
      The author believes that in the developing countries of today there is no correlation between industrialization and the emergence of a democratic tradition. In 19th century Europe industrialization created a democratic tradition. He says that it is true that "democracy is a game of wealthy nations, but there is no evidence that if developing nations become rich that they would adopt democracy as a way of life."

263. Eddison, John C., "Industrial Growth and Urban Land Requirements in East Pakistan," <u>The Pakistan Development Review</u>, 3(Winter 1963), 547-65.
      In surveying industrialization and urban growth in East Pakistan, the writer feels there has been an increase in the rate of development in the Second Five-Year Plan period. It is hoped that this pace can be accelerated during the Third Plan period. Before this can be achieved some major bottlenecks such as - an inadequate supply of suitable industrial land must be removed.

264. Eisenstadt, S. N., "Breakdown of Modernization," <u>Economic Development and Cultural Change</u>, 12(July 1964), 245-67.

265. _____, <u>Essays on Sociological Aspects of Political and Economic Development</u>, The Hague: Mouton, 1961.

(B1)

266. _____, "Modernization and Conditions of Sustained Growth," World Politics, 16(July 1964), 576-94.
An exposition and identification of the conditions which aid or impede sustained growth. There is a scholarly analysis of the broad socio-demographic and structural corolaries of modernization as they develop in the major institutional spheres.

267. _____, Modernization, Growth and Diversity, Bloomington, Ind.: Department of Government, University of Indiana, 1963.

268. Feldman, A. S., and W. E. Moore, "Industrialization and Industrialism: Convergence and Differentiation," Transactions of the Fifth World Congress of Sociology, 2, 151-69.

269. Fickett, Lewis, Jr., Problems of the Developing Nations, New York: Crowell, 1966.

270. Firth, Raymond, and B. S. Yamey (eds.), Capital Saving and Credit in Peasant Societies: Studies From Asia, Oceania, Caribbean and Middle America, Chicago: Aldine Publishing Company, 1964.
As a part of the growing concern among social scientists about the impact of a social system on economic development, anthropologists in this reader present their point of view, answering some of the questions which economists generally raise in discussing ramifications of social systems.

271. Friedman, Milton, "Foreign Economic Aid: Means and Objectives," Yale Review, 47(June 1958), 500-16.
Couched in terms of efficiency, the author makes the statement that government cannot contribute effectively to economic growth in developing areas.

272. Frost, Raymond, The Backward Society, New York: St. Martin's Press, 1961.

273. Galbraith, John K., Economic Development, Cambridge, Mass.: Harvard University Press, 1964.
The book (a revised and expanded version of Economic Development in Perspective, 1962) now consists of nine lectures, five of which are either new or thoroughly revised from the previous edition. Galbraith's contention is that countries which are in early stages of development should concentrate on the development of human and institutional resources. Education, efficient governmental machinery, transportation and communication are some of the basic prerequisites for development. In his opinion state initiative in development does not mean state ownership of the means of production. Central planning and institution of private property are not incompatible.

274. _____, "Economics: The Quality of Life," Encounter, 24, 1(January 1965), 31-39.
The author discusses the impact of economic circumstances on social attitudes of rich and poor countries. The influence is more intense in the poor countries where "there is obvious need to get as much as possible out of the productive resources that are available--to use the labor, capital, natural resources, and intelligence of the community with maximum efficiency."

(B1)

275. _____, "A Positive Approach to Economic Aid," <u>Foreign Affairs</u>, 39(April, 1961), 44-45.

    The prime difficulty of the present U. S. aid policy, according to the author, is that it is based on a convenient but largely erroneous view of the requirements for economic development. He thinks that contrary to prevailing thought capital is not the only factor missing in underdeveloped countries. He maintains that a certain degree of literacy, a certain degree of social justice, a reliable apparatus of government and public administration, and a clear and purposeful view of what development involves is also required.

276. Geertz, Clifford, <u>Peddlers and Princes: Social Change and Economic Modernization in Two Indonesian Towns</u>, Chicago: University of Chicago Press, 1963.

    In an effort to resolve the enigmatic problem and handling of socio-cultural factors in economic development, the author argues that change in socio-economic base is inescapable if a transitional society is to progress towards modernization. The study is an outcome of the material collected by the author in Java and Bali.

277. Goldschmidt, Arthur, "Technology in Emerging Countries," <u>Technology and Culture</u>, 3(Fall 1962), 286-92.

278. Goody, Jack (ed.), <u>Literacy in Traditional Societies</u>, London: Cambridge University Press, 1968.

279. Haberler, Gottfried, and Robert M. Stein (eds.), <u>Equilibrium and Growth in the World Economy</u>, Cambridge, Mass.: Harvard University Press, 1961.

280. Hagen, Everett E., "How Economic Growth Begins: A General Theory Applied to Japan," <u>Public Opinion Quarterly</u>, 22(Fall 1958), 373-90.

281. _____, "The Process of Economic Development," <u>Economic Development and Cultural Change</u>, 5(April 1957), 193-215.

282. Hall, C. P. (ed.), <u>Human Values and Advancing Technology</u>, New York: Friendship Press, 1967.

283. Hambidge, Gove (ed.), <u>Dynamics of Development: An International Development Reader</u>, New York: Frederick A. Praeger Co., 1964.

    As the first phase of the postwar era, marked by the emergence of new nations, nears its end, both new nations and old are confronted by the challenge of the second phase--the challenge of development.

    The struggle to achieve political independence is far easier than the long-range fight against economic, social, cultural, and psychological stagnation.

284. Hansen, Niles, "The Protestant Ethic as a General Precondition for Economic Development," <u>Canadian Journal of Economics and Political Science</u>, 29 (November 1963), 462-74.

285. Harbison, Frederick, and Charles A. Myers, <u>Education, Manpower and Economic Growth</u>, New York: McGraw-Hill Book Co., 1964.

    A general survey of the concepts and issues useful for economic planners, and students of political and social development. It is policy oriented. A quantitative analysis of indicators of human resource

(B1)

development and economic growth in 75 countries is the basis for a subsequent analysis of the countries grouped in four levels of human resource development. This provides an analytical framework for presenting appropriate strategies of human resource development at each level and for integrating planning.

287. _____, and Abdel Kadir Ibrahim, Human Resources for Egyptian Enterprise, New York: McGraw-Hill Book Co., 1959.
   The book is concerned with developments which have taken place in Egypt since the rise of President Nasser. Although from the title it appears to be a book on human resources alone, in substance it is a survey of Egypt's general economic growth. It also deals with the development of entrepreneurship, management, recruitment of labor for expanding industries, and educational system. The study is based on published English and Arabic material and 500 interviews with high officials.

288. Harrod, Sir Roy, "Economic Developments and Asian Regional Co-operation," The Pakistan Development Review, 2(Spring 1962), 1-22.
   Topics include: Methods for implementing the idea of "agreed specialization" in the Asian Region; an Asian buffer fund for steadying the incomes of primary producers in the face of world price oscillations; development of research in relation to the production of commodities which are of special importance in the Asian economy and which are not attracting sufficient research in institutions outside Asia; an Asian regional committee on methods of improving intra-Asian communication.

289. Hauser, Philip, "Cultural and Personal Obstacles to Economic Development," Human Organization, 18(Summer 1959), 78-84.

290. Helmer, Olaf, Social Technology, New York: Basic Books, 1966.

291. Henderson, Julia J., "The Challenge of World-Wide Social Conditions," The Annals of the American Academy of Political and Social Science, 329 (May 1960), 1-14.

292. Hershlag, Z. Y., Introduction to the Modern Economic History of the Middle East, Leyden: E. J. Brill, 1964.
   General review of the economic history of the Middle East from 1800 to Second World War. Primarily an analysis of the outside forces which have been moulding the economic destiny of this area.

293. Herskovits, Melville J., and Mitchell Harwitz (eds.), Economic Transition in Africa, (Northwestern University African Studies, No. 12), Evanston, Ill.: Northwestern University Press, 1964.

294. Hirschman, Albert O., and C. E. Lindblom, "Economic Development, Research and Development, Policy Making, Some Converging Views," Behavioral Science, 7(April 1962), 211-22.

295. _____, Journeys Toward Progress, Studies of Economic Policy-Making in Latin America, New York: The Twentieth Century Fund, 1963.
   A useful survey of the economic and social conditions in some of the countries of Latin America. There are discussions about the land

(B1)

reforms in Brazil and conditions of inflation in Chile. The author contends that change is being effected through what he calls "reform-mongering."

296. _____, *The Strategy of Economic Development*, New Haven, Conn.: Yale University Press, 1958.
    This study of the problems of economic growth in underdeveloped countries is chiefly concerned with the issue of balanced versus unbalanced growth and the search for inducements.

297. Hobhouse, Leonard, *Social Development*, London: Allen and Unwin, 1966.

298. Holt, Robert T., and John E. Turner, *The Political Basis of Economic Development: An Exploration in Comparative Analysis*, Princeton, N. J.: Van Norstrand, 1966.
    Applying their analysis to France, China, Japan, and England, the authors consider the impact of the political system upon economic development.

299. Holton, Gerald (ed.), *Science and Culture*, Boston, Mass.: Houghton, Mifflin, 1965.

300. Hong, Sung Chick, *The Intellectual and Modernization: A Study of Korean Attitudes*, Seoul: Daehan Textbook Co., 1967.

301. Hoselitz, Bert F., and Wilbert E. Moore (eds.), *Industrialization and Society*, Paris: UNESCO-Mouton, 1966; also The Hague: Mouton, 1963.

302. _____, "Non Economic Barriers to Economic Development," in *Economic Development and Cultural Change*, 1(March 1952), 8-21.

303. _____ (ed.), *The Progress of Underdeveloped Areas*, Chicago: University of Chicago Press, 1952.

304. _____, and others, *Theories of Economic Growth*, Glencoe, Ill.: The Free Press, 1960.

305. Hoselitz, R. B. (ed.), *The Role of Savings and Wealth in Southern Asia and the West*, Paris: UNESCO, 1963.

306. Hutchings, Edward and Elizabeth (eds.), *Scientific Progress and Human Values*, New York: American Elsevier, 1967.

307. International Bank for Reconstruction and Development, *A Public Development Program for Thailand*, Baltimore: Johns Hopkins Press, 1959.
    A report prepared at the request of the Government of Thailand. It contains a detailed study of general and administrative problems as Thailand develops at an accelerated pace.

308. *International Conference on the Problems of Modernization in Asia: Report*, Seoul: Asiatic Research Center, Korea University, 1966.
    Report of conference, including papers and discussions, held from June 28 to July 7, 1965 at Korea University under the chairmanship of Sang-eun Lee. More than 60 papers are presented within the following categories: Conceptual Problems of Modernization, Traditional Asian

(B1)

Society and Modernization, Modernization and Political Problems, Modernization and Economic Problems, and The Role of Various Population Strata in Modernization.

309. Johnson, Harry G., "The Ideology of Economic Policy in the New States," in Harry G. Johnson (ed.), _Economic Naturalism in Old and New States_, Chicago: University of Chicago Press, 1967, 124-41.

311. Kahl, Joseph A., _The Measurement of Modernism: A Study of Values in Brazil and Mexico_, Austin, Texas: University of Texas Press, 1968.

312. Kelley, Allen C., and Jeffrey G. Williamson, "Household Saving Behavior in the Developing Countries," _Economic Development and Cultural Change_, 16 (April 1968), 385-403.

313. Kerekes, Tibor (ed.), _The Arab Middle East and Muslim Africa_, New York: Frederick A. Praeger Co., 1961.
Aspects of the political, social and economic changes which have engulfed the Arab regions during the past decade are discussed. The role of Islam as a motivating factor is a prevalent theme.

314. Keyfitz, Nathan, "Age Distribution as a Challenge to Development," _American Journal of Sociology_, 70(May 1965), 659-68.
Age distribution plays a critical role in the development of less developed countries. In this paper, age distribution of Indonesia is analyzed and compared with other Asian countries. Economic and social consequences of changing age distribution also are examined.

315. Kunkel, John H., "Value and Behaviour in Economic Development," _Economic Development and Cultural Change_, 13(April 1965), 257-77.
Contemporary economic theories have assigned a prominent role to an individual as a lever of economic development. The author believes that this new theory will be workable only if the following problems are solved: (1) "What are the determinants of human behavior?" and (2) "What is the relationship between the individual and the societal context?"

317. Kuznets, Simon, "Economic Requirements of Modern Industrialization," in _Transactions of the Fifth World Congress of Sociology_, Belgium: International Sociological Association, 2(1962), 73-90.

318. Lamb, Robert K., "Political Elites and the Process of Economic Development," in Bertram F. Hoselitz (ed.), _The Progress of Underdeveloped Areas_, Chicago: University of Chicago Press, 1952, 30-53.

319. Lasswell, Harold D., "The Emerging Industrial Culture," in Richard J. Ward (ed.), _The Challenge of Development_, Chicago: Aldine Publishing Co., 1967.

320. Leibenstein, Harvey, _Economic Backwardness and Economic Growth: Studies in the Theory of Economic Development_, New York: John Wiley and Sons, 1957.

321. Levy, Marion J., Jr., _Modernization and the Structure of Societies_, Princeton, New Jersey: University Press, 1969.

(B1)

Attempts to set down a systematic, theoretical analysis of present day socio-economic-political institutions.

322. McLoughlin, P. F. M., "Population Growth Projections, 1906-2006, for Economic Development in Sudan," *The American Journal of Economics and Sociology*, 24(April 1965), 135-56.
Discusses population growth in the Republic of Sudan and indicates some of the more important economic pre-conditions and consequences of such growth. In the introduction the author explains the primary differences among the new economic regions of the country. Population projections both into the past and into the future are examined.

323. Madan, B. K., *Aspects of Economic Development and Policy*, Bombay: Allied Publishers Ltd., 1964.

324. Malenbaum, Wilfred, *Prospects for Indian Development*, Glencoe, Ill.: The Free Press, 1962.
A survey of the various development schemes in India, their execution and evaluation. The interplay of economic, social, and political factors which either motivate or retard the programmes of development are examined.

325. Mansfield, Edwin, *The Economics of Technological Change*, New York: Norton, 1968.

326. Meier, Gerald M., *The International Economics of Development, Theory and Policy*, New York: Harper and Row, 1968.

327. _____ (ed.), *Leading Issues in Development Economics*, New York: Oxford University Press, 1964.

328. Meier, Richard, *Science and Economic Development*, Cambridge, Mass.: M.I.T. Press, 1966.

329. Meynaud, Jean (ed.), *Social Change and Economic Development*, Paris: UNESCO, 1963.

330. Michael, Donald, "Some Speculations on the Social Impact of Technology," in Robert Perrucci and Marc Pilisuk (eds.), *The Triple Revolution*, Little-Brown, 1968. Also in Dean Morse and Aaron Warner (eds.), *Technical Innovation in Society*, New York: Columbia University Press, 1966.

331. Millikan, Max F., and Donald L. M. Blacker, *The Emerging Nations: Their Growth and United States Policy*, Boston: Little-Brown and Co., 1961.
The first of two parts has chapters concerned with: traditional society; the disruption of traditional society; resistance and conflict in the modernization process; some factors in social change; the process of economic modernization; and patterns and problems of political development. The second part contains an analysis of the various facets of American foreign policy with regard to less developed countries.

332. Millikan, Max F., and David Hapgood, *No Easy Harvest, The Dilemma of Agriculture in Underdeveloped Countries*, Boston: Little-Brown, 1967.

333. Mincer, Jacob, "Investment in Human Capital and Personal Income

Distribution," *Journal of Political Economy*, 66(August 1958), 281-302.

334. Moore, Wilbert E., *The Impact of Industry*, Englewood Cliffs, N. J.: Prentice-Hall, 1965.

335. Mountjoy, Allan B., *Industrialization and Underdeveloped Countries*, London: Hutchinson University Library, 1963.
  Enumerates various conditions of underdevelopment and problems of industrialization in less developed countries. These are illustrated by cases drawn from Ghana, Nigeria, Chile, Hong Kong, India, and Egypt.

336. Moussa, Pierre, *Underprivileged Nations*, Boston: Beacon Books, 1963.

337. Mudd, Stuart, *The Population Crisis and the Use of World Resources*, Bloomington, Ind.: Indiana University Press, 1964.
  The author is a microbiologist, whose main theme is the explosive increase in population, particularly in developing regions of the world, which is outpacing any practicable increase of resources and is a cause of grave concern to every thoughtful observer. The book consists of forty articles collected from magazines, papers, and speeches.

338. Mukerji, B., *Community Development in India*, Calcutta: Orient Longman, 1961.
  Considered one of the best treatise on this subject. Its scope is wide and comprehensive, and deals with practically all facets of community development. Development of programs, procedures and techniques, administration, relationship of community development program with local government, education and training and research are some of the salient discussions.

339. Muscat, Robert J., *Development Strategy in Thailand*, New York: Frederick A. Praeger Co., 1965.

340. Myint, H., *The Economics of Developing Countries*, London: Hutchinson, 1964.

341. Myrdal, Gunnar, *Asian Drama: An Inquiry into the Poverty of Nations*, New York: Twentieth Century Fund, 1968; also Pantheon Books, 1968.

342. _____, *Rich Lands and Poor*, New York: Harper and Row Publishers, 1957.
  An authoritative text on developmental economics. Attention is focussed on economic inequalities in the non-Soviet world--why and how they have come to exist and how these trends could be reversed.

343. Nash, Manning, "Multiple Society in Economic Development," *The American Anthropologist*, 59(October 1957), 825-33.

344. _____, *Primitive and Peasant Economic Systems*, Chicago: University of Chicago Press, 1966.

345. National Council of Applied Economic Research, *Rehabilitation and Development of Basti District: A Case Study in Economics of Depressed Areas*, Bombay: Asia Publishing House, 1959.
  In 1958 investigations were started to explore the problems of economic rehabilitation and development of Basti, one of the most backward

and depressed districts of Uttar Pradesh, a province of India. It examines forces which were responsible for the poverty and economic depression of this area. Part one is devoted to the life in Basti district, problems of economic development, and the programme for rehabilitation and development. Part two deals with problems of agriculture, industries, finance and credit, co-operatives population and manpower.

346. Novick, David E., and Robert Lekacchman, Development and Society, New York: St. Martin's Press, 1964.

347. Nurske, Ragnar, Problems of Capital Formation in Underdeveloped Countries, Oxford, England: Blackwell, 1953.

348. Okun, Bernard, and Richard Richardson (eds.), Studies in Economic Development, New York: Holt, Rinehart, and Winston, 1961.

349. Olson, Mancur, Jr., "Some Social and Political Implications of Economic Development," World Politics, 17, 3(April 1965), 525-54.
   This is a review article of the following books: Cyril A. Zebot, The Economics of Competitive Co-Existence, Convergence Through Growth; Zbigniew Brzezinski and Samuel P. Huntington, Political Power USA/USSR; Karl de Schweintiz, Industrialization and Democracy: Economic Necessities and Political Possibilities; Ronald Lersieth and Edgar Simkins, Corruption in Developing Countries; and Albert O. Hirschman, Journeys Toward Progress: Studies of Economic Policy-Making in Latin America.
   (These books have been annotated separately in this bibliography).

350. Palmier, Leslie H., "Improving Asia's Villages," Pacific Affairs, 36(Fall 1963), 283-89.
   A review article concerned with the problems of villages in a transitional society like that of Indonesia. The reviewer, however, has thrown considerable light on rural problems as they are being encountered in the emerging Asian nations in general.

350.1 Papanek, Gustav F. (ed.), Development Policy--Theory and Practice, Cambridge, Mass.: Harvard University Press, 1968.

351. Paul, Benjamin D. (ed.), Health, Culture and Community, New York: Russell Sage Foundation, 1955.

352. Pentony, Devere E., The Underdeveloped Lands: A Dilemma of the International Economy, San Francisco: Chandler Publishing Company, 1960.

353. Prasad, N., and B. N. Juyal (eds.), Impediments to Development in Developing Countries, Varanasi: Gandhian Institute of Studies, 1966.

353.1 Rakowski, Mieczyslaw (ed.), Efficiency of Investment in a Socialist Economy, New York: Pergamon Press.

354. Ramzani, R., The Middle East and the European Common Market, Charlottesville, Va.: University Press of Virginia, 1964.
   This is a critical evaluation of the decisions of E.E.C. with special emphasis on the demand of the European countries for Middle Eastern crude oil.

355. Raymond, Vernon, The Dilemma of Mexico's Development: The Roles of the

(B1)

Private and Public Sectors, Cambridge, Mass.: Harvard University Press, 1963.

    Raymond Vernon has examined the roles of the private and public sectors in Mexico, a crucial matter in today's world-wide effort to speed up economic development. An economist himself, his investigation leads him into the precincts of the political scientist, the sociologist, and the historian. Over the years, the ruling Mexican party has pursued two inconsistent objectives--universal consent for its action and the appearance of legitimacy in obtaining such consent. New governmental policies toward industry are called for today. But any change in the public sector's role in industry will provoke political reaction from part of the Mexican body politic, and Mexico's presidents seem determined not to risk a major shift in policy. By avoiding change, however, they court another danger--the risk of economic stagnation.

356. Reina, Ruben, "Political Crisis and Cultural Revitalization: The Guatemalan Case," *Human Organization*, 17(Winter 1958-1959), 14-18.

357. Robinson, Richard D., "Turkey's Agrarian Revolution and the Problem of Urbanization," *Public Opinion Quarterly*, 22(Fall 1958), 397-405.

358. Rosenstein-Rodan, P. N. (ed.), *Capital Formation and Development*, London: Allen and Unwin, 1964.

    Most of the contributors to this volume are from Harvard University or The Massachusetts Institute of Technology. The essays largely include mathematical models that are useful for planners.

359. _____, "Notes on the Theory of the Big Push," in Theodore Morgan (ed.), *Readings in Economic Development*, Belmont, Cal.: Wadsworth, 1963, 112-28.

360. Rostow, Walt W. (ed.), *The Economics of Take-off into Sustained Growth*, New York: St. Martin's Press, 1963.

361. _____, *The Stages of Economic Growth*, New York: Cambridge University Press, 1960.

362. Rubin, Vera, "The Anthropology of Development," *Biennial Review of Anthropology*, Stanford, 1961, 120-72.

363. Sametz, A. W., "Production of Goods and Services: The Measurement of Economic Growth," in Sheldon and Moore (eds.), *Indicators of Social Change*, New York: Russell Sage Foundation, 1968, 76-96.

365. Schaafhausen, Irma, *Development Through Mobilization of Own Resources Exemplified by Israel*, Hamburg, Germany: Hamburg Archives of World Economy, 1964.

366. Schickele, Rainer, *Agrarian Revolution and Economic Progress, A Primer for Development*, New York: Frederick A. Praeger Co., 1968.

367. Schramm, Wilbur, *Mass Media and National Development: The Role of Information in the Developing Countries*, Stanford, Cal.: Stanford University Press, 1964.

    The thesis of the author is that if the emerging nations want to develop economically and socially the adequate flow of information and proper use of the mass media are of indisputable significance. He discusses the intricate framework of cause and effect, the hurdles in the way of information flow, inadequacies of the present research, etc.

368. Schutz, Theodore W., <u>Transforming Traditional Agriculture: Comparative Economics</u>, New Haven, Conn.: Yale University Press, 1964.
The author's primary contention is that traditional agriculture can become a powerful vehicle of growth.

369. Shannon, Lyle W., <u>Underdeveloped Areas</u>, New York: Harper and Brothers, 1957.

370. Silcock, T. H., and E. K. Fisk (eds.), <u>The Political Economy of Independent Malaya: A Case Study in Development</u>, Canberra: Australian National University Press, 1963.
The book originated from the contributions of nine experts who participated in a seminar held at the Australian National University in 1963. All facets of Malaya's economy such as industrialization, rural development, rubber plantations, demography, exports, imports, balance of payments have been discussed with scholarly insight.

371. Silj, Alessandro, "Down with the year 2000," <u>Interplay</u>, 2(May 1969), 25-28.
People are becoming too interested in the "fallout of the post-industrial society" and too little interested in the problems that "the industrial society has dumped on us."

372. Sinai I. R., <u>The Challenge of Modernization: The West's Impact on the Non-Western World</u>, New York: W. W. Norton and Co., 1964.
West and the non-West are at cross-purposes on many accounts. Leaders of many underdeveloped countries are in revolt against western values and the west's position of dominance in the world. Mr. Sinai, journalist lecturer, has isolated many of the complex issues involved in this problem. The book is divided into five topics: the West and Asia, imperialism and its consequences, the Burmese dilemma, the irrelevance of Asian socialism, and the challenge of modernization.

373. Sisger, H. W., <u>International Development Growth and Change</u>, New York: McGraw-Hill Book Co., 1964.

374. Society for International Development, <u>Motivations and Methods in Development and Foreign Aid; Proceedings of the Sixth World Conference, March 16-18, 1964</u>, Washington, D. C.: Society for International Development, 1964.

375. Spengler, J. J., "Economic Development: Political Preconditions and Political Consequences," <u>Journal of Politics</u>, 22(August 1960), 387-416.
According to the writer's views, governments in less developed countries, over and above law and order function, must actively participate in the private and the public sectors.

376. _____, and Ralph Braibanti (eds.), <u>Traditions, Values, and Socio-Economic Development</u>, Durham, N. C.: Duke University Press, 1961.

377. Staley, Eugene, <u>The Future of Underdeveloped Countries: Political Implications of Economic Development</u>, New York: Harper and Brothers, 1961.
The book is divided into the following parts: "What is successful

(B1)

development?," "The communist path of development," "Democratic paths to development," and "Development in the sixties."

378. _____, and Richard Morse, <u>Modern Small Industry for Developing Countries</u>, New York: McGraw-Hill Book Company, 1965.

379. Stewart, Charles F., <u>The Economy of Morocco, 1912-1962</u>, Harvard Middle Eastern Monographs, 12, Cambridge, Mass.: Harvard University Press, 1964.

380. Strassmann, Paul W., <u>Technological Change and Economic Development: The Manufacturing Experience of Mexico and Puerto Rico</u>, Ithaca, N. Y.: Cornell University Press, 1968.

381. Tinbergen, Jan, <u>Central Planning</u>, New Haven, Conn.: Yale University Press, 1964.

382. Tsantis, Andreas C., "Political Factors in Economic Development," <u>Comparative Politics</u>, 2(October 1969), 63-78.

383. Turner, Roy (ed.), <u>India's Urban Future</u>, Berkeley: University of California Press, 1962.
   A compilation of twenty-three papers plus one editorial postscript prepared for a seminar on urbanization in India held at Berkeley in 1960. Participants included planners, social scientists, administrators, architects, politicians, and government officials from both India and the United States. The book examines two conflicting purposes of economic planning in developing countries: planning as the optimum use of men and materials for economic growth, and planning as initiation of non-economic values for overall national development.

384. United Nations, <u>The United Nations Development Decade: Proposals for Actions</u>, New York: United Nations, 1962.
   On December 19, 1961, the General Assembly designated the 1960s "The United Nations Development decade." In pursuance of this resolution, the Secretary General prepared a report for the consideration of the Economic and Social Council.

385. United Nations, <u>Co-operation for Economic Progress</u>, New York: United Nations, 1962.
   The booklet consists of the purposes, composition, and organization of the Four Economic Commissions for Europe, Asia and the Far East, Latin America and Africa. It is a general review of the activities of these international bodies and mention is also made of some of their accomplishments.

386. Vanek, Jaroslav, "A Theory of Growth with Technological Change," <u>American Economic Review</u>, 57(March 1967), 73-89.

387. _____, "Towards a More General Theory of Growth with Technological Change," <u>Economic Journal</u>, 76(December 1966), 841-54.

388. Vernon, Raymond, "Conflict and Resolution between Foreign Direct Investors and Less Developed Countries," <u>Public Policy</u>, 17, Cambridge, Mass.: John Fitzgerald Kennedy School of Government, Harvard University, 1968.

389. _____, "The Role of U. S. Enterprise Abroad," Daedalus, 98 (Winter 1969), 113-33.

390. von Vorys, Karl, "Some Political Incentives for Economic Development in India, Pakistan, Burma and Ceylon," Western Political Quarterly, 4 (December 1959), 1057-76.
   A general survey of the effect of political forces in the course of economic development in these four countries. The author's opinion is that leadership in planning in these countries is held by the civil servants who, in addition to their efficiency and competence, will have to create an image of a nation-state among the people.

391. Walinsky, Louis J., Social Development in Burma, 1951-60, Twentieth Century Fund, Inc., 1962.

392. Walterhouse, Harry F., A Time to Build Military Civic Action: Medium for Economic Development and Social Reform, Columbia, S. C.: The University of South Carolina Press, 1964.

393. Ward, Barbara, The Rich Nations and the Poor Nations, New York: W. W. Norton and Company, 1962.
   This is a compilation of the lectures given by the writer for the Canadian Broadcasting Corporation. The subjects include: "The rich nations," "The poor nations," "Communism's blueprint," "The economics of development," "The politics of development," and "Not by bread alone."

394. Ward, Robert E., and Dankwart A. Rustov (eds.), Turkey and Japan: A Comparative Study of Modernization, Princeton: Princeton University Press, 1964.

395. Weinberg, Ian, "The Problem of the Convergence of Industrial Societies: A Critical Look at the State of the Theory," Comparative Studies in Society and History, 2(January 1969), 1-15.

396. Weiner, Myron (ed.), Modernization: The Dynamics of Growth, New York: Basic Books, 1966.

397. Weisbrod, Burton A., and W. Lee Hansen, "An Income-Net Worth Approach to Measuring Economic Welfare," American Economic Review, 58(December 1968), 1315-29.
   Develops a way of measuring "current economic welfare" based on a combination of current income and current net worth and demonstrates ways in which this measure can affect public policy.

398. Wellisz, Stanislaw, The Economics of the Soviet Bloc: A Study of Decision Making and Resource Allocation, New York: McGraw-Hill Book Company, 1964.

399. Whyte, William F., and Lawrence Williams, Toward an Integrated Theory of Development, Ithaca, N. Y.: School of Industrial and Labor Relations, Cornell University, 1968.

400. Wickwar, W. Hardy, "Food and Social Development in the Middle East," The Middle East Journal, 19(Spring 1965), 177-93.
   "Life is not far above the subsistence level and much often below it." Ten years ago these remarks were made by a World Bank mission

(B1)

about Iraq. Such judgments are often passed about the countries of the Middle and Near East - Mr. Wickwar examines "some of the considerations and some of the evidence that lead to these conclusions, as well as such positive steps as have been taken to augment the food resources of the region."

401. Winsemius, Albert, and John A. Pincus, *Methods of Industrial Development With Special Reference to Less Developed Areas*, Paris: Organization for Economic Cooperation and Development, 1962.

    Contains the proceedings of a Conference organized by the European Productivity Agency of O.E.E.C. at Madrid April 10-15, 1961. Some of the papers deal with general problems of industrial development and others are case studies of countries such as Puerto Rico, Israel, Yugoslavia, Great Britain, and Turkey.

402. Wolf, Charles, and Sidney C. Sufrin, *Capital Formation and Foreign Investment in Underdeveloped Areas*, Syracuse, N. Y.: Syracuse University Press, 1955.

403. Younger, Kenneth, "Trained Manpower for New States: The Scope for International Action," *Public Administration: Journal of the Royal Institute of Public Administration* (London), 38(Spring 1960), 17-26.

    Trained manpower is a basic necessity for the development of new states. The transitional societies in addition to problem of educating their own people, have the special responsibility and problem of retaining older civil servants.

404. Zebot, Cyril A., *The Economics of Competitive Co-Existence: Convergence Through Growth*, New York: Frederick A. Praeger Co., 1964.

    The book proposes the thesis that the western nations, the Soviet bloc, and the underdeveloped nations have possibilities of resembling one another, if economic growth is continuous in these blocs.

2. POLITICAL AND ADMINISTRATIVE DEVELOPMENT

a. General

405. Adams, Richard N., The Second Sowing: Power and Secondary Development in Latin America, San Francisco: Chandler Publishing Co., 1967.

406. Adelman, Irma, and Cynthia Taft Morris, Society, Politics and Economic Development: A Quantitative Approach, Baltimore: Johns Hopkins University Press, 1967.

407. Adu, A. L., "Problems of Government in Emergent African States," International Review of Administrative Sciences, 26(1, 1960), 61-66.
    In the author's opinion, independence has given a tremendous impetus to economic growth of African countries. He emphasizes the role of leadership in an analysis of the situation in Ghana where competent leadership has been responsible for the economic progress of the country.

408. Agpalo, Remigio E., "Interest Groups and their Role in the Philippine Political System," Philippine Journal of Public Administration, 9(April 1965), 87-106.

409. Ahmad, J. M., The Intellectual Origins of Egyptian Nationalism, New York: Oxford University Press, 1960.
    A comprehensive survey of the contributions of the men of letters during the reawakening between 1850-70. He points out that the leaders during the formative period showed commitment to imported ideas of western liberalism for the establishment of nation-state in Egypt. The dominant theme of the book is that the early reformers believed that "no political revolution could take the place of a general transformation of the mind and heart of Egypt." An excellent account of the intellectual antecedents of Egyptian nationalism is presented.

410. Ahmad, Mushtaq, Government and Politics in Pakistan, Karachi: Pakistan Publishing House, 1963.
    A cogent account is given of the three phases of political and constitutional development in Pakistan including parliamentary democracy from the inception of Pakistan to its ultimate failure in 1958, an analysis of the various achievements of the Revolution, and an analytical survey of the presidential system.

411. Alderfer, Harold F., Local Government in Developing Countries, New York: McGraw-Hill Book Company, 1964.
    A general survey of the theory and practice of local government in developing countries. In his opinion most of the less developed countries in planning the framework of their local bodies keep in view four

(B2a)

models: British, French, Russian, and Traditional.

412. _____, and others, <u>Local Government in the United Arab Republic</u>, Cairo: Institute of Public Administration, 1963.
　　In 1960 local government was reorganized, and Central Ministry of Local government was constituted to supervise the work of local bodies in the country. Other legislative measures have strengthened the ideological approach of the government. Effort has been made to decentralize authority so that people can participate effectively.

413. _____, <u>Public Administration in New Nations</u>, New York: Frederick A. Praeger Co., 1967.

414. Almond, Gabriel A., <u>The Appeal of Communism</u>, Princeton, N. J.: Princeton University Press, 1966.

415. _____, and Sidney Verba, <u>The Civic Culture: Political Attitudes and Democracy in Five Nations</u>, Princeton, N. J.: Princeton University Press, 1963.

416. _____, and S. Bingham Powell, Jr., <u>Comparative Politics: A Developmental Approach</u>, Boston: Little-Brown & Co., 1966.

417. _____, "A Development Approach to Political System," <u>World Politics</u>, 17(January 1964), 183-214.

418. _____, "Political Development: Analytical and Normative Perspectives," <u>Comparative Political Studies</u>, 1(January 1969), 447-69.

419. _____, and James Coleman (eds.), <u>The Politics of the Developing Areas</u>, Princeton: Princeton University Press, 1960.

420. Anderson, Charles W., <u>Politics and Economic Change in Latin America: The Governing of Restless Nations</u>, Princeton, N. J.: Van Nostrand, 1967.

421. _____, and Fred R. Von der Mehden, and Crawford Young, <u>Issues of Political Development</u>, Englewood Cliffs, N. J.: Prentice-Hall, 1967.

422. Andrain, Charles, and David E. Apter, "Comparative Government: Developing New Nations," <u>Journal of Politics</u>, 30(May 1968), 372-412.

423. Angus, N. C., and others, <u>The Expert and Administration in New Zealand</u>, Wellington: New Zealand Institute of Public Administration, 1959.

424. Appleby, Paul H., <u>Public Administration for a Welfare State</u>, London: Asia Publishing House, 1961.
　　The book consists of four lectures which Paul H. Appleby delivered at the Indian Institute of Public Administration in December 1961: (1) "Individual initiation in a welfare state," (2) "The politician and the administrator," (3) "The generalist and the specialist in administration," and (4) "Character of the good administrator."

425. Apter, David E., <u>The Politics of Modernization</u>, Chicago: University of Chicago Press, 1965.

426. _____, "The Role of Traditionalism in the Political

(B2a)

Modernization of Ghana and Uganda," <u>World Politics</u>, 13(October 1960), 45-68.

427. _____, <u>Some Conceptual Approaches to the Study of Modernization</u>, Englewood Cliffs, N. J.: Prentice-Hall, 1968.

428. Ashford, Douglas E., "Contradiction of Nationalism and Nation-Building in the Muslim World," <u>The Middle East Journal</u>, 18(Autumn 1964), 421-30.
   The author believes that during the past decade the Muslim World has been making a hectic drive towards modernization, and contends, "The differences among generations, social classes, political groups, and economic interests appear to be expanding rather than contracting with modernization."

429. _____, "Patterns of Group Development in a New Nation: Morocco," <u>The American Political Science Review</u>, 55(June 1961), 321-32.
   An inquiry into the basic principle of group theory "that important political characteristics are regularly associated with the number of nationally active groups." For the purpose of analysis the author has divided Morocco into three regions according to their level of development and awakening in national politics. Assessment was made of seven nationally active groups in these regions.

430. Austin, Dennis, <u>Politics in Ghana 1946-1960</u>, London: Oxford University Press, 1964.

431. Bailey, F. G., <u>Politics and Social Change</u>, Berkeley: University of California Press, 1963.

432. Baldwin, G. B., "The Foreign Educated Iranian: A Profile," <u>Middle East Journal</u>, 17(Summer 1963), 264-78.

433. Banks, Arthur S., and Robert B. A. Texter, <u>Cross-Polity Survey</u>, Cambridge, Mass.: The M.I.T. Press, 1963.
   Through the use of a computer the authors (Banks is a Political Scientist and Texter an Anthropologist) have used the data from 115 independent polities to establish an intellectual base for verifying and testing important generalizations about social and political systems.

434. Barnett, A. D. (ed.), <u>Communist Strategies in Asia: A Comparative Analysis of Governments and Parties</u>, New York: Frederick A. Praeger Co., 1963.
   A study of the communist regimes and parties in Asia. Through comparison, similarities and differences have been carefully examined. Efforts are also expended to investigate relations among them and their impact on the Sino-Soviet dispute.

435. Bayley, David H., "The Effects of Corruption in a Developing Nation," <u>Western Political Quarterly</u>, 19(December 1966), 719-32.

436. _____, "The Pedagogy of Democracy: Coercive Public Protest in India," <u>The American Political Science Review</u>, 57(September 1962), 663-72.
   Since the beginning of the 20th century, the public opinion in India has been dominated by the idea that institutional and constitutional means are inadequate to remedy grievances, frustrations and wrongs. The result has been that agitation, hungerstrikes, black flag demonstrations

have become regular features of India's political process. The author has remarked that since the British withdrawal the basic suspicion persists that government is still alien and elite although now the separation is based upon indigenous social division rather than upon foreign conquest and race.

437. _____, *Public Liberties in the New States*, Chicago: Rand McNally, 1964.

438. Behrendt, R. F., "The Emergence of New Elites and New Political Integration Forms and Their Influence on Economic Development," *Transactions of the Fifth World Congress of Sociology*, 2, 3-32.

439. Bendix, Richard, *Nation-Building and Citizenship*, New York: John Wiley and Sons, 1964.

440. Bienen, Henry, *Violence and Modernization*, Chicago: University of Chicago Press, 1968.

441. Binder, Leonard, *Religion and Politics in Pakistan*, Berkeley, California: University of California Press, 1961.
   The author has examined various religio-political forces which retarded the progress of constitution-making.

442. Black, Cyril Edwin, *The Dynamics of Modernization: A Study in Comparative History*, New York: Harper & Row, 1966.

443. Bobrow, Davis B., "Soldiers and the Nation-State," *The Annals of American Academy of Political and Social Science*, 358(March 1965), 65-76.

444. Braibanti, Ralph, and Joseph Spengler (eds.), *Administrative and Economic Development in India*, Durham, N. C.: Duke University Press, 1963.

445. Braibanti, Ralph, "The Civil Service of Pakistan: A Theoretical Analysis," *South Atlantic Quarterly*, 58(Spring 1959), 258-303.

446. _____ (ed.), *Politics and Administrative Development*, Durham, N. C.: Duke University Press, 1969.

447. Brausch, Georges, *Belgian Administration in the Congo*, London: Oxford University Press, 1961.

448. Brecher, Michael, *The New States of Asia: A Political Analysis*, New York: Oxford University Press, 1963.
   The volume consists of six essays concerning various aspects of national and international transactions of the new states of Asia. There are chapters on colonialism, neutralism, and political stability.

449. Bretton, Henry L., *Power and Stability in Nigeria: The Politics of Decolonization*, New York: Frederick A. Praeger Co., 1962.

450. Brockway, Fenner, *African Socialism*, London: Bodley Head, 1963.

451. Brzezinski, Zbigniew, and Samuel P. Huntington, *Political Power: USA/USSR*, New York: Viking Press, 1964.
   The authors support W. W. Rostow's view that as the USA and USSR

become societies of high mass consumption, they would attain general resemblance. But after making a thorough examination of the two political systems, they come to the conclusion that even if the two countries attain economic resemblance, they will never be able to reduce their political differences.

452. Burke, Fred G., *Local Government and Politics in Uganda*, Syracuse, New York: Syracuse University Press, 1964.

453. _____, "Public Administration in Africa--The Legacy of Inherited Colonial Institutions," *Journal of Comparative Administration*, 1 (November 1969), 345-78.

454. Caiden, Gerald, "Coping with Turbulence--Israel's Administrative Experience," *Journal of Comparative Administration*, 1(November 1969), 259-80.

455. Caplow, Theodore, and Kurt Finsterbusch, "Development Rank: A New Method of Rating National Development," unpublished paper, New York: Columbia University Bureau of Applied Social Research, 1966.

456. Carlson, Sune, *Development Economics and Administration*, Bonniers: Svenska Bok for Laget, 1964.

457. Christoph, James B. (ed.), *Cases in Comparative Politics*, Boston: Little-Brown & Co., 1965.

458. Coleman, James S. (ed.), *Education and Political Development*, Princeton, N. J.: Princeton University Press, 1965.

460. The Congress for Cultural Freedom, *Problems of Administration*, Cairo: Dar-al-Maaref, 1959.

461. Cottam, Richard, *Nationalism in Iran*, Pittsburgh: University of Pittsburgh Press, 1964.

462. Cutright, Philip, "National Political Development: Measurement and Analysis," *American Sociological Review*, 28(April 1963), 253-64.
    Applying comparative methods to national political systems, the author attempts to build an index of political development which can be correlated with other system variables. The level of political development is highly correlated with the level of communication, economic development, education and urbanization. The author believes that "Analysis of the errors of prediction of what the level of political development should be, given its level of communications and urbanization development, allows the testing of certain theories of social change." The author considers the extent to which a nation diverges from its predicted level of political development and possible ways to utilize these errors of prediction. He also discusses the ability of social scientists to test theories concerning revolution, mass movements, and political change.

463. Daalder, H., *The Role of the Military in Emerging Countries*, S'Gravenhage, Netherlands: Mouton, 1962.

464. Daland, Robert T., *Comparative Urban Research: The Administration and Politics of Cities*, Beverly Hills, Cal.: Sage Publications, 1969.

(B2a)

465. _____, "Development Administration and the Brazilian Political System," *Western Political Quarterly*, 21(June 1968), 335-39.

466. Dang, Nghiem, *Vietnam: Politics and Administration*, Honolulu, Hawaii: East-West Center Press, 1966.
    The author traces events and forces that have formed the traditional Vietnamese concept of government. These include nine centuries of Confucian and Taoist emphases under Chinese domination; nine centuries of independence and expansion southward where Indian and Buddhist influences were encountered; nearly a century of French colonialism; and, following World War II, independence.

467. de Guzman, Raul P. (ed.), *Patterns in Decision-Making, Case Studies in Philippine Public Administration*, Manila: Graduate School of Public Administration, University of the Philippines, 1963.
    A collection of fifteen administrative studies prepared by staff members of the Graduate School of Public Administration. The cases have been carefully selected so that the reader can gain a substantial amount of information on various aspects of Philippine administration.

467.1 Department of Economic and Social Affairs, Public Administration Division, *Appraising Administrative Capability for Development*, *A Methodological Monograph Prepared by the International Group for Studies in National Planning* (Interplan), New York: United Nations, 1969.

468. de Smith, S. A., *The New Commonwealth and Its Constitutions*, London: Stevens, 1964.
    Surveys constitutional developments of member nations of the commonwealth. Emphasis is on countries which have acquired their constitutions since 1957.

469. Deutsch, Karl W., Philip E. Jacob, Henry Teune, James V. Toscano, and William L. C. Wheaton, *The Integration of Political Communities*, Philadelphia: J. B. Lippincott, 1964.
    Integration of political behavior at the metropolitan and international levels is explored in ten essays. These essays concern such items as communication, planning and regional science, local government, and social structure.

470. Deutsch, Karl W., and William J. Foltz (eds.), *Nation-Building*, New York: Altherton Press, 1963.

471. Dey, S. K., *Panchayati Raj: A Synthesis*, Bombay: Asia Publishing House, 1962.

472. Dix, Robert H., *Columbia, The Political Dimensions of Change*, New Haven, Conn.: Yale University Press, 1967.

473. du Sautoy, Peter, "Some Administrative Aspects of Community Development," *Journal of Local Administration Overseas*, 1(January 1962), 39-46.

474. Dusek, Val, "Falsifiability and Power Elite Theory," *Journal of Comparative Administration*, 1(August 1969), 198-212.

475. Dwarkadas, R., *Reflections on Indian Administration*, Delhi: Kitab Mahal, 1960.

476. Eckstein, J., and David Apter, <u>Comparative Politics</u>, New York: Free Press, 1963.
    A detailed and comprehensive reader on the subject of comparative politics covering such topics as: (1) present trends in comparative politics, (2) constitutional and representative government, (3) electoral systems, (4) political parties, (5) pressure and interest groups, (6) totalitarianism and autocracy, (7) political change, and (8) non-western government and politics.

477. Ehrmann, Henry W. (ed.), <u>Democracy in a Changing Society</u>, New York: Frederick A. Praeger Co., 1964.

478. _____ (ed.), <u>Interest Groups on Four Continents</u>, Pittsburgh: University of Pittsburgh Press, 1960.
    This book contains proceedings and reports from nine countries at a roundtable conference held by International Political Science Association in Pittsburgh in 1957. These include discussions of the identification, internal organization and public relations of pressure groups, the consideration of interest groups, influence on political parties and the governmental process, and the overall effects of groups on consensus and decision-making.

479. Eisenstadt, S. N., "Initial Institutional Patterns of Political Modernizations, a Comparative Study," <u>Civilizations</u>, 12(1962), 461-72.

480. _____, "Political Modernization; Some Comparative Notes," <u>International Journal of Comparative Sociology</u>, 5(March 1964), 3-24.

481. _____, "Transformation of Social, Political, and Cultural Orders in Modernization," <u>American Sociological Review</u>, 30(October 1965), 810-825.

482. Eldersveld, S. J., V. Jagannadham, and A. P. Barnabas, <u>The Citizen in a Developing Democracy: An Empirical Study in Delhi State, India</u>, Glenview, Ill.: Scott, Foresman & Co., 1968.

483. Emerson, Rupert, <u>From Empire to Nation: The Rise to Self-Assertion of Asian and African Peoples</u>, Cambridge, Mass.: Harvard University Press, 1960.
    A detailed and scholarly account of the processes and procedures by which colonial people are now moving towards nationalism and democracy.

483.1 _____, <u>Political Modernization: The Single-Party System</u>, Denver: University of Denver, 1963.

484. Esman, Milton J., "The Politics of Development Administration," Chicago: Comparative Administration Group of American Society for Public Administration, 1963 (mimeographed).
    A novel approach to implementing institutional changes in developing societies.

485. Ezera, Kalu, <u>Constitutional Developments in Nigeria</u>, London: Cambridge University Press, 1960.
    A historical account of the post World War II constitutional conferences and changes which led to the independence of Nigeria. The author gives an objective view of the various internal and external forces

(B2a)

which from time to time influenced the course of constitutional events. The last chapter enumerates the problems and difficulties which developed in the wake of independence.

486. Fallers, L. A. (ed.), The Kings Men: Leadership and Status in Buganda on the Eve of Independence, New York: Oxford University Press, 1964.
The book begins with a detailed and insightful essay on the economic structure of Buganda by C. C. Wrigley. This is followed by chapters on social stratification, authority in a village community, and attitudes towards authority.

487. Feith, Herbert, The Decline of Constitutional Democracy in Indonesia, Ithaca, N. Y.: Cornell University Press, 1962.
The author spent four years in Indonesia to collect data for this book and has unearthed an impressive mass of data on all aspects of Indonesia's political and constitutional history. The study gives an almost month to month account of the events from 1949 to the emergence of guided democracy in 1957.

488. Ferkiss, Victor C., "The Coexistent Universes of Comparative Administration," Journal of Comparative Administration, 1(August 1969), 177-92.

489. Field, Lowell G., Comparative Political Development: The Precedent of the West, Ithaca, N. Y.: Cornell University Press, 1967.

490. Finer, S. E., The Man on Horseback, New York: Frederick A. Praeger Co., 1962.
An account of the role of military in developing societies. In the opinion of the author "every country gets the degree of military intervention it deserves." His contention is that the military has the monopoly of force in every modern nation. Through superior discipline and organization it is always in a position to take over machinery of government.

491. Finkle, Jason, and Richard Gable (eds.), Political Development and Social Change, New York: John Wiley and Sons, 1966.

492. Fischer, J., "Universities and the Political Process in Southeast Asia," Pacific Affairs, 36(Spring 1963), 3-15.
The role of the University in the political transformation of the developing countries is analyzed. Their University relationships with government policies and nation-building processes are also examined, and an investigation is made about the impact of University education on the training and behavior of a political and administrative elite.

493. Fox, Guy H., and Charles A. Joiner, "Perceptions of the Vietnamese Administrative System," Administrative Science Quarterly, 8(March 1964), 443-48.
The article is based on interviews with top level Vietnamese civil servants. The Vietnamese administration is permeated with the mandarin philosophy. The results of the inquiry show that at present the top civil servants believe that for purposes of development centralization of administration was essential. However, ascriptive leadership in a country breeds irrationality in administration.

494. Froman, Lewis A., Jr., People and Politics, Englewood Cliffs, N. J.: Prentice-Hall, Inc., 1962.
Especially useful for his definition of terms.

(B2a)

495. Furse, Sir Ralph, <u>Aucuparious: Recollections of a Recruiting Officer</u>, London: Oxford University Press, 1962.
An autobiography of a man who was solely responsible for the recruitment of colonial civil servants of Great Britain during the inter-war period. The book furnishes insights into the policy-making procedures at the colonial office.

497. Gant, George F., "A Note on Applications of Development Administration," <u>Public Policy</u>, 15(1966), 199-211.

498. Gaus, John M., and others, <u>Frontiers of Public Administration</u>, Chicago: Public Administration Service, 1936.

499. Geertz, Clifford (ed.), <u>Old Societies and New States: A Quest for Modernity in Asia and Africa</u>, New York: Free Press, 1963.
Contents include articles by McKin Marriott on cultural policies of new states, David Apter on political religion, Clifford Geertz on civil politics, Lloyd Fallers on modernity and democracy, Max Rheinstein on legal problems, Mary Joan Bowman and C. Arnold Anderson on the role of education in development, and Robert Levine on the process of political socialization.

500. Ginsburgh, R. N., "The Challenge to Military Professionalism," <u>Foreign Affairs</u>, 42(January 1964), 255-68.

501. Glickman, Harvey, "One-Party System in Tanganyika," <u>The Annals of the American Academy of Political and Social Science</u>, 358(March 1965), 136-59.
Nation-Building in Tanganyika is being piloted by a one-party system with the Tanganyika African National Union (TANU) dominating every sphere of national life. As a party in power it controls all projects of economic development and social change; it supervises every segment of national economy. Bureaucracy for all practical purposes is integrated into the party structure.

502. Gluckman, Max, <u>Politics, Law and Ritual in Tribal Society</u>, Chicago: Aldine Publishing Company, 1965.
An examination of the political systems of tribal societies. Contents include: (1) data and theory, (2) property rights and economic activity, (3) stateless societies, (4) the state and civil strife, (5) dispute and settlement, (6) mystical disturbance and ritual adjustment, and (7) custom and stability and change.

504. Guenther, H. P., "The Beirut Management College, An Experiment in Management Training for a Developing Nation," <u>The Middle East Journal</u>, 7 (Autumn 1963), 368-82.

505. Gutheridge, William F., <u>Military Institutions and Power in the New States</u>, New York: Frederick A. Praeger Co., 1965.

506. Halpern, Manfred, <u>The Politics of Social Change in the Middle East and North Africa</u>, Princeton, N. J.: Princeton University Press, 1963.
The author in his foreword states: "The area from Morocco to Pakistan is in the midst of a profound revolution. The book attempts to analyze the ideas, and institutions now in motion, and estimate the

(B2a)

direction which politics may take in the future in the Middle East and North Africa." The range and depth of the material can be indicated by the titles of the parts - (1) the legacy of the past, (2) the change structure of society, (3) the range of political choices, (4) the instruments of modernization, and (5) the cost and the consequences of choices.

507. _____, "The Rate and Costs of Political Development," <u>The Annals of the American Academy of Political and Social Science</u>, 358 (March 1965), 20-28.

"Increments of power, substance or efficiency, alone are not sufficient to create strength among social systems to conduct change in modern times. Nations which are undergoing radical changes require an inherent and continuous capacity to assimilate transformation." The author also discusses the role of ideology as a major instrument for creating a new political culture. A discussion of alternative costs of failing and succeeding in modernization leads to the conclusion that for most nations success will depend on the capacity of international society to deal with system transformation.

508. Harris, Richard L., "Administrative Systems of Canada and Ceylon," <u>Administrative Science Quarterly</u>, 8(December 1963), 339-60.

Ecological approach in recent years has been fruitful instrument for the comparative study of administrative systems. This is a pioneer study within this frame of reference.

509. Heady, Ferrel, and Sybil L. Stokes (eds.), <u>Papers in Comparative Public Administration</u>, Ann Arbor, Mich.: Institute of Public Administration, University of Michigan, 1962.

Most of the articles are of a theoretical nature. The author and titles are: (1) "Comparative public administration: concerns and priorities" by Heady, "An ecological approach: the Sala Model" by Riggs, "An information-energy model" by Dorsey, "The political role of field administration" by Fesler, and "Control and responsibility in administration comparative aspects" by Morstein Marx. Other articles cover the nations of Nigeria, Ghana, Thailand and Israel.

510. Heady, Ferrel, <u>Public Administration: A Comparative Perspective</u>, Englewood Cliffs, N. J.: Prentice-Hall, 1966.

511. Heaphey, James, and Philip Kronenberg, <u>Toward Theory Building in Comparative Public Administration: A Functional Approach</u>, Occasional Paper, Washington, D. C.: Comparative Administration Group of the American Society for Public Administration, 1966.

512. Heckscher, Gunnar, <u>The Study of Comparative Government and Politics</u>, London: Allen and Unwin Ltd., 1960.

A report of a roundtable conference on research methods and teaching procedures in comparative government held by the International Political Science Association in Florence, Italy, in 1954.

513. Henderson, Keith M., "Comparative Public Administration: The Identity Crisis," <u>Journal of Comparative Administration</u>, 1(May 1969), 65-84.

514. _____, "The Old Public Administration: Five British

Instances," <u>Journal of Comparative Administration</u>, 1(August 1969), 249-55.

515. Heussler, Robert, <u>Yesterday's Rulers: Making of British Colonial Service</u>, Syracuse, N. Y.: Syracuse University Press, 1963.
   Gives a historical and critical account of the British colonial service. After a brief chapter on the pre-World War I establishment, the author devotes most of the book to the inter-war development of the colonial service. The chapters on the educational background of the colonial civil servants are particularly insightful.

516. Hicks, Ursula K., <u>Development From Below, Local Government and Finance in Developing Countries of the Commonwealth</u>, Oxford: Claredon Press, 1961.

517. Honey, John C., <u>Toward Strategies of Public Administration Development in Latin America</u>, Syracuse, N. Y.: Syracuse University Press, 1968.

518. Horowitz, Irving, <u>Three Worlds of Development: The Theory and Practice of International Stratification</u>, New York: Oxford, 1966.

519. Hsueh, S. S. (ed.), <u>Public Administration in South and Southeast Asia</u>, Brussels: International Institute of Administrative Sciences, 1962.
   A book of readings which was compiled at the request of the International Institute of Administrative Sciences. The thesis is that for the proper understanding of the people it is essential to know the administrative environments in which they live. The countries examined include Burma, Cambodia, Indonesia, Japan, Korea, Malaya, Nepal, Pakistan, Philippines, Thailand, Vietnam, and Ceylon.

520. Humes, Samuel, and Eilean H. Martin, <u>The Structure of Local Governments Throughout the World</u>, The Hague: Nijhoff, 1961.
   Contains materials on the problems of local government in forty-three countries. The first half makes a comparative analysis of the organization and structures of local governments. The second deals with individual countries.

521. Hunter, Guy, <u>Education for A Developing Region--A Study in East Africa</u>, London: Allen and Unwin, 1963.

521.1 _____, <u>Modernizing Peasant Societies</u>, London: Overseas Development Institute, 1969.

522. Huntington, Samuel P., "Political Development and Political Decay," <u>World Politics</u>, 17(April 1965), 386-430.

523. _____, "Political Modernization: America vs. Europe," <u>World Politics</u>, 18(April 1966), 378-414.

524. _____, <u>Political Order in Changing Societies</u>, New Haven, Conn.: Yale University Press, 1968.

525. Hyman, Herbert, <u>Political Socialization: A Study in the Psychology of Political Behavior</u>, New York: The Free Press, 1962.

526. Ilchman, Warren F., "The Unproductive Study of Productivity: Public

(B2a)

Administration in Developing Nations," <u>Comparative Political Studies</u>, 1 (July 1968), 227-49.

527. Janowitz, Morris, <u>The Military in the Political Development of New Nations: An Essay in Comparative Analysis</u>, Chicago: The University of Chicago Press, 1964.

528. Jennings, Sir Ivor, <u>Democracy in Africa</u>, London: Cambridge University Press, 1963.

529. Johnson, John J., <u>The Military and Society in Latin America</u>, Stanford: Stanford University Press, 1964.

530. _____ (ed.), <u>The Role of the Military in Underdeveloped Countries</u>, Princeton, N. J.: Princeton University Press, 1962.

531. Jowitt, Kenneth, "The Relevance of Comparative Public Administration to American Political Life," <u>Journal of Comparative Administration</u>, 1(May 1969), 85-93.

532. Katz, Saul M., <u>Guide to Modernizing Administration for National Development</u>, Pittsburgh: Graduate Institute of Public and International Affairs, 1965.

533. Kautsky, John H. (ed.), <u>Political Change in Underdeveloped Countries: Nationalism and Communism</u>, London: John Wiley and Sons, 1962.
    In the first part of the book the editor has written a long essay on the politics of development. It throws light on industrialization, nationalism, communism and totalitarianism. Part two has twelve articles on various aspects of political processes in the developing countries.

534. Kebschull, Harvey G. (ed.), <u>Politics in Transitional Societies</u>, New York: Appleton-Century-Crofts, 1968.

535. Khan, Muhammad Ayub, "A New Experiment in Democracy in Pakistan," <u>The Annals of the American Academy of Political and Social Science</u>, 358 (March 1965), 109-13.
    The parliamentary system, which was the legacy of the British, was not adequate to the needs of the new state. In 1958 President Ayub assumed responsibility for running the government. The article gives the views of the President on Basic Democracies and the 1962 Constitution.

536. Khera, S. S., <u>District Administration in India</u>, New Delhi: Indian Institute of Public Administration, 1960.
    Consists of three lectures which the author delivered at the Indian Institute of Public Administration in November 1957. The district is still one of the pivotal territorial administrative units in South Asia. At the time when the author delivered these lectures he was Secretary to the Government of India. The narrative draws upon the experience he had as a district officer.

537. Kilson, Martin L., "Authoritarian and Single-Party Tendencies in African Politics," <u>World Politics</u>, 16(January 1963), 262-94.
    There is a growing tendency among African countries to establish one-party rule. The author explores the causes of this tendency, and

(B2a)

discusses the future prospects of opposition in these countries.

538. Kingsbury, Joseph B., and Tahir Aktan, *The Public Service in Turkey*, Brussels: International Institute of Administrative Sciences, 1955.
    An introduction to Turkish Civil Service. The booklet starts with geography, people and historical background of social and political reforms. The rest of the narrative is devoted to the structural aspects of the government administration, dealing with problems of personnel administration, education, and training discussed briefly.

538.1 Kriesberg, Martin (ed.), *Public Administration in Developing Countries*, Washington, D. C.: The Brookings Institution, 1963.

539. Kriesberg, Martin, "Senior Civil Servants and the Teaching of Public Administration in Underdeveloped Countries," *International Review of Administrative Sciences*, 23(1959), 336-39.
    The author begins his analysis by pointing out that in most developing countries emphasis is laid on the training of young recruits who have joined the government service. The training of senior civil servants is generally overlooked. The writer makes suggestions which can be used for inculcating extra initiative and efficiency among senior civil servants.

540. Kroll, Morton, "Social Science, Scientism and Coexistent Universes: Comments on the Gunnell and Ferkiss Papers," *Journal of Comparative Administration*, 1(August 1969), 193-97.

541. Lane, Robert, "The Decline of Politics and Ideology in a Knowledgeable Society," *American Sociological Review*, 31(October 1966), 649-62.

542. La Palombara, Joseph, and Myron Weiner (eds.), *Political Parties and Political Development*, Princeton, N. J.: Princeton University Press, 1966.

543. Lasswell, Harold D., "The Policy Sciences of Development," *World Politics*, 17(January 1965), 286-310.

544. Leach, E., *Political Systems of Highland Burma*, (2nd ed.), Boston: Beacon Press, 1965.
    In this book techniques of sociological analysis have been used to examine political systems of developing societies.

545. Lee, Hahn-Been, *Korea: Time, Change, and Administration*, Honolulu: East-West Center Press, 1968.
    A "time orientation approach" is developed and utilized to study the various aspects of Korea's governmental, environmental and program changes from 1945 to 1960. "Developmentalist time," an attitude involving positive, future orientation operating in the proper ecological atmosphere is seen as an essential ingredient for proper country development.

546. Lerner, Daniel, and Richard D. Rolinson, "The Turkish Army as a Modernizing Force," *World Politics*, 13(October 1960), 19-44.

547. Levy, Marion J., Jr., "Patterns (Structures) of Modernization and Political Development," *The Annals of the Academy of Political Science*, 358(March 1965), 29-40.

"Degrees of modernization are defined by the ratio of inanimate to animate sources of power." The conclusion is that modernization will mitigate the differences between the advanced and less advanced societies and creates fundamental resemblances.

548. Lieuwen, Edwin, *Aims and Politics in Latin America*, New York: Frederick A. Praeger Co., 1961.
    The first part of the book deals with the political and social role of the armed forces of Latin America and the second with the military aspects of United States policy toward Latin America. The book analyzes the transitional process as these countries strive to shed the "shackles" of militarism. Criticizing current United States policy, the book points out that basing political gains upon military ties is a dangerous game.

549. McClelland, D., *The Achieving Society*, Princeton, N. J.: Van Nostrand Co., 1961.

551. Macridis, Roy C., *The Study of Comparative Government*, New York: Random House, 1962.

552. Mair, Lucy P., *New Nations*, Chicago: University of Chicago Press, 1963.
    Examines emergent Africa in terms of the changes taking place in the structure of society. Entry into large-scale society is an expansion of the existing fields of choice in the matter of rights and obligations. The choice is not between different customs but between the authority of village headman and that of employer, between the community of kin and age-mates and that of church or trade union, between dependence on the family herds and on the market for cattle. The entry into new relationships often brings disregard of pre-existing ones and a resultant conflict of values. This interpretation of the process of social change in underdeveloped countries helps to explain the slow acceptance of technological change in African and other "new" nations.

553. Malenbaum, Wilfred, "Economic Factors and Political Development," *The Annals of the American Academy of Political and Social Science*, 358 (March 1965), 41-51.
    Traditionally, scholars associate political, social, and cultural advancement with economic growth, and economic growth is deemed to generate from "inputs of capital and technology of the right type and proportion." More than money and physical resources, "administrative guidance and devoted leadership" should be procured for stability and development.

554. Mansur, Fatima, *Process of Independence*, New York: Humanities Press, 1962.

556. Micaud, Charles A., and others, *Tunisia: The Politics of Modernization*, London: Pall Mall Press, 1964.
    The contributors to this volume acquired their information during their stay in Tunisia in 1960 and 1961. An article by Leon Carl Brown traces the history of Tunisia between 1881 and 1933. It shows the effects and consequences of the French contact. Clement Henry-Moore deals with the New-Dastour movement since 1934, and Charles A. Micaud gives an account of the social and economic changes since the disappearance of the Protectorate in 1956.

(B2a)

558. Miles, Arnold, and Alan L. Dean, <u>Issues and Problems in the Administrative Organization of National Governments</u>, Brussels: International Institute of Administrative Sciences, 1959.
   This booklet deals with such concepts as responsibility, authority, delegation, organization, leadership, and form of organization.

559. Millen, Bruce H., <u>The Political Role of Labor in Developing Countries</u>, Washington, D. C.: The Brookings Institute, 1963.
   This small treatise attempts to analyze the role of trade unions in politics of the developing countries of Asia and Africa. Primarily a handbook for the U. S. A. officials who work with these trade unions, the focus is on the future of these labor organizations, rather than on their present conditions.

560. Millikan, Max F., <u>The Role of Popular Participation in Development: Report of a Conference on the Implementation of Title IX of the Foreign Assistance Act, June 24 to Aug. 2, 1968</u>, Cambridge: The M.I.T. Press, 1969.

561. Milne, R. S., "Differentiation and Administrative Development," <u>Journal of Comparative Administration</u>, 1(August 1969), 213-33.

562. Montgomery, John D., and William J. Siffin (eds.), <u>Approaches to Development: Politics, Administration and Change</u>, New York: McGraw-Hill Book Co., 1966.

563. Montgomery, John D., <u>Forced To Be Free: The Artificial Revolution in Germany and Japan</u>, Chicago: University of Chicago Press, 1957.

565. Morris, G. M., <u>Modernizing Government Budget Administration--The Application of Technical Co-operation in Improving Budget Administration in the Governments of Developing Countries</u>, Washington: Agency for International Development, 1962.
   The monograph has been prepared for the Public Administration Division of Agency for International Development. The first purpose is to assist AID officials in understanding budgetary procedures, and second to help the officials of the host country to understand some of the modernized techniques for better perspective. In an effort to do so, it deals with the following topics: the budget in modern governments, budgeting and government development, the essential elements of an effective budget system, organization and staffing of the budget agency, techniques of budget administration, and technical assistance in budget modernization.

566. Mosher, Frederick C., <u>Democracy and the Public Service</u>, New York: Oxford University Press, 1968.
   Addresses "the question of how a protected public service, removed from direct electoral control, can be made to operate in a manner compatible with democracy, and kept responsive to the public."

567. National Institute of Public Administration, <u>Wheeler Report: Report of the Government of India Secretariat Committee 1935-36</u>, Karachi: National Institute of Public Administration, 1963.
   This is a comprehensive survey of the philosophy and structure of the British-India secretariat system. The Committee spent six months in studying the central and provincial secretariats and made pertinent observations and recommendations on procedures and practices; some of

(B2a)

which were as old as 1772 when Warren Hastings first established a secretariat on the sub-continent.

568. National Institute of Public Administration, <u>Maxwell Report: Report of the Government of India Secretariat Organization and Procedure 1937</u>, Karachi: National Institute of Public Administration, 1963.
    The Government of India Act 1935 envisaged a federation for Indo-Pakistan sub-continent. Hoping that the federal part of the Act would be implemented, the Government of India appointed the Maxwell Committee to review the position of the Central Departments under Federation. Since administrative structure of Pakistan is still basically patterned on the British India model, Maxwell Report provides historical perspective.

569. Nettle, J. P., <u>Political Mobilization: A Sociological Analysis of Methods and Concepts</u>, New York: Basic Books, 1967.

570. Nsarkoh, J. K., <u>Local Government in Ghana</u>, Accra: Ghana University Press, 1964.

571. Organski, A. F. K., <u>The Stages of Political Development</u>, New York: Alfred A. Knopf, 1965.

573. Packenham, Robert A., "Approaches to the Study of Political Development," <u>World Politics</u>, 17(October 1964), 108-21.

574. Pennock, J. Roland, "Political Development, Political Systems and Political Goods," <u>World Politics</u>, 18(April 1966), 415-34.

575. _____ (ed.), <u>Self-Government in Modernizing Nations</u>, Englewood Cliffs, N. J.: Prentice-Hall, 1964.

576. Potter, David C., <u>Government in Rural India--An Introduction to Contemporary District Administration</u>, London: Bell and Co., 1964.

577. Pye, Lucian W., <u>Aspects of Political Development</u>, Boston: Little-Brown, 1966.

578. _____ (ed.), <u>Communications and Political Development</u>, Princeton, N. J.: Princeton University Press, 1963, 1965.

579. _____, "The Concept of Political Development," <u>The Annals of American Academy of Political and Social Science</u>, 358(March 1965), 1-13.
    The concept of political development is a subject of unending controversy among political scientists. The confusion has increased in recent years because political and economic developments are so closely linked. The author has analyzed ten definitions of political development and gives a summary view of the dimensions of the concept which are being encountered in developing societies.

580. _____, <u>Guerrilla Communism in Malaya: A Study in Political Behavior</u>, Princeton, N. J.: Princeton University Press, 1956.

581. _____, "The Non-Western Political Process," <u>Journal of Politics</u>, 20(August 1958), 468-86.

(B2a)

582. _____, and Sidney Verba (eds.), <u>Political Culture and Political Development</u>, Princeton, N. J.: Princeton University Press, 1964.

583. _____, <u>Politics, Personality, and Nation Building: Burma's Search for Identity</u>, New Haven, Conn.: Yale University Press, 1963. Attempts to link personality development with the broader social context of nation building.

584. Raphaeli, Nimrod, <u>Readings in Comparative Public Administration</u>, Rockleigh, N. J.: Allyn & Bacon, 1967.

585. Rehman, A. T. R., <u>Basic Democracies at the Grass Roots--A Study of the Three Union Councils of Kotwali, Thana, and Comilla</u>, Comilla: Pakistan Academy for Village Development, 1962.

586. Retzlaff, Ralph H., <u>Village Government in India: A Case Study</u>, Bombay: Asia Publishing House, 1962.

587. Riggs, Fred W., <u>Administration in Developing Countries: The Theory of Prismatic Society</u>, Boston: Houghton Mifflin Company, 1964.

588. _____, "Administrative Development: An Elusive Concept," in John D. Montgomery and William J. Siffin (eds.), <u>Approaches to Development Administration and Change</u>, New York: McGraw-Hill Book Co., 1966, 225-55.

589. _____, "Administrative Development: Notes on an Elusive Concept and the 'KEF-PRI' Model," Chicago: Comparative Administration Group of the American Society of Public Administration, 1964 (mimeographed).

590. _____, <u>The Ecology of Public Administration</u>, Bombay: Asia Publishing House, 1961.

591. _____, "Modernization and Political Problems: Some Developmental Prerequisites," (paper prepared for the International Conference on the Problem of Modernization in Asia, Asiatic Research Center, Korea University, July 1965).

592. _____, "Political Aspects of Developmental Change" in Art Gallaher, Jr. (ed.), <u>Perspectives in Developmental Change</u>, Lexington, Ky.: University of Kentucky Press, 1968.

593. _____, "Professionalism, Political Science, and the Scope of Public Administration," <u>Theory and Practice of Public Administration</u>, Monograph no. 8, Philadelphia: American Academy of Political and Social Science, October 1968, 32-62.

594. _____, "Public Administration: A Neglected Factor in Economic Development," <u>The Annals of the American Academy of Political and Social Science</u>, 305(May 1956), 70-80.

595. _____, "Relearning an Old Lesson: The Political Context of Development Administration," <u>Public Administration Review</u>, 25(March 1965), 70-79.

(B2a)

596. _____, *Thailand: The Modernization of a Bureaucratic Polity*, Honolulu: East-West Center Press, 1966.
   Dr. Riggs carefully traces the processes of change that have taken place in Thai politics and administration from the mid-nineteenth to the mid-twentieth century with a close look at contemporary Thai government as a bureaucratic polity. The final chapters are devoted to a more microscopic view of bureaucratic life in Thailand, focusing on administration of the rice program to examine the cultural and social changes now taking place.

597. _____, "The Theory of Developing Politics," *World Politics*, 16 (October 1963), 147-72.
   Review of Leonard Binder, *Iran: Political Development in a Changing Society*, Berkeley and Los Angeles: University of California Press, 1962; and Myron Weiner, *The Politics of Scarcity: Public Pressure and Political Response in India*, Chicago: University of Chicago Press, 1962.

598. _____, "Trends in the Comparative Study of Public Administration," *International Review of Administrative Sciences*, 28(1, 1962), 9-15.

599. Rivkin, Arnold, "The Politics of Nation-Building Problems and Preconditions," *Journal of International Affairs*, 16(2, 1962), 131-43.

600. Roberts, James S. "Language and Development Administration," *Public Administration Review*, 29(May, June 1969), 255-63.

601. Rokkan, Stein, and others, *Citizens, Elections, Parties: Approaches to the Comparative Study of the Processes of Development*, New York: David McKay Co., 1969.

602. Samuel, Viscount (ed.), *Public Administration in Israel and Abroad*, Jerusalem: Israel Institute of Public Administration, 1964.

603. Sayeed, Khalid Bin, "Religion and Nation Building in Pakistan," *The Middle East Journal*, 17(Summer 1963), 279-91.
   Religion still plays a very decisive role in the life and history of modern developing societies. Reforms, which are innovative and anti-traditional in nature, have to be conducted in the name and through the interpretation of religion. Pakistan is used as a case study.

604. Scarrow, Howard A., *The Higher Public Service of the Commonwealth of Australia*, Durham, N. C.: Duke University Commonwealth Studies Center, 1957.
   It is the contention of Dr. Scarrow that, in spite of their British origin, the administrative institutions of Australia have developed distinctive features. Emphasis is on the growth, development, composition, and the role of the higher public services in Australia.

605. Schacter, Ruth, "Single-Party Systems in West Africa," *The American Political Science Review*, 55(June 1961), 294-307.
   Examines the rise of single-party systems in West Africa with reference to "social structures and historical circumstances." It is the opinion of the author that mass parties in Africa have been created by

(B2a)

leaders out of egalitarian forces which are associated with democratic traditions.

606. Schapera, I., <u>Government and Politics in Tribal Societies</u>, London: C. A. Watts and Co., 1956.

    This is a comparative study of political institutions and organizations in primitive societies and includes such topics as: "Political Community," "The Framework of Government," "The Activities of Tribal Government," "The Privileges and Powers of Office," "Rulers and Subjects," and "Forms of Tribal Governments."

607. Seligman, L. G., "Elite Recruitment and Political Development," <u>Journal of Politics</u>, 26(August 1964), 612-26.

    The discussion of elite in developing societies is divided into three categories: elite legislation, career paths and mobility, and elite representatives.

608. Shils, Edward, "The Intellectuals in the Political Development in the New States," <u>World Politics</u>, 12(April 1960), 329-68.

    In the history of western political institutions intellectuals played an insignificant role. On the contrary, intellectuals have been piloting nationalist and revolutionary movements in the new states. They frame the constitutions and set political precedents and as such their part in political developments is very important. According to Shils, after creating the new state, the intellectuals will continue to dominate the national life.

609. _____, "The Military in Political Development in the New States" in John J. Johnson (ed.), <u>The Role of the Military in Underdeveloped Countries</u>, Princeton, N. J.: Princeton University Press, 1962, 7-67.

610. _____, <u>Political Development in the New States</u>, S'Gravenhage, Holland: Mouton, 1962.

611. Siffin, William J., "The Civil Service System of the Kingdom of Thailand," <u>International Review of Administrative Sciences</u>, 26(March 1960), 255-68.

    An account of the origin and growth of civil services in Thailand. According to Siffin, Thai administration has a long history of modernization including the late 19th century civil service reforms. However, because of accelerated development and population growth it is felt that the administrative machinery will require further changes.

612. _____ (ed.), <u>Toward the Comparative Study of Public Administration</u>, Bloomington, Ind.: Indiana University Press, 1959.

    This book of readings begins with an article by William J. Siffin on the merits of the comparative method in the study of public administration and is followed by a long article by Riggs, entitled, "Agraria and Industria--Toward a Typology of Comparative Administration." Also included are case studies on Turkey, Egypt, France, Bolivia, Philippines, and Thailand.

613. Sigmund, Paul E. (ed.), <u>The Ideologies of the Developing Nations</u>, New York: Frederick A. Praeger Co., 1963.

(B2a)

614. Silvert, K. H., "Parties and the Masses," The Annals of the American Academy of Political and Social Science, 358(March 1965), 101-8.

615. _____ (ed.), Expectant Peoples: Nationalism and Development, New York: Random House, 1964.
A symposium of 12 area studies conducted by American Universities Field Staff. Each study examines a distinct facet of nationalism.

616. Singer, M. R., The Emerging Elite: A Study of Political Leadership in Ceylon, Cambridge, Mass.: The M.I.T. Press, 1964.

617. Sjoberg, Gideon, M. Donald Hancock, and Orion White, Jr., Politics in the Post-Welfare State: A Comparison of the United States and Sweden, Bloomington, Ind.: Department of Government, Indiana University, 1967.

618. Sklar, Richard L., Nigerian Political Parties: Power in an Emergent African Nation, Princeton, N. J.: Princeton University Press, 1963.

619. Smith, T. E., Elections in Developing Countries, London: Macmillan & Co.,

620. Spiro, Herbert J., "Comparative Politics: A Comprehensive Approach," The American Political Science Review, 56(September 1962), 517-95.
It is a tentative outline of the author's approach to comparative politics. In essence, the basic concepts of the paper stem from the author's thesis that all political systems have four goals--1) stability, 2) flexibility, 3) efficiency, and 4) effectiveness. In his opinion, the relative success of political systems can be gauged by the degree to which they manage to sustain a dynamic equilibrium among the four basic goals. The paper is profusely illustrated by graphs and figures.

620.1 _____, "New Constitutional Forms in Africa," World Politics, 13(October 1960), 69-76.

621. Stauffer, Robert B., "The Biopolitics of Underdevelopment," Comparative Political Studies, 2(October 1969), 361-88.

622. _____, The Development of an Interest Group: The Philippine Medical Association, Quezon City: University of the Philippines Press, 1966.

623. _____, "Philippine Interest Groups: An Index of Political Development," Asian Studies (Philippines), 3(August 1965), 193-200.

624. Stedman, Murray, Jr. (ed.), Modernizing American Government, Englewood Cliffs, N. J.: Prentice-Hall, 1968.

625. Stein, Harold (ed.), Modernizing American Government: A Case Book, New York: Harcourt, Brace and World, 1952.

626. Stone, Donald C., "Government Machinery Necessary for Development" in Martin Kriesberg (ed.), Public Administration in Developing Countries, Washington, D. C.: Brookings Institution, 1965.

(B2a)

627. Swerdlow, Irving (ed.), <u>Development Administration: Concepts and Problems</u>, Syracuse, New York: Syracuse University Press, 1963.

628. Taylor, J. Clagett, <u>The Political Development of Tanganyika</u>, Stanford: Stanford University Press, 1963.
   Mr. Taylor, as an educational missionary, was supervisor of twenty-eight village schools in Southern Rhodesia. His book is a political history of Tanganyika from 1880 to December 1961. The study is comprehensive and sympathetic. At the end there is an excellent bibliography which covers practically all aspects of Tanganyika's history, life and character.

629. Theobald, Robert (ed.), <u>Social Policies for America in the Seventies</u>, New York: Doubleday, 1968.

630. Tinker, Hugh, <u>Ballot Box and Bayonets: People and Governments in Emergent Asian Countries</u>, London: Oxford University Press, 1964.

631. Tucker, Robert C., "Towards a Comparative Politics of Movement Regimes," <u>The American Political Science Review</u>, 55(June 1961), 231-69.
   The regimes which are born out of revolutions try to maintain revolutionary momentum, even after their leaders are firmly entrenched. The author has defined movement regime as "the revolutionary mass movement regime under single-party auspices."

632. Udyanin, Kasem, and Rufus D. Smith, <u>The Public Service in Thailand: Organization, Recruitment and Training</u>, Brussels: International Institute of Administrative Sciences, 1954.

633. Ulman, A. Haluk, and Frank Tachau, "Turkish Politics: The Attempt to Reconcile Rapid Modernization with Democracy," <u>The Middle East Journal</u>, 19 (Spring 1965), 153-68.

634. Vatikiotis, P. J., "Dilemmas of Political Leadership in the Arab Middle East: The Case of the United Arab Republic," <u>American Political Science Review</u>, 55(March 1961), 103-11.
   The new states are using traditional symbols to achieve unity and consensus among the people. The military leaders who have assumed political authority in several Middle Eastern countries are striving for modernization. But modernization depends on "ideology, order and system." The article examines the Islamic religious background of the new military leaders who hold power in the United Arab Republic.

635. Von der Mehden, Fred R., <u>Politics of the Developing Nations</u>, Englewood Cliffs, N. J.: Prentice-Hall, 1964.
   Dealing with political problems common to all developing nations, Von der Mehden views the role of political disunity and instability in relation to leadership groups, social and political environment, and ideologies. He classifies parties, ideologies, and military activity throughout the developing world. The appendix offers complete data on the date of independence, party system, ideological framework, manner of independence, and criteria of stability of fifty developing countries.

636. von Vorys, Karl, "Toward a Concept of Political Development," <u>The Annals of the American Academy of Political and Social Science</u>, 358(March 1965), 14-19.

(B2a)

In the opinion of the author the way to understand political development is to identify the basic ingredients of the political processes which are emerging in the newly independent states. The focus of such a study would be on economic disequilibrium which generally prevails in these states. At this stage the new states do not possess the capacity to mould the course of social and economic change. The cultivation of this capacity depends on the balanced use of coercion and persuasion.

637. Waldo, Dwight, Comparative Public Administration: Prologue, Problems and Promise, Chicago: Comparative Administration Group of the American Society for Public Administration, 1963.

639. Ward, Robert E., and Roy C. Macridis, Modern Political Systems, Englewood Cliffs, N. J.: Prentice-Hall, 1963.

640. Weiner, Myron, "Political Integration and Political Development," The Annals of the American Academy of Political and Social Science, 358(March 1965), 52-64.
   The problem of national and political integration is rooted in the history of every state. In transitional periods nations have to handle problems of national integration which involve, national identity, territorial control, the establishment of norms for the handling of public conflict, and above all, establishment of amicable and workable relations between the rulers and the ruled, which includes motivating individuals for the prosecution of the common purposes of the community.

641. _____, The Politics of Scarcity, Public Pressure and Political Response in India, Chicago: University of Chicago Press, 1962.

642. _____ (ed.), Studies in Political Change, Chicago: Rand McNally & Co., 1967.

643. Welch, Claude E. (ed.), Political Modernization: A Reader in Comparative Political Change, Belmont, Cal.: Wadsworth Publishing Co., 1968.

644. Westwood, Andrew F., "Politics of Distrust in Iran," The Annals of the American Academy of Political and Social Science, 358(March 1965), 123-35.
   According to the author, Iran suffers from intense and deep distrust of the possessors of power. He examines the careers of Iran's two outstanding post-war politicians, Ahmad Ghavan and Muhammad Massadagh. The article points out that the present regime "has proven resistant to major political change in the short run, and perhaps incapable of important change over the long run."

645. Whitten, Norman E., Jr., "Power Structure and Socio-Cultural Change in Latin American Communities," Social Forces, 43(March 1965), 320-29.
   The proposition explored in this article is that "as community power becomes increasingly rationalized, the local socio-cultural system will become less parochial and increasingly similar to national system."

646. Wickwar, W. Hardy, The Modernization of Administration in the Near East, Beirut: Khayats, 1963.
   Modernization of administration in the Near East can be understood only in the light of the impact of market economy. The administrative transformation in various countries of the regions is discussed in terms

of the framework of power, economic development, social development, and public finance. Assessment is made of the past, and hopes and prospects of the future are presented.

647. Wilcox, Wayne, Pakistan: The Consolidation of a Nation, New York: Columbia University Press, 1963.
A study of the integration of the princely states into the new state of Pakistan. It also treats the problems which the Central Government faces in modernizing the regions and the provinces.

648. _____, "Politicians, Bureaucrats and Development in India," The Annals of the American Academy of Political and Social Science, 358 (March 1965), 114-22.
The forces of political development, including the elite who are working for modernization, are alien to India's indigenous thinking or traditions. Although Nehru, the Congress, and the bureaucracy dominated the first decade of independence, the author is of the opinion that in view of the needs of development, the bureaucracy is weak. "The democratic system of social change has been more effective in India than the bureaucratic system of economic planning."

649. Wilkinson, Rupert, Gentlemanly Power: British Leadership and the Public School Tradition. A Comparative Study in the Making of Rulers, New York: Oxford University Press, 1964.
A treatise on the comparative sociology of education. The book is primarily concerned with the idea that role of the public schools during the last Victorian period in England was to produce political leaders and bureaucratic elites. He compares this system and philosophy of public school education with the Chinese Confucian educational system.

650. Willner, Ann Ruth and Dorothy, "The Rise and Role of Charismatic Leaders," The Annals of the American Academy of Political and Social Science, 358 (March 1965), 77-88.
Charisma is the mystique of inspiring loyalty among followers. It is something beyond formal position or status. Conscience, belief or faith are the sources which legitimatize it. Among many emerging societies, the disappearance of traditional values plus the demands of modernization create a sense of "historical dislocation" among the people. This is the most conducive atmosphere for the rise of charismatic leaders.

651. Wraith, Ronald, and Edgar Simpkins, Corruption in Developing Countries, New York: W. W. Morton and Company, 1964.
Partly devoted to the moral ramifications of corruption, a long list of examples of corruption in many underdeveloped countries is given. Most of the evidence is drawn from the former British Colonies in West Africa with the assumption that the situation is similar in other developing countries.

652. Wriggins, W. Howard, "Impediments to Unity in New Nations: The Case of Ceylon," The American Political Science Review, 55(June 1961), 313-20.
Emancipation from foreign rule does not automatically bring nationhood. Independence, religious, regional, and linguistic differences hamper process toward national unity as this case study verifies.

653. Zinkin, Maurice, Development of Free Asia, New York: Oxford University Press, 1963.

b. Bureaucracy

654. Ahmad, Munir, <u>The Civil Service of Pakistan: A Study of the Background and Attitudes of Public Servant in Lahore</u>, Karachi: Oxford University Press, 1964.

654.1 Alford, Robert F., <u>Bureaucracy and Participation: Political Cultures in Four Wisconsin Cities</u>, Chicago: Rand McNally & Co., 1969.
This is a comparative study of community power, classifying four cities according to the degree of bureaucratization and professionalization of their local governments and also the level of participation and inter-group activity. Alford develops a theory relating the growth of cities to changes in economic base and the processes of local government and politics.

654.2 Anderson, James G., <u>Bureaucracy in Education</u>, Baltimore: The Johns Hopkins Press, 1968.
This is an analysis of the functions and effects of bureaucratic controls in a large metropolitan school system. The author finds that centralization of authority and standardization of rules, while reducing teachers' anxieties, may also lead to their losing commitment to the goals of the institution.

655. Apter, David E., <u>The Political Kingdom in Uganda: A Study in Bureaucratic Nationalism</u>, Princeton, N. J.: University Press, 1969.

656. Aronson, Sidney H., <u>Status and Kinship in the Higher Civil Service</u>, Cambridge: Harvard University Press, 1964.

657. Ashford, Douglas E., "Bureaucrats and Citizens," <u>The Annals of the American Academy of Political and Social Science</u>, 358(March 1965), 89-100.
The demands of development have changed the role of administrators in developing countries. In this article Professor Ashford uses the typology of Apter to compare the impact of a modernizing autocracy (Morocco), a mobilization regime (Tunisia), and a reconciliation regime (Pakistan) on the administrator. The crux of the argument is that rapid progress is not possible without an enlightened citizenry.

658. Bennis, Warren G., "Beyond Bureaucracy," <u>Trans-Action</u>, 12(July and August 1965), 31-35.

659. _____, "Organizational Developments and the Fate of Bureaucracy," <u>Industrial Management Review</u>, 7(Spring 1966), 41-56.

660. Bent, Frederick T., "The Turkish Bureaucracy as an Agent of Change," <u>Journal of Comparative Administration</u>, 1(May 1969), 47-64.

661. Berger, Morroe, <u>Bureaucracy and Society in Modern Egypt: A Study of Higher Civil Service</u>, Princeton: Princeton University Press, 1957.
An empirical study based on the interviews of 249 higher civil servants of Egypt. Efforts have been made to comprehend the salient aspects of the Egyptian bureaucracy. The social setting, the background of the civil servants, attraction, status, prestige of the civil service for the educated man, initiative, subservience and the range of bureaucratic behavior are some of the salient discussions of this book.

(B2b)

662. Blank, Blanche Davis, "A Proposal for a Statistical Approach to Comparative Administration: The Measurement of National Bureaucracies," Washington, D. C.: Comparative Administration Group of the American Society for Public Administration, 1965 (mimeographed).

663. Blau, Peter M., Wolf V. Heydebrand, and Robert E. Stauffer, "The Structure of Small Bureaucracies," American Sociological Review, 31(April 1966), 179-92.

664. Braibanti, Ralph, "Administrative Modernization," in Myron Weiner, Modernization: The Dynamics of Growth, New York: Basic Books Inc., 1966, 29-48.

665. _____ (ed.), Asian Bureaucratic Systems, Durham, N. C.: Duke University Press, 1966.

666. _____, "Public Bureaucracy and Judiciary in Pakistan," in Joseph La Palombara (ed.), Bureaucracy and Political Development, Princeton, N. J.: Princeton University Press, 1963, 360-440.

667. Burton, Ralph, and Edward B. Strait, The Central Machinery of Government, Its Role and Functioning, Brussels: International Institute of Administrative Sciences, 1960.

668. Chapman, Brian, The Profession of Government: The Public Service in Europe, London: Allen and Unwin, 1959.

669. Chaudhri, Muzaffer Ahmad, "The Organization and Composition of the Central Divil Services in Pakistan," International Review of Administrative Sciences, 26(March 1960), 279-92.

670. Delany, William, "The Development and Decline of Patrimonial and Bureaucratic Administration," Administrative Science Quarterly, 7(March 1963), 458-501.
    The author believes that Max Weber's theory of bureaucratic structure and efficiency has been a chief source of inspiration for organizational research by contemporary American sociologists as well as their primary object of criticism. With few exceptions, however, they have ignored the problems of development and the cross-cultural comparisons of administration which Weber had in mind in developing his typology of primitive, patrimonial, and bureaucratic authority. The author attempts to relate Weber's theory of administrative development to careful empirical work done since and thus assess the current scientific status of this theory. He indicates modifications suggested by research and points out alternative research designs. He concludes that although Weber's theory is still useful it needs reinterpretations and adaptations according to new research. He thinks Weber did not anticipate the inefficiencies of of bureaucracy in the long-run and beyond certain upper limits of size and complexity.

671. Diamant, Alfred, "Bureaucracy in Development Movement Regimes: A Bureaucratic Model for Developing Societies," Washington, D. C.: Comparative Administrative Group of the American Society for Public Administration, 1964 (mimeographed).

672. _____, and Blanche D. Blank, "Measuring National Bureaucracies, The Interaction of Theory and Research (Research Note)," Journal

of Comparative Administration, 1(May 1969), 114-27.

673. Dimock, Marshall E., Administrative Vitality, London: Routledge and Kegan Paul, 1960.

674. Downs, Anthony, Inside Bureaucracy, Boston: Little-Brown and Co.
Using the axiom that all bureaucratic officials act in their own self-interest, the author develops a realistic and concrete theory of bureaucratic behavior which encompasses a wide range of activities.

674.1 Dube, S. C., "Bureaucracy and Nation Building in Transitional Societies," International Social Science Journal, 16(2, 1964), 229-36.

675. Egger, Rowland A., "Ministerial and Departmental Organization and Management in the Government of Pakistan," Public Administration: Journal of the Royal Institute of Public Administration, (London), 39(Summer 1961), 149-72.
This paper is a summary of the author's report on administrative reorganization which he submitted to the government of Pakistan in 1953.

676. Eisenstadt, S. N., The Political System of Empires: The Rise and Fall of the Historical Bureaucratic Societies, Glencoe, Ill.: The Free Press, 1963.

677. _____, "Problems of Emerging Bureaucracies in Developing Areas and New States," in Bert F. Hoselitz and Wilbert E. Moore (eds.), Industrialization and Society, Paris: UNESCO-Mouton, 1966, 159-74.

678. Fulton, Lord, The Civil Service, six volumes, London: Her Majesty's Stationery Office, 1967.

679. Goodnow, Henry Frank, The Civil Service of Pakistan: Bureaucracy in a New Nation, New Haven, Conn.: Yale University Press, 1964.
A study of the superior bureaucracy called the Civil Service of Pakistan. Part one of the book is devoted to the theoretical concept of bureaucracy and political power in emerging societies. Part two is a case study of the Civil Service of Pakistan. Part three comprises the author's view on bureaucracy and its role in the development of democratic institutions.

680. Graham, Lawrence S., Civil Service Reform in Brazil: Principles versus Practice (Latin American Monographs, No. 13, Institute of Latin American Studies, University of Texas), Austin, Texas: University of Texas Press, 1968.

681. Guyot, James F., "Bureaucratic Transformation in Burma," in Ralph Braibanti (ed.), Asia Bureaucratic Systems Emergent from the British Tradition, Durham, N. C.: Duke University Press, 1966, 354-443.

682. Harr, John Ensov, The Professional Diplomat, Princeton, N. J.: Princeton University Press, 1969.

683. Hopkins, Jack W., "Comparative Observations on Peruvian Bureaucracy," Journal of Comparative Administration, 1(November 1969), 301-20.

684. Howton, F. William, Functionaries, Chicago: Quadrangle Books, 1969.

(B2b)

685. Inayatullah, Bureaucracy and Development in Pakistan, Peshawar: Pakistan Academy for Rural Development, 1963.
   A book of readings on various aspects of public administration in Pakistan. The book has been divided into the following parts: (1) bureaucracy in a developing state, (2) administrative structure of Pakistan, (3) structure of bureaucracy in Pakistan, (4) bureaucracy, local government and rural development, and (5) reorientation of bureaucracy for development.

686. Johnson, John J. (ed.), The Role of the Military in Underdeveloped Countries, Princeton, N. J.: University Press, 1969.
   This book provides information, comparative analyses and balanced judgements by a number of experts on such topics as: "The Military in the Political Development of the New States," "Armies in the Process of Political Modernization," "The Latin-American Military as a Politically Competing Group in Transitional Society," "Militarism and Politics in Latin America, and Indonesia, Thailand, Burma, and the Middle East."

687. Kearney, Robert N., "Ceylon: The Contemporary Bureaucracy," in Ralph Braibanti (ed.), Asian Bureaucratic Systems Emergent from the British Imperial Tradition, Durham, N. C.: Duke University Press, 1966, 485-549.

688. LaPalombara, Joseph (ed.), Bureaucracy and Political Development, Princeton, N. J.: Princeton University Press, 1964.
   This is the second in a series of studies in political development sponsored by the Committee on Comparative Politics of the Social Sciences Research Council. LaPalombara, Morstein Marx, S. N. Eisenstadt, Fred Riggs, Bert Hoselitz, Joseph Spengler and Merle Fainsod, Carl Beck, Donald Kingsly, John Dorsey, Ralph Braibanti, and Walter Sharp are contributors.

689. Lee, Hahn-Been, "The Role of the Higher Civil Service Under Rapid Social and Political Change," Washington, D. C.: Comparative Administration Group of the American Society for Public Administration, 1966 (mimeographed).

690. Leiserson, Avery, "Scientists and the Policy Process," American Political Science Review, 59(June 1965), 408-16.

691. Mars, David, "Creativity and Administration," Public Administration Review, 27(September 1967), 120-28.

692. Marx, Fritz Morstein, The Administrative State: An Introduction to Bureaucracy, Chicago: The University of Chicago Press, 1957.

693. Meyer, Marshall, "Automation and Bureaucratic Structures," American Journal of Sociology, 74(November 1968), 256-64.

694. Mouzelis, Necos P., Organization and Bureaucracy: An Analysis of Modern Theories, London: Routledge & Kegan Paul, 1967.

695. National Institute of Public Administration, Llwellyn Smith Report: Report of the Government of India Secretariat Procedure Committee 1920, Karachi: National Institute of Public Administration, 1963.
   A reprint of the original report submitted in 1920. It is named

after the President of the Committee. The report has an excellent account of the principles of organization. In their opinion, because of rigidity of the formal procedures, officers generally resort to informal communications. The committee advocated the reform of formal procedures to eliminate excessive use of informal devices in government offices. Some of the most important recommendations of the Committee were as follows: appointment of an 'Inspector of office procedures, creation of an Imperial Secretariat Service, centralization of recruitment of the secretariat, and establishment of a central staff selection board.

696. Oching, Adonijah, *A Comparative Analysis of the East African Bureaucracies Through Periods of Colonization and Decolonization* (John W. Donner Fund Publication No. 28, School of Public Administration), Los Angeles: University of Southern California, 1964.

697. Peabody, Robert L., and Francis E. Rourke, "Public Bureaucracies," in James S. March (ed.), *Handbook of Organization*, Chicago: Rand McNally, 1965, 801-37.

698. Perlmutter, Amos, "The Praetorian State and the Praetorian Army: Toward a Taxonomy of Civil-Military Relations in Developing Politics," *Comparative Politics*, 1(April 1969), 382-404.

699. Presthus, Robert V., "Weberian vs. Welfare Bureaucracy in Traditional Society," *Administrative Science Quarterly*, 6(June 1961), 1-24.
A study of Turkish coal industry in which the author has pointed out the operational limitations of the Weberian model in less developed societies. Weber's emphasis on rationality and efficiency is based on value premises which is alien to traditional societies.

699.1 Rao, Lakshmana, "Bureaucrats and Political Development: A Paradoxical View," in Joseph LaPalombara (ed.), *Bureaucracy and Political Development*, Princeton: Princeton University Press, 1963, 120-67.

700. Riggs, Fred W., "Bureaucratic Politics in Comparative Perspective," *Journal of Comparative Administration*, 1(May 1969), 5-38.

701. Roos, Leslie L., and P. Noralou, "Bureaucracy in the Middle East--Some Cross-Cultural Relationships," *Journal of Comparative Administration*, 1 (November 1969), 281-300.

702. Rourke, Francis E., *Bureaucracy, Politics, and Public Policy*, Boston: Little, Brown and Company, 1969.
The central concern of this work is the role of the bureaucracy in the policy-making process. Rourke believes that much of public policy is determined by negotiation between appointed and not elected officials. He examines how bureaucracies derive and use power, and the processes of making policy.

703. Singh, K. N., "Analysis of the Community Development Administration at Village, Block, and District Level," *Journal of Local Administration Overseas*, 4(April 1965), 99-108.

704. Sisson, Richard, "Bureaucratic Politics in Comparative Perspective: A Commentary and Critique," *Journal of Comparative Administration*, 1(May 1969), 39-46.

705. Spengler, Joseph J., "Public Bureaucracy, Resource: Structure and Economic Development: A Note," *Myklos*, 11(4, 1958), 459-87.

706. Tilman, Robert O., "Bureaucratic Development in Malaysia," in Ralph Braibanti (ed.), *Asian Bureaucratic Systems Emergent from the British Imperial Tradition*, Durham, N. C.: Duke University Press, 1966, 550-604.

707. _____, "Emergence of Black-Market Bureaucracy: Administration, Development and Corruption in the New States," *Public Administration Review*, 27(September-October 1968), 437-44.

708. *Tottenham Report: Reports on the Re-organization of Central Government, 1945-46*, Karachi: National Institute of Public Administration, 1963.

709. Tullock, Gordon, *The Politics of the Bureaucracy*, Washington, D. C.: Public Affairs Press, 1965.

710. United Nations, *Handbook of Civil Service Laws and Practices*, New York: United Nations, 1966.

711. Williams, V., "Bureaucratic Proliferation: Theoretical Approach," *American Journal of Economics and Sociology*, 22(July 1963), 337-45.
    Under the general theory of social change, the author has discussed the processes by which bureaucratic structures undergo changes.

712. Wittfogel, Karl, *Oriental Despotism*, New Haven: Yale University Press, 1956.

C. CHANGE

(C1)

1. ORGANIZATIONAL THEORY AND BEHAVIOR

713. Abegglen, J. C., <u>The Japanese Factory: Aspects of Its Social Organization</u>, Glencoe, Ill.: The Free Press, 1958.
    Three main features of organization are noted: (1) the organization is elaborately divided into separate, formally distinct groupings, (2) a small proportion of people hold formal positions and titles, and (3) the complexity of the organization is heightened by the presence of large numbers of deputies and assistants to department and section chiefs. The Japanese firms closely relate to their workers and their family lives. Employment tends to be for a lifetime.

713.1 Albers, Henry H., <u>Principles of Management: A Modern Approach</u>, third edition, New York: John Wiley and Sons, Inc., 1969.
    Presents a systematic study of management practice. The heart of the book is concerned with the fundamental elements of managerial action: planning, communication, and motivation. Hierarchy, process, perspective, and economy are underlying themes.

714. Allen, Louis A., <u>Management and Organization</u>, New York: McGraw-Hill Book Co., 1958.
    Emphasizes the nature of management, organization for management, the designing of the company organization structure, divisionization, the process of delegation, and staff and line relationship. The last part treats the changing of organizational structures and the dynamics of change.

715. _____, <u>The Management Profession</u>, New York: McGraw-Hill Book Co., 1964.
    Treats the conventional wisdom of management within the terms of four related functions: planning, organizing, leading, and controlling.

716. Applewhite, Philip D., <u>Organizational Behavior</u>, Englewood Cliffs, N. J.: Prentice-Hall, 1965.

717. Arensberg, C. M. (ed.), <u>Research in Industrial Human Relations: A Critical Appraisal</u>, New York: Harper & Row, 1957.

718. Argyris, Chris, <u>Diagnosing Human Relations in Organization: A Case Study of a Hospital</u>, New Haven, Conn.: Yale University Press, 1956.

719. _____, <u>Integrating the Individual and the Organization</u>, New York: John Wiley and Sons, 1964.
    Analyzes the causes of human problems within organizations and presents a theoretical framework for changing the structure of the organizations.

(C1)

720. _____, <u>Interpersonal Competence and Organizational Effectiveness</u>, Homewood, Ill.: Richard D. Irwin Co., 1962.
   Successful change in top executive behavior is described. Presents a model that relates interpersonal competence and organizational effectiveness.

721. _____, <u>Organization of a Bank</u>, New Haven, Conn.: Labor and Management Centre, Yale University, 1954.

722. _____, <u>Personality and Organization</u>, New York: Harper & Row, 1957.

723. _____, <u>Some Causes of Organizational Ineffectiveness Within the Department of State</u>, Washington, D. C.: Department of State, 1967.
   A short, but insightful treatise, directing attention to major organizational problems of the United States Department of State. The conclusion is reached that the "living system" is characterized as one dominated by lack of interpersonal openness and trust, confrontation, high withdrawal, mistrust of aggressive behavior, and blindness to superior authority.

724. _____, <u>Understanding Organizational Behaviour</u>, Homewood, Ill.: Dorsey Press, 1960.

725. Astin, Alexander W., <u>The College Environment</u>, Washington, D. C.: The American Council of Education, 1967.
   Provides a solid framework against which to examine the environment of U. S. institutions of higher learning.

726. Athos, Anthony G., and Robert E. Coffey, <u>Behavior in Organizations: A Multidimensional View</u>, Englewood Cliffs, N. J.: Prentice-Hall, 1968.
   This work, a combination of text, readings, and cases, offers a conceptual scheme for a humanistic, experimental, multidimensional approach to behavior in organizations. The emphasis is on what people experience in organizations, the demands of each facet on experience, and the conflicts that arise among the several dimensions.

727. Avery, Robert S., <u>Experiment in Management: Personnel Decentralization in the Tennessee Valley Authority</u>, Knoxville, Tenn.: University of Tennessee Press, 1954.

728. Bales, Robert F., <u>Interaction Process Analysis: A Method for Study of Small Groups</u>, Cambridge, Mass.: Addison-Wesley Press, 1950.
   Deals with experimentation and observation of social behavior and interaction in small face-to-face groups. It describes the method of experimentation, the theoretical framework, and follows the training of observers and the analysis and interpretation of the results of observation.

729. Barnard, Chester I., <u>The Functions of the Executive</u>, Cambridge, Mass.: Harvard University Press, 1938.
   A classical treatment of formal organization as a social process. Highly useful in providing insights on how to gain "conscious, deliberate, purposeful" cooperation and in depicting factors relating to stability and instability in organizations.

(C1)

730. Barton, Allen H., *Communities in Disaster: A Sociological Analysis of Collective Stress Conditions*, New York: Doubleday, 1969.

731. _____, *Organizational Measurement and Its Bearing on the Study of College Environment*, New York: College Entrance Examination Board, 1961.
   Discusses key principles and practices required for the effective measurement of organizational performance within an American University environment.

732. Bass, Bernard, *Leadership, Psychology, and Developmental Behavior*, New York: Harper & Brothers, 1960.

733. Bauer, Raymond, "Social Psychology and the Study of Policy Formation," *American Psychologist*, 21(October 1966), 933-42.

734. _____, and Kenneth Gergen (eds.), *The Study of Policy Formation*, New York: The Free Press, 1968.

735. Belknap, D., and J. G. Steinle, *The Community and Its Hospitals: A Comparative Analysis*, Syracuse, New York: University of Syracuse Press, 1963.
   Examines why some American communities have good general hospitals and others do not. Concludes that differences in hospital quality and service are derived not from quality of personnel or from community income, but rather from the way in which the hospital is defined by a small group of leaders in the community. A good study in the problems of system linkages.

736. Bell, Earl H., *Social Foundations of Human Behavior*, New York: Harper & Row, 1961.
   This book is particularly useful in applying the concepts of gemeinschaft and gesellschaft to the analysis of society.

737. Belshaw, C., *Traditional Exchange and Modern Markets*, Englewood Cliffs, N. J.: Prentice-Hall, 1965.

738. Bendix, Reinhard, *Work and Authority in Industry*, New York: John Wiley and Sons, 1957.

739. Bennis, Warren G. (ed.), *Interpersonal Dynamics: Essays and Readings on Human Interaction*, Homewood, Ill.: Dorsey Press, 1964 and 1968.

740. _____, and Philip E. Slater, *The Temporary Society*, New York: Harper & Row, 1969.

741. _____, "Toward a 'Truly' Scientific Management: The Concept of Organizational Health," *Industrial Management Review*, 4(Fall 1962), 1-27.

742. Berrelson, Bernard, and Gary A. Steiner, *Human Behavior: An Inventory of Scientific Findings*, New York: Harcourt, Brace and World, Inc., 1964.
   Over 1050 findings on human behavior are classified, covering a wide range of subjects including organizations, groups and change.

(C1)

743. Black, Max (ed.), <u>The Social Theories of Talcott Parsons</u>, Englewood Cliffs, N. J.: Prentice-Hall, Inc., 1961.
The article included in this work, "Parsons's Sociological Theory," by Edward C. Devereux, Jr., is especially useful in providing a board construct of social organization.

744. Blau, Peter M., <u>Exchange and Power in Social Life</u>, New York: John Wiley & Sons, Inc., 1965.
A study which treats in comprehensive detail the application of social exchange in associational life. The work is particularly useful in indicating how complex organizational relationships arise from the simple process of social exchange. The sections on the dynamics of change and adjustment are extremely insightful and useful for scholars of planned change.

745. _____, and W. Richard Scott, <u>Formal Organizations: A Comparative Approach</u>, San Francisco: Chandler Publications, 1962.

746. Blau, Peter M., "Theories of Organizations," in David L. Sills (ed.), <u>International Encyclopedia of the Social Sciences</u>, New York: The Macmillan Comp., and The Free Press, 1968, 11, 297-305.

747. Boulding, Kenneth E., <u>Conflict and Defense: A General Theory</u>, New York: Harper Torchbooks, 1963.

748. _____, <u>The Image</u>, Ann Arbor, Michigan: The University of Michigan Press, 1961.
A study based upon the assumption that human behavior depends upon the image--"the sum of what we think we know and what makes us act the way we do." Chapter Two, "The Image in the Theory of Organization" is especially useful in providing background information on organizational change.

749. _____, <u>The Organizational Revolution</u>, New York: Harper & Brothers, 1953.

750. _____, "Some Questions on the Measurement and Evaluation of Organization," in Hendrik M. Ruitenbeek (ed.), <u>The Dilemma of Organizational Society</u>, New York: Dutton, 1963.

750.1 Bradburn, Norman, and David Caplovitz, <u>Reports on Happiness: A Plot Study of Behavior Related to Mental Health</u>, Chicago: Aldine, 1965.

750.2 Cantril, Hadley, <u>The Pattern of Human Concerns</u>, New Brunswick, N. J.: Rutgers University Press, 1966.

751. Caplow, Theodore, <u>Principles of Organization</u>, New York: Harcourt, Brace & World, 1964.

752. _____, <u>The Sociology of Work</u>, Minneapolis, Minn.: University of Minnesota Press, 1954.

753. Cartwright, Dorwin, and Alvin Zander (eds.), <u>Group Dynamics: Research and Theory</u>, New York: Harper & Row, 1968.
Two chapters place the field of group dynamics in historical and theoretical perspective. The intellectual and social origins of group

dynamics and the basic theoretical and methodological issues encountered by those working in the field are described. The determinants and consequences of group cohesiveness are then discussed. This is followed by articles on the nature of group pressures and the operation of group standards. Individual motives and the formation of group goals' as well as leadership and group performance are considered. The final section deals with group structure, concentrating on communication, power and status, and interpersonal attractions and repulsions.

754. Carzo, Rocco, and John N. Yanouzas, *Formal Organizations: A Systems Approach*, Homewood, Ill.: R. D. Irwin, 1967.

755. _____, "Some Effects of Organization Structure on Group Effectiveness," *Administrative Science Quarterly*, 7(March 1963), 393-424.

756. Chamberlain, Neil W., *Enterprise and Environment*, New York: McGraw-Hill, 1968.

757. Chandler, Alfred D., Jr., *Strategy and Structure*, Cambridge, Mass.: The M.I.T. Press, 1962.

758. Chernoff, Herman, and Lincoln Moses, *Elementary Decision Theory*, New York: John Wiley and Sons, Inc., 1959.

759. Collins, Alan Keith, *The Dynamics of Organization*, Melbourne: Sem Books, 1968.

760. Cooper, Joseph D., *The Art of Decision-Making*, Garden City, N. Y.: Doubleday & Co., 1961.

761. Cooper, William W., Harold J. Leavitt, and Maynard W. Shelly II, *New Perspectives in Organization Research*, New York: John Wiley and Sons, Inc., 1964.

762. Crozier, Michel, *The Bureaucratic Phenomenon*, Chicago: University of Chicago Press, 1964.

763. Curry, Robert L., and L. L. Wade, *A Theory of Political Exchange: Economic Reasoning in Political Analysis*, Englewood Cliffs, N. J.: Prentice-Hall, 1968.
    Conceptualizes political interaction through economic and social theory.

764. Cyert, Richard M., and James C. March, *A Behavioral Theory of the Firm*, Englewood Cliffs, N. J.: Prentice-Hall, 1963.
    A theory of the firm based on an empirical study of decision-making is developed. Taking a methodological approach, the authors: (a) show how computer simulation can be used, (b) use data based on empirical observation, (c) combine organization theory and economic theory, (d) use laboratory experiments, and (e) develop a number of new concepts such as organization slack and estimation bias. Contents: "Antecedents of the Behavioral Theory of the Firm," "Organizational Goals," "Organizational Expectations," "Organizational Choice," "A Summary of Basic Concepts in the Behavioral Theory of the Firm," "A Specific Price and Output Model," "A General Model of Price and Output Determination," "A Model of Rational Managerial Behavior," "A Model of Trust Investment

(C1)

Behavior," "Some Implications," "Assumptions, Prediction, and Explanation in Economics," and "Computer Models in Dynamic Economics."

765. Dahl, Robert A., and Charles E. Lindblom, <u>Politics, Economics, and Welfare</u>, New York: Harper Brothers, 1953.

766. Dale, Ernest, <u>Organization</u>, New York: American Management Association, 1967.

767. Dalton, Gene W., <u>The Distribution of Authority In Formal Organizations</u>, Boston: Harvard Graduate School of Business Administration, 1968.

768. Danhardt, Robert B., "Organizational Citizenship and Personal Freedom," <u>Public Administration Review</u>, 28(January/February 1968), 47-53.

769. Deutsch, Karl W., <u>The Nerves of Government: Models of Political Communication and Control</u>, New York: The Free Press, 1963.

770. Diamant, Alfred, <u>The Temporal Dimension in Models of Administration and Organization</u>, Chicago: Comparative Administration Group of the American Society for Public Administration, 1966 (mimeographed).

770.1 Dill, W. R., "Environment as Influence in Managerial Autonomy," <u>Administrative Science Quarterly</u>, 2(March, 1958), 409-443.

771. Dobzhansky, Theodosius, <u>The Biological Basis of Human Freedom</u>, New York: Columbia University Press, 1955.

772. _____, "Changing Man," <u>Science</u>, 155(January 27, 1967), 409-15.

773. Doxiadis, Constantinas, <u>Ekistics: An Introduction to the Science of Human Settlements</u>, New York: Oxford University Press, 1968.

774. Drabek, Thomas E., and J. Eugene Haas, "Laboratory Simulation of Organizational Stress," <u>American Sociological Review</u>, 34(April 1969), 223-38.

775. Drucker, Peter, <u>Managing for Results</u>, New York: Harper and Brothers, 1964.
    A treatment on "what to do" in management. Especially useful in discussing the entrepreneurial role of both private and public managers.

776. Eckstein, Harry, "Authority Relations and Governmental Performance: A Theoretical Framework," <u>Comparative Political Studies</u>, 2(October 1969), 269-326.

777. Eisenstadt, N. B., "Communication Systems and Social Structure: An Exploratory Comparative Study," <u>Public Opinion Quarterly</u>, 19(Summer 1955), 153-67.

778. Emery, F. E., and E. L. Trist, "The Causal Texture of Organizational Environments," <u>Human Relations</u>, 18(1, 1965), 26-48.
    A treatise on the processes through which parts of the environment become related to each other, constituting what may be called its causal texture--the area of interdependencies that belong within the environment itself. These processes are contextual, i. e., ecological. They involve characteristics of aid forces in the wider society. "The processes which connect parts of the environment to each other are often

unlike these connecting parts of the organization to each other, or even with those which relate the environment to the organization. A major fallacy has been to assume their identity.

778.1 Emery, James C., *Organizational Planning and Control Systems*, New York: The Macmillan Company, 1969.
This book is a synthesis of the field of information relating to organizational planning. It studies the organization as a system, how information is processed, and the economics of information.

779. England, George W., "Organizational Goals and Expected Behavior of American Managers," *Academy of Management Journal*, 10(June 1967), 107-17.

780. Etzioni, Amitai, *The Active Society: A Theory of Societal and Political Process*, New York: The Free Press, 1968.

781. _____, "Authority, Structure and Organizational Effectiveness," *Administrative Science Quarterly*, 4(June 1959), 43-67.

782. _____, *A Comparative Analysis of Complex Organizations*, New York: The Free Press, 1961.
Analyzes complex organizations in terms of their compliance relationships; that is, the relationships between the kind of power used by the organization to enforce control and the organizational members' attitudes of involvement toward this power. The analysis cuts across a variety of organizational "types" and looks at the relationships between compliance relations and other organizational characteristics such as goals, consensus, socialization, cohesion, etc.

783. _____, *Complex Organizations: A Sociological Reader*, New York: Holt, Rinehart and Winston, Inc., 1969, 1961.
Presents material about the structure and functioning of organizations, organizational theories, relevant research findings, and some selections on organizational research methodologies. Considerable attention is paid to organizational goals, research techniques, comparative study, organizational change, and the interactions between organization and society.

784. _____, *Modern Organizations*, Englewood Cliffs, N. J.: Prentice-Hall, Inc., 1964.
A succinct treatise on the general theories of organizational theory and behavior.

785. _____, *Political Unification*, New York: Holt, Rinehart and Winston, Inc., 1965.

788. _____, "Two Approaches to Organizational Analysis: A Critique and a Suggestion," *Administrative Science Quarterly*, 5(September 1960), 257-78.
A study of models that deal with measurement of organization effectiveness. It is critical of goal models and favors systems model for such purposes. The article is not directly related to planned organizational change, as it never touches these aspects. However, it is useful inasmuch as it points out why goal model is preferred by those who are committed to social change.

(C1)

789. Eulau, Heinz, <u>The Behavioral Persuasion in Politics</u>, New York: Random House, 1963.
    A discussion of the behavioral approach to the study of politics, stressing methodology and pointing out some of the difficulties and limitations of behavioral research.

790. Forrester, J. W., <u>Industrial Dynamics</u>, Cambridge, Mass.: The M.I.T. Press, 1961.

791. Foundation for Research on Human Behavior, <u>Modern Organization Theory</u>, New York: John Wiley and Sons, Inc., 1959.
    Eleven papers read at a symposium held at Ann Arbor, Michigan, in February, 1959, sponsored by the Foundation for Research on Human Behavior. Topics include recurrent themes and general issues in organization theory; concept of the social organization; behavioral theory of organizational objectives; understanding human behavior in a motivation approach to a theory of organization and management; stability of organizations; contribution of graph theory to organization theory; and biological models and empirical histories of organizational growth.

792. Frank, Andrew Gunder, "Goal Ambiguity and Conflicting Standards: An Approach to the Study of Organization," <u>Human Organization</u>, 17(Winter 1958-59), 9-13.
    This analysis of decision-making and management conducted in Soviet industry provides an example of the consequences of goal ambiguity and resultant conflicting standards in organizations. Some hypotheses about behavior and system organization under such conditions are suggested.

793. Freilich, Morris, "Ecology and Culture: Environmental Determinism and the Ecological Approach in Anthropology," <u>Anthropological Quarterly</u>, 40 (January 1967), 26-43.

794. _____, "Toward an Operational Definition of Community," <u>Rural Sociology</u>, 28(June 1963), 117-27.

795. Friedman, John, "A Conceptual Model for the Analysis for Planning Behavior," <u>Administrative Science Quarterly</u>, 12(September 1967), 225-52.

796. Gamson, William A., "Rancorous Conflict in Community Politics," <u>American Sociological Review</u>, 31(February 1966), 71-81.

797. Gardner, Burleigh, and David G. Hoore, <u>Human Relations in Industry: Organizational and Administrative Behavior</u>, Homewood, Ill.: Richard D. Irwin, Inc., 1964.
    Treatment of fundamental concepts of organization and management principles in business settings. The work is weak on change, although certain aspects of this subject are discussed.

798. Garthrop, Louis C., <u>Bureaucratic Behavior in the Executive Branch</u>, New York: The Free Press, 1969.
    Provides a theoretical analysis of bureaucratic behavior in the executive branch and examines this subject in terms of organizational responses to both internal and external change. Conflict resolution, decision-making, organizational loyalty, and the interrelationship of these three to organizational change are the four basic topics evaluated.

798.1 Garvey, Gerald, "The Domain of Politics," The Western Political Quarterly, 23(March 1970), 120-37.
   An excellent treatise on factors other than power to explain political relationships, and especially useful for explaining exchanges within marginal analysis.

799. Gellner, Ernest, Thought and Change, Chicago: University of Chicago Press, 1965.

799.1 Geoffrey, Sir Vickers, The Art of Judgement, London: Chapman and Hall, 1966.
   An extremely perceptive book dealing with organizations in decision-making terms.

800. Gerth, H. H., and C. Wright Mills (trans. and eds.), From Max Weber: Essays in Sociology, New York: Oxford University Press, 1958. (Galaxy Paperback).

801. Gibb, J. R., Grace N. Platts, and Lorraine F. Miller, Dynamics of Participative Groups, Washington, D. C.: National Training Laboratories, 1951.

802. Gilpin, Robert, and Christopher Wright (eds.), Science and National Policy-Making, New York: Columbia University Press, 1964.

803. Glass, David C. (ed.), Environmental Influences, New York: The Rockefeller University Press and Russell Sage Foundation.
   The third of three volumes in a Biology and Behavior Series presenting research of biologists and social scientists. (Volume I: Neurophysiology and Emotion; Volume II: Genetics). Volume III includes sections on: Early Nutritional Deficiencies; Infrahuman Studies of Social Isolation; Social Implications of Early Environmental Influences; Reinforcement and Interpersonal Relations; and The Effects of Cultural Deprivation.

804. Gluckman, Max (ed.), Closed Systems and Open Minds: The Limits of Naivety in Social Anthropology, Chicago: Aldine Publishing Company, 1965.
   A collection of five essays which depict the consequences of interdependence among social sciences. Each essay is devoted to a specific problem encountered in field research. Contents: introduction, symbols in Ndembu ritual, the villages in Orissa (India), urban communities in Africa, workshop behavior, social mobility and social class in industrial communities, conclusions.

805. _____, "The Utility of the Equilibrium Model in the Study of Change," American Anthropologist, 70(April 1968), 219-37.

806. Golembiewski, Robert T., Behavior and Organization--O and M and the Small Groups, Chicago: Rand McNally and Co., 1962.
   The author declares that he is not at all satisfied with the textbooks on organization widely used in most schools of business and public administration. He judges most of them to be lamentably slow in incorporating new research findings and, more seriously, to lack a framework compatible with the presentation of such materials. The book attempts to remedy the situation by integrating materials derived from the traditional organization and methods approach with findings from the new behavioral research, in particular, small group analysis. He asserts that

all goals based on empirical theories are prescriptive and, hence, his typology puts organization goals outside the domain of organization science.

807. _____, and Frank Gibson (eds.), <u>Managerial Behavior and Organizational Demands</u>, Chicago: Rand McNally & Co., 1967.

808. _____, <u>Men, Management, and Morality: Toward A New Organizational Ethics</u>, New York: McGraw-Hill Book Co., 1965.

809. _____, <u>Organizing Men and Powers</u>, Chicago: Rand McNally & Co., 1967.

810. Gore, William J., <u>Administrative Decision-Making: A Heuristic Model</u>, New York: John Wiley and Sons, 1964.
    Offers a careful and detailed analysis of policy-making in open-ended and problematic situations and develops a model of the policy-making process.

811. _____, "Administrative Decision-Making in Federal Field Offices," <u>Public Administration Review</u>, 16(Autumn 1956), 281-91.
    Develops a model which comprehends the similarities of and explain the differences between the decision-making processes of federal field offices in the State of Washington. Four phases of the decision-making process in these offices were: (1) perception of the need for change in policy, (2) interpretation, i. e., determination of initial objectives behind which the power and influence of the field office will be mobilized, (3) negotiation with power centers outside the office to procure sufficient support to sustain the course of action adopted, and (4) formalization.

812. Gouldner, Alvin Ward, "Organizational Analysis," in Robert K. Merton and others (eds.), <u>Sociology Today--Problems and Prospects</u>, New York: Basic Books, Inc., 1959, 112-22.

813. _____ (ed.), <u>Studies in Leadership: Leadership and Democratic Action</u>, New York: Harper & Brothers, 1959.
    A collection of thirty-three papers centering on leadership behavior. Topics include types of leaders, group settings, minority groups, ethics of leadership, and techniques of leadership.

814. Greer, Scott A., <u>Social Organization</u>, New York: Random House, 1955.
    A short treatise on the essential characteristics of social organization. The sections on groups are particularly useful relating to the theoretical construct of planned organizational change.

815. Grimshaw, Austin, and John W. Hennessy, Jr., <u>Organization Behavior: Cases and Readings</u>, New York: McGraw-Hill Book Co., 1960.
    A collection of cases on organizational behaviour supplemented by selected readings. It is designed to present a broad variety of situations and problems in which administrative decisions must be made and to offer some general insights about key administrative processes.

816. Gross, Bertram M., "The City of Man: A Social Systems Accounting," in William R. Ewald, Jr. (ed.), <u>Environment for Man: The Next Fifty Years</u>, Bloomington: Indiana University Press, 1967, 136-56.

(C1)

816.1 _____, The Managing of Organizations, Vols. I and II, New York: The Free Press of Glencoe, 1964.

817. _____, Organizations and Their Managing, New York: The Free Press, 1968.
    The two volume edition of this work, as noted above, has now been restructured and condensed to provide the student of organizations with the essence of Professor Gross pioneering study. This edition focuses on the new systems concepts needed for successful management in the 1970's.

818. Haas, Michael, "Comparative Analysis," Western Political Quarterly, 15(June 1962), 294-303.
    The author attempts to outline some of the key problems of "evidence and inference" inherent in comparative analysis. He feels that no formal statement has been made hitherto on the methodology of comparative method itself, in spite of rich theoretical and methodological developments of recent decades. He describes the configurative approach, which involves comparison of functions and processes of large units in order to infer broad conclusions on the basis of the pattern of trait distribution, and the nominalist approach, which takes many small structural units, finds co-variation between traits and makes inferences to accept or reject middle-gauge null hypotheses. The author believes that the conclusions of the former type are usually "metaphysical," and the latter may be too artificial and procrustean. He suggests that intensive deviant case analysis may avoid both problems. He emphasizes the use of more rigorous data collection procedures and more care in data inference.

819. Haire, Mason, and others, Managerial Thinking, New York: John Wiley & Sons, 1966.

820. _____ (ed.), Modern Organization Theory, New York: John Wiley & Sons, 1959.

821. _____, Organizational Theory in Industrial Practice, New York: John Wiley & Sons, 1962.

822. Hall, Edward T., The Hidden Dimension, Garden City, N. Y.: Doubleday, 1966.
    Utilizing information from animal studies and human observations, anthropologist Hall demonstrates that animals and humans have a sense of psychic space which differs from species to species and among peoples of the human race. Crowding creates stress situations at varying rates with one result seen in animals being a lowering of the birth rate and a rise in the death rate.

823. Hall, Richard H., J. Eugene Haas, and Norman J. Johnson, "An Examination of the Blau-Scott and Etzioni Typologies," Administrative Science Quarterly, 12(June 1967), 118-39.

824. Halpin, Andrew W., and D. B. Croft, The Organizational Climate of Schools, Chicago: Midwest Center, University of Chicago, 1963.
    Analyzes the organizational climate of 71 schools. The result was the development and description of six school climates classified as: open, autonomous, controlled, familiar, paternal, and closed.

(C1)

825. _____, *Theory and Research in Administration*, New York: The Macmillan Co., 1966.

826. Harbison, F. H., and J. R. Coleman, *Goals and Strategy in Collective Bargaining*, New York: Harper & Brothers, 1951.

827. Hardwich, Clyde T., and Bernard F. Landuyt, *Administrative Strategy*, New York: Simmons-Boardman, 1961.

828. Harvey, E., "Technology and the Structure of Organizations," *American Sociological Review*, 33(April 1968), 247-58.

829. Hawley, Willis D., and Frederick M. Wirt, *Search for Community Power*, Englewood Cliffs, N. J.: Prentice-Hall, 1968.
   Traces substantive and methodological developments of elitist and pluralistic structural conflicts.

829.1 Helmer, Olaf, Theodore Gordon, and Bernice Brown, *Social Technology*, New York: Basic Books, 1966.

830. Herskovits, Melville J., "The Organization of Work," in W. E. Moore and A. S. Feldman (eds.), *Labor Commitment and Social Change in Developing Areas*, New York: Social Science Research Council, 1960, 123-35.

831. Hicks, Herbert G., *The Management of Organizations*, New York: McGraw-Hill, 1968.

832. Hollander, Samuel, *The Sources of Increased Efficiency: A Study of Du Pont Rayon Plants*, Cambridge, Mass.: The M.I.T. Press, 1965.

833. Homans, George Casper, *The Human Group*, New York: Harcourt, Brace, & Co., 1950.
   Emphasizes role relationships in terms of superior-subordinate activity examined from a sociological viewpoint. Social change is examined through the study of equilibrium and the interaction of internal-external system relationships.

834. _____, *Sentiments and Activities: Essays in Social Sciences*, New York: The Free Press, 1962.

835. _____, "Social Behavior as Exchange," *American Journal of Sociology*, 63(May 1958), 597-606.

836. _____, *Social Behavior: Its Elementary Forms*, New York: Harcourt, Brace and World, 1961.
   This book may be read as a sequel to the author's, *The Human Group*, or independently as a systematic statement of a theory of interaction. The author attempts to show that generalizations at one level are instances of generalizations at a more inclusive level. Explanatory framework, borrowed from economics, defines interaction as exchange in which each participant seeks fair value received for value given. A set of propositions from learning theory is used to augment prediction at various points.

837. Hopkins, Terence K., *The Exercise of Influence in Small Groups*, Totowa, N. J.: The Bedminster Press, 1965.

(C1)

Provides an insightful analysis of influence in small group behavior. It appears that many of the propositions advanced also apply to certain types of change agents, particularly small groups internal to an organization.

838. Horowitz, Irving Louis, "Professionalism and Disciplinarianism," *Philosophy of Science*, 31(July 1964), 275-81.

839. _____, "The Search for a Development Ideal: Alternative Models and Their Implications," *Sociological Quarterly*, 8(Autumn 1967), 427-38.

840. Huntington, Samuel P., *The Common Defense*, New York: Columbia University Press, 1961.

841. Hutchinson, John G., *Organization: Theory and Classical Concepts*, New York: Holt, Rinehart, and Winston, 1967.

842. Ilchman, Warren, and Todd R. LaPorte, *Comparative Administration: Synthesis and Analysis* (in the press).

843. Jasinski, Frank J., "Adapting Organization to New Technology," *Harvard Business Review*, 37(January-February 1959), 79-86.
    Integration between technology and organization can be brought about in several ways: by changing the technology; by changing the organization, and by introducing mechanisms. Difficulties usually occur when attempts at integration lack a systematic and purposeful approach. Systematic analysis of technology and organization might include the following: (1) determine relations required by work flow of the technology, (2) identify points where formal organization meets and does not meet these requirements, (3) determine existing nonformal relationships in the organization, (4) determine existing formal structure for coping with unusual relationships, (5) decide which informal relationships might profitably be formalized, and (6) take measures to facilitate desirable existing nonformal relationships which had best remain nonformal.

844. Johnson, Richard, and others, *The Theory and Management of Systems*, New York: McGraw-Hill Book Co., 1968.

845. Johnson, Walter L. (ed.), *The Management of Aerospace Programs*, Tarzana, Cal.: American Astronautical Society, 1967.

846. Jones, Edward E., *Ingratiation: A Social Psychological Analysis*, New York: Appleton-Century Crofts, 1964.

847. Kahn, Robert L., and Elise Boulding, *Power and Conflict in Organizations*, New York: Basic Books Co., 1964.

848. Kahn, Robert S., and others, *Organizational Stress: Studies in Role Conflict and Ambiguity*, New York: John Wiley and Sons, 1964.
    Utilizing the framework of role theory, this book examines the pressures that occur in various echelons of modern, large scale organizations.

849. Katz, Daniel, and Robert L. Kahn, *The Social Psychology of Organization*,

(C1)

New York: John Wiley and Sons, 1966.
   The authors attempt a synthesis of recent work of social scientists in organizational theory through the extension of the open system theory, especially in terms of roles.

850. Katz, Elihu, and Paul F. Lazaesfeld, <u>Personal Influence, The Part Played by People in Mass Communications</u>, Glencoe, Ill.: The Free Press, 1955.

851. Katz, Elihu, Herbert Hamilton, and Martin Levin, <u>Problems in Social Psychology</u>, New York: McGraw-Hill Book Co., 1966.

852. Katz, Fred E., <u>Autonomy and Organization: The Limits of Social Control</u>, New York: Random House, 1968.

853. Kaufman, Herbert, "Organization Theory and Political Theory," <u>American Political Science Review</u>, 58(March 1964), 5-14.
   A solid article reviewing the common features and problem of organization and political theory. Especially useful in presenting a short overall survey of organizational theory, its growth and development. In doing so, the article points out contributions and problem areas of current organizational theory to an understanding of men in social settings.

854. Kelley, Harold H., <u>The Social Psychology of Groups</u>, New York: John Wiley and Sons, 1959.

855. Kelly, Joe, <u>Organizational Behavior</u>, Homewood, Ill.: R. D. Irwin, 1969.

856. Kerr, Clark, and others, <u>Industrialism and Industrial Man</u>, Cambridge, Mass.: Harvard University Press, 1960.

857. Konig, Rene, <u>The Community</u> (translated from German by Edward Fitzgerald), London: Routledge & Kegan Paul, Ltd., 1968.

858. Krech, David, Richard S. Crutchfield, and Egerton S. Ballachery, <u>Individual in Society</u>, New York: McGraw-Hill Book Co., 1962.

859. Krupp, Sherman, <u>Pattern on Organizational Analysis: A Critical Examination</u>, Philadelphia: Chilton Co., 1961.

860. Kudson, Harry R., Jr., <u>Human Elements of Administration</u>, New York: Holt, Rinehart & Winston, 1963.
   The author has compiled an excellent selection of readings, cases and exercises related to the human side of enterprise. The articles stress organizational theory. Topics covered are: administrative climate, motivation and behavior, leadership and authority, communication in the organization, administration of change, and administrative control.

861. Kuhn, Thomas S., <u>The Structure of Scientific Revolutions</u>, Chicago: University of Chicago Press, 1962.

862. Kunkel, John H., "Some Behavioral Aspects of the Ecological Approach to Social Organization," <u>American Journal of Sociology</u>, 73(July 1967), 12-29.

863. Lawrence, Paul R., and Jay W. Lorsch, <u>Organization and Environment, Managing Differentiation and Integration</u>, Cambridge, Mass.: Harvard University Business School, 1967; also Homewood, Ill.: R. D. Irwin, 1969.

(C1)

Central theme is that different kinds of organizations are needed to cope with different environmental conditions. In investigating this theme, light is thrown on another critical organization issue: "How do organizations respond to changing technology and how do they organize for innovation?"

864. Lawrence, Paul R., and others, <u>Organizational Behavior and Administration</u>, New York: The Dorsey Press, 1965.
   This book is composed of seven sections: The Human Problems of Administration, Work Group Behavior, Supervisor Behavior, Diagnosing and Proposing Remedial Action, Inter-Group Behavior, Organizational Behavior and Wider Culture, and the Administrator as An Agent of Organizational Change. The last section consists of case studies on change as well as concepts and research findings on various aspects of change and the change agent, including: Gene W. Dalton, "Criteria for Planning Organizational Change;" Paul R. Lawrence, "Resistance to Change;" Robert R. Blake and others, "A Study of Organizational Development;" Kenneth D. Benne, "Changes in Institutions and the Role of the Change Agent;" and James E. Richard, "A President's Experience with Democratic Management."

865. Learned, Edmund Philip, and Audrey T. Sproat, <u>Organizational Theory and Policy</u>, Homewood, Ill.: R. D. Irwin, 1966.

866. Leavitt, Harold J., <u>Managerial Psychology</u>, Chicago: University of Chicago Press, 1968.

867. _____ (ed.), <u>The Social Science of Organizations: Four Perspectives</u>, Englewood Cliffs, N. J.: Prentice-Hall, Inc., 1963.
   Consists of an excellent collection of essays drawn from several social science disciplines on organizational behavior. The book is especially good on the growth and development of leading concepts of organizational theory and change.

868. Le Breton, Preston P., and William G. Scott (eds.), <u>Academy of Management 28th Annual Meeting: Organization Structure and Behavior</u>, Eugene, Ore: Academy of Management, 1969.
   Partial contents -"Social systems analysis and industrial humanism: awareness without revelation," by R. A. Smith III. "Introducing technological change in a bureaucratic structure: a case study," by R. Hoffman and R. W. Archibald. "Achieving integration through information systems," by J. R. Galbraith. "Managerial motivation: the impact of role diversity, job level, and organizational size," by A. M. Elsalmi and L. L. Cummings. "The economics of executive mobility," by W. F. Glueck.

869. _____, <u>Administrative Intelligence--Information Systems</u>, Boston: Houghton Mifflin Co., 1969.

870. _____ (ed.), <u>Comparative Administrative Theory</u>, Seattle, Wash.: University of Washington Press, 1968.

871. Leibenstein, Harvey, <u>Economic Theory and Organizational Analysis</u>, New York: Harper & Brothers, 1960.
   A theoretical discussion of integrating microeconomic theory and organizational analysis. The author largely deals with organizational analyses in the terms of Chester Barnard and Herbert A. Simon. Leading concepts in organizational theory are presented in a simple and

forthright manner. His general model is based upon organizational equilibrium.

872. Leighton, Alexander H., <u>The Governing of Men</u>, Princeton, N. J.: Princeton University Press, 1946.
   Deals with observations and analyses that have bearing on general problems of administration derived from the experiences at a Japanese relocation camp when 110,000 Japanese were moved in the Spring of 1942. Emphasis is on remedial change operating under stress situations.

873. Levine, Soloman, and Paul E. White, "Exchange as a Conceptual Framework for the Study of Interorganizational Relationships," <u>Administrative Science Quarterly</u>, 5(March 1961), 583-601.

874. Levy, Marion J., Jr., <u>Modernization and the Structure of Societies: A Setting for International Affairs</u>, two volumes, Princeton, N. J.: Princeton University Press, 1966.
   An extremely detailed treatment of the structure of societies following a continuum traditional-modern structures. Especially useful in the broader analysis of society as a social system.

875. _____, <u>The Structure of Society</u>, Princeton, N. J.: Princeton University Press, 1952.
   Intended to be an initial step in a long-range program of comparative social analysis, offering a tentative and very abstract system for analysis of any society, and a process by which segments of a society can be analyzed and related to the whole society.

876. Likert, Rensis, <u>The Human Organization: Its Management and Value</u>, New York: McGraw-Hill Book Co., 1967.
   The original theory was presented in his earlier volume, <u>New Patterns of Management</u>. Further research and field tests have enabled him to add to the theory and to describe more fully a workable management system which can be used by any enterprise to achieve high productivity, above average financial success, and improved labor relations. He has substituted a systems approach for the piece-meal methods usually employed in efforts to improve an organization. The result is a highly effective management system whose parts are mutually compatible.

877. _____, <u>New Patterns of Management</u>, New York: McGraw-Hill Book Co., 1961.
   Presents an improved organization theory based on techniques of managers achieving the best results in American business and government, and draws upon research done in voluntary organizations. The focus is predominantly on business enterprises. More important subjects oriented toward change are effective supervision, nature of highly effective groups, the interaction-influence system, and the function of measurements.

878. Lindblom, Charles E., "The Science of 'Muddling Through,'" <u>Public Administration Review</u>, 19(Spring 1959), 79-88.

879. Litterer, Joseph (ed.), <u>Organizations: Structure and Behavior</u>, New York: John Wiley and Sons, 1963.
   A book of readings and commentaries on organizational theory largely from the behavioral approach. Part IV, dealing with "organizational

adaptation," is particularly useful in studying planned organizational change.

880. Loomis, Charles P., and Allen J. Beagle, <u>Rural Social Systems</u>, New York: Prentice-Hall, Inc., 1950.
    A treatise on the structure of rural society and as such it is concerned with social groups which are styled "social systems." The first three parts deal with the family and informal groups, locality groups and social strata. The last three deal with religious, educational, political and occupational groups and service agencies.

881. Lyden, Fremont J., George A. Shipman, and Morton Kroll (eds.), <u>Policies, Decisions, and Organization</u>, New York: Appleton-Century Crofts, 1969.
    A selection of interdisciplinary readings, with comment, focussed squarely on the dynamics of decision-making in the administrative situation. In a field in which the very volume and variety of the literature threaten to overwhelm both the student and practitioner, the text develops a needed analytic framework in which to study the decision-making process.

882. Lynch, Charles J., "A Communication Revolution," <u>Science and Technology</u>, 76 (April 1968), 30-40.

883. McGregor, Douglas, <u>The Human Side of Enterprise</u>, New York: McGraw-Hill Book Co., 1960.

884. _____, <u>The Professional Manager</u>, New York: McGraw-Hill Book Co., 1967.
    A vital book that concerns itself with the various means by which the manager can grow and realize his basic goals while at the same time furthering the goals of the organization itself. In this new book McGregor has linked some of the main concepts of his earlier text, <u>The Human Side of Enterprise</u>, to the basic concepts of the behavioral sciences, notably social psychology and psychiatry, while at the same time developing methodologies for changing organizations.

885. MacKenzie, W. J. M., <u>Politics and Social</u>, Baltimore: Penguin Books, 1967.

886. Maier, Norman R. F., <u>Frustration: The Study of Behavior Without A Goal</u>, Ann Arbor, Mich.: The University of Michigan Press, 1961.
    A study of human behavior in situations where no goal is prevalent.

887. Mailick, Sidney, and Edward A. Van Ness (eds.), <u>Concepts and Issues in Administrative Behavior</u>, Englewood Cliffs, N. J.: Prentice-Hall, Inc., 1962.
    This book presents a collection of essays on administrative behavior. The following articles are particularly useful on the subject of planned organizational change: William R. Dill, "The Impact of Environment on Organizational Development;" Norton E. Long, "The Administrative Organization as a Political System;" and Daniel Katz, "Human Interrelationships and Organizational Behavior."

888. Maniha, John, and Charles Perrow, "The Reluctant Organization and the Aggressive Environment," <u>Administrative Science Quarterly</u>, 10(September 1965), 256-57.

(C1)

889. March, James G. (ed.), <u>Handbook of Organizations</u>, Chicago: Rand McNally & Co., 1965.
    Encyclopaedia treatment of the rapidly expanding scholarship on organizational theory and behavior.

890. _____, and Herbert A. Simon, <u>Organizations</u>, New York: John Wiley and Sons, Inc., 1958.
    This classic represents an attempt to integrate and codify much of the relevant information about organization theory into a set of testable hypothesis and propositions.

891. Marrows, Alfred J., David G. Bowers, and Stanley E. Seashore, <u>Management By Participation</u>, New York: Harper & Row Publishers, 1967.

892. Marsh, Robert M., "The Bearing of Comparative Analysis on Sociological Theory," <u>Social Forces</u>, 43(December 1964), 188-96.
    According to the author if a researcher compares data from two or more societies, he can make four major contributions. They are as follows: (1) to broaden the range of variations in variables, thereby requiring theory to explain more than it has heretofore; (2) to replicate studies done in one society in other similar societies; (3) to generalize propositions from one type of society to other types of societies, and (4) to specify apparently discrepant findings from different societies by developing new positions which account for the originally discrepant findings.

893. Meier, Richard F., "Explorations in the Realm of Organization Theory IV: The Simulation of Social Organization," <u>Behavioral Science</u>, 6(July 1961), 232-48.
    This article places emphasis upon the synthesis of organizations, reviews recent literature on simulation studies of social organizations, and explores ideas leading to further expansion of this method for studying social organizations.

894. Meier, Richard L., <u>A Communication Theory of Urban Growth</u>, Cambridge, Mass.: The M.I.T. Press, 1962.

895. Melton, A. W., and G. E. Briggs, "Engineering Psychology" in <u>Annual Review of Psychology</u>, Vol. 2, Palo Alto, Cal.: Annual Reviews, Inc., 1960.

896. Merton, R. K., <u>Social Theory and Social Structure: Toward the Codification of Theory and Research</u>, Glencoe, Ill.: The Free Press, 1949.

897. Michaels, Donald, "Some Long-Range Implications of Computer Technology for Human Behavior in Organizations," <u>American Behavioral Scientist</u>, 9(April 1966), 29-35.

898. Miller, David, and Martin Starr, <u>The Structure of Human Decisions</u>, Englewood Cliffs, N. J.: Prentice-Hall, 1967.

899. Miller, Eric, and A. K. Rice, <u>Systems of Organization</u>, London: Tavistock Publications, 1967.

900. Miller, Eric, <u>Systems of Organization: The Control of Task and Sentient Boundaries</u>, New York: Barnes & Noble, 1967.

901. Miller, G. A., E. Galenter, and K. H. Pribram, <u>Plans and the Structure of Behavior</u>, New York: Holt, 1960.

902. Millett, John D., <u>Organization for the Public Service</u>, New York: Van Nostrand, 1966.

903. Moore, Wilbert E., <u>Order and Change: Essays in Comparative Sociology</u>, New York: John Wiley and Sons, 1967.

903.1 National Research Council, Advisory Committee on Government Programs in the Behavioral Sciences, <u>The Behavioral Sciences and the Federal Government</u>, Washington, D. C.: National Academy of Sciences Publication 1680, 1968.

904. Newman, A., <u>Organizational Analysis</u>, Carbondale, Ala.: Southern University Press, 1968.

905. Noville, Pierre, "Technical Elites and Social Elites," <u>Sociology of Education</u>, 37(Fall 1963), 27-29.

906. Olmsted, Donald W., <u>Social Groups, Roles and Leadership: An Introduction to the Concepts</u>, East Lansing, Mich.: Institute of Community Development and Services, Michigan State University, 1961.
    A short treatment of group theory with special application of community social organizations. The definitions of essential concepts are succinct and precise, and are particularly useful in designing research constructs on planned organizational change.

907. Olsen, Marvin E., <u>The Process of Social Organization</u>, New York: Holt, Rinehart and Winston, 1968.

908. Parsons, Talcott, "A Sociological Approach to the Theory of Organization," <u>Administrative Science Quarterly</u>, 1(June, September 1956), 63-85, 225-39.

909. _____, and Edward A. Shils (eds.), <u>Toward A General Theory of Action: Theoretical Foundations of Social Science</u>, New York: Harper Torchbook, 1962.
    A treatise on the behavioral foundation for a general theory in social science. The sections dealing with concepts of the social system are particularly useful.

910. _____, R. F. Bales, and E. A. Shils (eds.), <u>Working Papers in the Theory of Action</u>, Glencoe, Ill.: The Free Press, 1953.

911. Peabody, Robert L., <u>Organizational Authority</u>, New York: Atherton Press, 1964.

912. Pennock, J. Roland, and John W. Chapman (eds.), <u>Voluntary Associations</u>, New York: Atherton Press, 1969.

913. Perrow, Charles, "The Analysis of Goals in Complex Organizations, <u>American Sociological Review</u>, 26(December 1961), 854-65.

914. _____, "Organizational Goals" in David Sills (ed.), <u>International Encyclopedia of Social Sciences</u>, New York: Macmillan and The

Free Press, 1968, 11, 305-11.

Derived goals are distinguished from system goals, which relate to system characteristics of the organization, such as its emphasis upon growth, stability, risk, and from product goals, which relate to the type and characteristics of the goods or services produced, such as the emphasis upon quality, quantity, variety, etc. Derived goals may, in time, become system or product goals.

915. Pfiffner, John M., and Frank P. Sherwood, Administrative Organization, New York: Prentice-Hall, Inc., 1960.

916. Porter, Lyman W., and Edward E. Lawler, Managerial Attitudes and Performance, Homewood, Ill.: Richard D. Irwin, 1968.

The concern of this book is the relationship between job attitudes of managers and their on-the-job performance. The study is pursued first by construction of a theoretical model in which the key variables are identified and related to one another, and second by analysis of empirical data collected to test and evaluate the model. The authors conclude with an evaluation of their model and some suggested implications of their findings for practical applications by organizations.

917. Presthus, Robert, Behavioral Approach to Public Administration, Birmingham, Ala.: University of Alabama Press, 1965.

Discusses the leading scholarly thoughts, concepts, and possible trends in the use of the behavioral approach.

918. _____, Men at the Top, New York: Oxford University Press, 1964.

A study of the exercise of power in two small communities in New York State. It attempts to integrate concepts of political pluralism and community hierarchy. Chapter Eleven, dealing with power structure and organizational defectiveness, particularly provides insights which pertain to planned organizational change on a community level.

919. _____, The Organizational Society, New York: Alfred Knopf, 1962.

Large scale organizations as miniature social systems employ similar mechanisms to induce socialization. The pattern of accommodation in the large scale organization depends upon the nature of individual experiences and background both within and outside the family environment. The patterns, according to Presthus, are of three types: upward mobile, indifferent, and ambivalent.

920. Price, James, Organizational Effectiveness, Homewood, Ill.: Richard D. Irwin, 1968.

921. Pugh, D. S., "A Conceptual Scheme for Organizational Analysis," Administrative Science Quarterly, 8(December 1963), 289-315.

A detailed review of the literature on bureaucracy. Examines its shortcomings and deals with them by postulating a conceptual framework for analyzing the structure and functioning of organizations which serve as predictive instruments.

922. _____, D. J. Hickson, and C. R. Hinings, Writers on Organizations, London: Hutchinson & Co., 1964.

(C1)

923. Raiffa, Howard, <u>Decision Analysis: Introductory Lectures on Choices Under Uncertainty</u>, Reading, Mass.: Addison-Wesley, 1968.

924. Ramsoy, Odd, <u>Social Groups as System and Subsystem</u>, New York: The Free Press of Glencoe, 1963.
    This book focuses on the relationship between a subsystem and an inclusive social system; describes a number of empirical occurrences in modern and developing cosieties; proposes a theoretical structure to handle the analysis of complex system; and lists a number of tentative generalizations.

925. Rapaport, Anatol, <u>Strategy and Conscience</u>, New York: Harper & Row, 1964.

926. Rogers, Carl, and B. F. Skinner, "Some Issues Concerning the Control of Human Behavior: A Symposium" <u>Science</u>, 124(November 30, 1956), 1057-65.

927. Ross, Murray G., <u>Community Organization: Theory and Principles</u>, New York: Harper & Row Publishers, 1955.
    A discussion of the theory underlying community planning services and the principles involved in the understanding and the use of community organization process.

928. Roth, J. A., "Ritual and Magic in Control and Contagion," <u>American Sociological Review</u>, 22(June 1957), 310-14. See E. Kuginka for comment and Roth's reply in 22(December 1957), 726-27.

929. Rubenstein, Albert H., and Chadwick J. Heverstroh (eds.), <u>Some Theories of Organization</u>, Homewood, Ill.: The Dorsey Press, Inc., and Richard D. Irwin, Inc., 1960.

930. Ruitenbeck, Hendrick M., <u>The Dilemma of Organizational Society</u>, New York: E. P. Dulton & Co., 1963.

931. Schein, Edgar H., <u>Organizational Psychology</u>, Englewood Cliffs, N. J.: Prentice-Hall, 1965.

932. Schelling, Thomas C., <u>The Strategy of Conflict</u>, Oxford: Galaxy Books, 1963.

933. Schramm, Wilbur L. (ed.), <u>Mass Communication: A Book of Readings</u>, Urbana, Ill.: The University Press, 1949.

934. Scott, William G., <u>Organizational Theory: A Behavioral Analysis for Management</u>, Homewood, Ill.: Richard D. Irwin, Inc., 1967.
    Scott creates a theoretical model centered around the importance of human relations in organizational behavior. The body of the volume is divided into four parts: the history of management values and human relations in organizations, the "human territory of administration," processes within the "social territory," and the problems and issues in the human territory. The author readily admits that the book is value-laden, but feels that knowledge of these values and their implications is essential to enlightened administrative action.

935. Seashore, Stanley E., <u>Assessing Organizational Performance with Behavioral Measurements</u>, Ann Arbor, Mich.: Foundation for Research on Human Behavior, 1964.

(C1)

936. Seiler, John A., System Analysis in Organizational Behavior, Homewood, Ill.: Richard D. Irwin, Inc., 1967.

937. Selznick, Philip, Leadership in Administration, Evanston, Ill.: Row, Peterson and Co., 1957.

938. _____, The Organizational Weapon, Glencoe, Ill.: The Free Press, 1960.

939. _____, TVA and the Grass Roots, Berkeley and Los Angeles: University of California Press, 1949; New York: Harper & Row, 1966.
    Selznik analyzes the concept of grass roots administration as it operated in the context of the functions and dilemmas of official doctrine of the Tennessee Valley Authority.

940. Sherif, Muzafer (ed.), Intergroup Relations and Leadership, Norman, Okla.: Institution of Group Relations, University of Oklahoma Press, 1962.
    A collection of papers originating from an inter-disciplinary symposium held at the University of Oklahoma in 1961; makes available some highlights of intergroup research. The collection is divided into three sections: problems of approach and theory, inter-system and intra-system relations, and their reciprocal impact. It brings out some intergroup problems related with social change. In his chapter Sherif develops the concept of "superordinate goals," as means of reducing conflicts between groups.

941. Sherwood, Frank P., "Devolution as a Problem of Organization Strategy," in Robert T. Daland (ed.), Comparative Urban Research: The Administration and Politics of Cities, Beverly Hills, Cal.: Sage Publications, 1969, 60-87.

942. Shipman, George A., "Complexities of Goal Attainment," Public Administration Review, 29(March/April 1969), 210-13.

943. _____, "Measurement of Agency Effectiveness," Public Administration Review, 29(March/April 1969), 206-7.

944. Simon, Herbert A., Administrative Behavior, New York: Macmillan Co., 1958.
    A leading study of decision-making in administrative organization. Chapter Six, dealing with "The Equilibrium of the Organization" is particularly useful for theoretical constructs on planned organizational change.

945. _____, "Man's New Information Environment," Far Horizons, 2 (May 1969), 1-6.
    Discusses factors to consider when designing an information system.

946. _____, Models of Man: Social and Rational, New York: John Wiley & Sons, 1957.
    A mathematical treatment of human behavior in social settings. The sections on rational goal determination are particularly useful.

947. _____, The New Science of Management Decision, New York: Harper, 1960.

948. _____, "On the Concept of Organizational Goal," <u>Administrative Science Quarterly</u>, 9(June 1964), 1-22.
    Defines organizational goal without reifying the organization. The term is used to refer to constraints or set of constraints, imposed by the organizational goal, that have only an indirect relation with the personal motives of the individual who fills the role.

949. _____, Donald W. Smithburg, and Victor A. Thompson, <u>Public Administration</u>, New York: Alfred A. Knopf, 1962.
    This book is largely built on a few concepts of human behavior. Chapter 18, "The Struggle for Existence: Organizational Equilibrium," is particularly useful on the subject of planned organizational change.

950. _____, "Theories of Decision-Making in Economics and the Behavioral Sciences," <u>American Economic Review</u>, 49(June 1959), 253-83.

951. Simpson, Richard L., and William H. Gulley, "Goals, Environmental Pressures, and Organizational Characteristics," <u>American Sociological Review</u>, 27 (1962), 344-50.
    A study of the relationship of authority structure and organizational goals in voluntary organizations. Both are examined in connection with internal and external pressures. The general hypothesis that organizations with many goals and subject to community demands will exhibit less bureaucratization than those of few goals and little connection.

952. Sjoberg, Gideon, "Contradictory Functional Requirements and Social Systems," <u>Conflict Resolution</u>, 4(June 1960), 198-208.
    The article suggests a modification in the existing structural-functional theory which will enable it to better incorporate sociological findings with respect to both social change and the recurrent tensions within and among social systems. The author concentrates his attention on the outstanding weakness of "harmony" of "self consistency" in social systems with little attention given to the processes of change as a result of this formulation. The crux of argument is a social system is an exceedingly complex entity, whose structural arrangements reflecting mutually contradictory functional demands upon it are often at odds with one another. As a result, no particular social pattern can ever be fully realized.

953. Skinner, B. F., <u>Science and Human Behavior</u>, New York: Macmillan, 1953.

955. Spann, R. N., "The Study of Organization," <u>Public Administration</u>, 40(Winter 1962), 387-405.

956. Steiner, Gary A. (ed.), <u>The Creative Organization</u>, Chicago: University of Chicago Press, 1965.

957. Stover, Carl F. (ed.), <u>The Technological Order</u>, Detroit, Mich.: Wayne State University Press, 1963.

958. Sutermeister, Robert A., <u>People and Productivity</u>, New York: McGraw-Hill Book Co., 1963.
    A book of cases, readings, articles and commentaries on the ways to work with people in organizational settings.

(C1)

959. Tannenbaum, Arnold S., "Control in Organizations: Individual Adjustment and Organizational Performance," *Administrative Science Quarterly*, 7 (September 1962), 236-57.
   A synthesis of recent research. Evidence suggests that increased control exercised at all levels of the organizational hierarchy is associated with increased organizational effectiveness.

959.1 _____, *Social Psychology of the Work Organization*, Belmont, Cal.: Wadsworth, 1966.

960. Tannenbaum, Robert, and others (eds.), *Leadership and Organization*, New York: McGraw-Hill Book Co., 1961.
   This book analyzes the functions of leadership in organizations. Its social-psychological orientation has as one of its major dimensions the problems of innovation and change within organizational structures.

960.1 Tausky, Curt, *Work Organizations: Major Theoretical Perspectives*, Iasca, Ill.: Peacock Publishers, 1970.
   This text critically discusses the major theories of work organization--classical theory, human relations and structuralism--and the basic processes in organization. The link between individual and organizational goals, hierarchical controls, immobility and productivity are discussed.

961. Thibaut, John W., and Harold H. Kelly, *The Social Psychology of Groups*, New York: John Wiley and Sons, 1967.
   A basic text and treatise on the subjects of dyadic relationships and complex relationships. Nearly every section contains useful data on the behavior of agents involved in the planned change process. The sections on the social exchange process are especially useful.

962. Thompson, James D. (ed.), *Approaches to Organizational Design*, Pittsburgh: University of Pittsburgh Press, 1966.
   Consists of a set of five carefully prepared papers on the following subjects: (1) dimensions of organizational theory, (2) design of organizations, (3) organization as a system of constraints, (4) organizational set, toward a theory of inter-organizational relations, and (5) innovations in organizations.

963. _____, and others, *Comparative Studies in Administration*, Pittsburgh: University of Pittsburgh Press, 1959.
   Book consists of twelve comparative studies gleaned from the literature of sociology, anthropology, and administration. Cross-cultural as well as cross-institutional subjects are discussed.

964. _____, and William J. McEwen, "Organizational Goals and Environment: Goal Setting as an Interaction Process," *American Sociological Review*, 23(February 1958), 23-30.

965. _____, *Organizations in Action: The Social Sciences Bases of Administration Theory*, New York: McGraw-Hill Book Co., 1967.

966. Thompson, Victor A., *Modern Organization*, New York: Alfred A. Knopf, 1961.
   Modern organization attempts to fit specialization into the older hierarchical framework. There is a growing gap between the right to

decide, which is authority, and the power to do so, which is specialized ability. This gap is growing because technological change, with resulting increase in specialization, occurs at a faster rate than the change in cultural definitions of hierarchical roles. This situation produces tensions and strains the willingness to co-operate. Much bureaucratic behavior can be understood as a reaction to these tensions. In sum, a symptomatic characteristic of modern bureaucracy is the growing imbalance between "ability" and "authority."

967. Tonnies, Ferdinand, Community and Society: Gemeinschaft and Gesellschaft (Translated and edited by Charles P. Loomis), New York: Harper Torchbooks, 1957).

968. Torgersen, Paul E., A Concept of Organization, New York: American Book, Van Nostrand, 1969.

968.1 Trist, E. L., and others, Organizational Choice, London: Tavistock, 1963.

969. Udy, Stanley H., Jr., "'Bureaucracy and Rationality' in Weber's Organization Theory: An Empirical Study," American Sociological Review, 24 (December 1959), 791-95.

970. _____, "The Comparative Analysis of Organizations" in James G. March (ed.), Handbook of Organizations, Chicago: Rand McNally & Co., 1965, 678-709.

971. Van Ness, E. H., Concepts and Issues in Administrative Behavior, Englewood Cliffs, N. J.: Prentice-Hall, 1963.

972. Verba, Sidney, Small Groups and Political Behavior: A Study of Leadership, Princeton, N. J.: Princeton University Press, 1961.
    The book concentrates on an analysis of three problems: the relationship between effective leadership and instrumental leadership, the interrelation between the norms of the groups and social change, and participation in decisions and acceptability. Verba's careful treatment of small group experiments provides an understanding of leader-follower relationships.

973. Vickers, Geoffrey, Value Systems and Social Process, Basic Books, 1968.

974. Vogt, Evon Z., and Thomas F. O'Dea, "A Comparative Study of the Role of Values in Social Action in Two South-Western Communities," American Sociological Review, 18(December 1953), 645-53.

975. Vroom, Victor H. (ed.), Methods of Organizational Research, Pittsburgh: University of Pittsburgh, 1967.
    Consists of four quality papers upon the following subjects: organizations in the laboratory, organizational change and field experiment methods, comparative study of organizations, and computer simulation models for organizational theory. This publication contains many useful sections on the theoretical aspects of organizational change and offers a number of constructive proposals.

976. Waldo, Dwight, The Administrative State: A Study of the Political Theory of American Public Administration, New York: The Ronald Press, 1948.

(C1)

A classical study of the public administration movement from the viewpoint of political theory and the history of ideas. Chapter Nine, "Principles, Theory of Organization and Scientific Method," and Chapter Ten, "Economy and Efficiency," are particularly useful in providing background information pertaining to planned organizational change.

977. _____, "Organizational Theory: An Elephantine Problem," Public Administration Review, 21(Autumn 1961), 210-25.
An excellent review article of six leading works on organizational theory published in 1959 or 1960. A basic reference for gaining an overall perspective of organizational theory as it relates to planned change.

978. _____, and Martin Landau, The Study of Organizational Theory, Status Problems, and Trends, Washington, D. C.: Comparative Administrative Group of American Society for Public Administration, 1966.

979. Warner, Aaron W. (ed.), The Environment of Change, New York: Columbia University Press, 1968.

980. _____, and A. Eugene Havens, "Goal Development and the Intangibility of Organizational Goals," Administrative Science Quarterly, 12 (March 1968), 539-55.
Excellent treatment on goals. For a commentary see George A. Shipman, "Complexities of Goal Attainment," Public Administration Review, 24 (March/April 1969), 210-13.

981. Weiss, Robert S., Process of Organization, Ann Arbor, Mich.: Survey Research Center, 1956.

982. Wertheim, W. F., "A Sociological Approach to Problems of Underdevelopment," East-West Parallels, The Hague: W. Van Hoeve, 1964, 3-22.

983. Westcott, John H., An Exposition of Adaptive Control, New York: Macmillan Co., 1962.

984. Whitehill, Arthur M., Jr., and Shinichi Takezawa, The Other Worker: A Comparative Study of Industrial Relations in the United States and Japan, Honolulu: East-West Center Press, 1969.

985. Whyte, William Foote, Men at Work, Homewood, Ill.: Richard D. Irwin Co., 1961.
Deals with the human problems of work at the levels of the individual, the group, and the organization. Cases are used to illustrate behavioral patterns in organizations. The last part, "A Theoretical Statement" is a good summary.

986. Wickesberg, Albert K., Management Organization, New York: Appleton Century Crofts, 1966.

987. Wiener, Norbert, The Human Use of Human Beings, New York: Houghton, Mifflin, 1950.

987.1 Wilensky, Harold L., "Organizational Intelligence" in David L. Sills (ed.), International Encyclopedia of the Social Sciences, New York: Macmillan and The Free Press, 1968, 11, 319-34.

(C1)

987.2 _____, <u>Organizational Intelligence: Knowledge and Policy in Government and Industry</u>, New York: Basic Books, 1967.

988. Young, Stanley, "Organization as a Total System" <u>California Management Review</u>, 10(Spring 1968), 21-32.

989. Zetterberg, Hans, <u>Social Theory and Social Practice</u>, New York: Bedminister Press, 1962.

2. SOCIAL CHANGE

990. Adams, Richard N., and others, Social Change in Latin America Today: Its Implications for United States Policy, New York: Harper & Row, Publishers, 1961.
    Six leading students of Latin American society analyze the social forces that are reshaping the societies of Latin America and highlight their meaning for American policy.

991. Albert, Ethel M., "Socio-Political Organization and Receptivity to Change: Some Differences between Ruanda and Urundi," Southwestern Journal of Anthropology, 16(Spring 1960), 46-74.
    A comparative socio-political study of the neighboring African kingdoms of Ruanda and Urundi in terms of their historical factors, traditional political organization, the kingships, social status, and kinship.

992. Allen, Francis R., and others, Technology and Social Change, New York: Appleton-Century Crofts, 1957.

993. Arensberg, Conrad M., and Arthur H. Niehoff, Introducing Social Change, Chicago: Aldine Publishing Company, 1964.

994. Armand, Louis, "Machines, Technology, and the Life of the Mind," Impact of Science on Society, 3(Autumn 1952), 155-70.

995. Ashby, Eric, "Technological Humanism," Impact of Science on Society, 9 (Spring 1958), 45-58.

996. Banfield, Edward C. and Laura, The Moral Basis for Backward Society, New York: The Free Press, 1958.

997. Barbichon, Guy, "Social Change: Innovation or Conformity?" International Social Science Journal, 20(3,1968), 412-30.

998. Bardis, P. D., "Synopsis of Theories of Social Change," Social Science, 37 (June 1962), 181-88.

999. Barnett, H. G., Anthropology in Administration, Evanston, Ill.: Row, Peterson & Co., 1956.

1000. Barnett, Harold, "Laws of Socio-Cultural Change," International Journal of Comparative Sociology, 6(September 1965), 207-30.

1001. Barringer, Herbert, and others (eds.), Social Change in Developing Areas, Schenkman, 1966.

1002. Barth, Frederik, "On the Study of Social Change," <u>American Anthropologist</u>, 69(December 1967), 661-69.

1003. Basu, T. K., <u>The Bengal Peasant From Time to Time</u>, Calcutta: Statistical Publishing Society, 1962.
   Gives an account of the impact of change on faith and behavior. There have been sharp changes from tradition occupations but social restrictions between castes remain entrenched as do most of the daily customs within each caste. The ritual structure of the village has been least affected.

1004. Beaglehole, Earnest, "Cultural Factors in Economic and Social Changes," <u>International Labor Review</u>, 69(May 1954), 415-32.

1005. Beals, Alan R., "Change in the Leadership of a Mysore Village," <u>The Economic Weekly</u> (Bombay), 5(April 1953), 487-92.
   An analysis of factors leading to change with attention given to the priestly castes and the money lenders.

1006. _____, and Bernard J. Sugel, <u>Divisiveness and Social Conflict: An Anthropological Approach</u>, Stanford, Cal.: Stanford University Press, 1966.
   A comparative study of social conflict as shown in two villages, Taos, New Mexico, and Namhalli, India. Useful study in the application of the anthropological approach to the study of social change.

1007. Bell, Daniel, "The Measurement of Knowledge and Technology" in Eleanor B. Sheldon and Wilbur E. Moore (eds.), <u>Indicators of Social Change</u>, New York: Russel Sage Foundation, 1968, 145-246.

1007.1 Bell, Daniel (ed.), <u>Toward the Year 2000</u>, New York: Houghton Mifflin, 1968.
   Includes articles by Herman Kahn, Anthony Wiener, Donald Schon, Martin Shubik, Fred Ickle, Leonard Duhl, Harvey Perloff, Daniel Moynihan, Laurence Frank, Stephen Graubard, Harold Orlans, Ernest Mayr, Gardner Quarton, Krister Stendahl, Erik Erikson, Margaret Mead, Harry Kalven, Jr., George Miller, David Riessman, John Pierce, Eugene Rostow, Samuel Huntington, Ithiel de Sola Pool, Daniel Bell, and James Wilson on all aspects of planning and development in the next thirty years. Originally published in <u>Daedalus</u> 96(Summer 1967).

1008. Belshaw, Cyril S., <u>Changing Melanesia</u>, Wellington: Oxford University Press, 1954.
   An account of the society of Eastern Melanesia--the three colonies of New Caledonia, the New Hebrides, and the British Solomon Island--as it has developed as a result of contact with the West.

1009. Benedict, Ruth, <u>Patterns of Culture</u>, Boston: Houghton Mifflin Compnay, 1934.

1009.1 Berry, Brian, <u>Strategies, Models, and Economic Theories of Development in Rural Regions</u>, Washington, D. C.: U. S. Department of Agriculture, Economic Research Service, Agricultural Economic Report No. 127, December, 1967.

1010. Bienen, Henry, *Violence and Social Change*, Chicago: University of Chicago Press, 1968.

1011. Bock, Kenneth E., "Evolution, Function, and Change," *American Sociological Review*, 28(April 1963), 229-37.

1012. Boguslaw, Robert, *The New Utopians: A Study of System Design and Social Change*, Englewood Cliffs, N. J.: Prentice-Hall, 1965.

1013. Bordis, P. D., "Synopsis of Theories of Social Change," *Social Science*, 37 (June 1962), 181-88.

1014. Borkner, Lloyd, *The Scientific Age: The Impact of Science on Society*, New Haven, Conn.: Yale University Press, 1964.

1015. Brickman, William (ed.), *Automation, Education, and Human Values*, New York: School and Society Books, 1966.

1016. Cahnman, Werner J., "Toennies and Social Change," *Social Forces*, 47(December 1968), 136-44.

1017. Carneiro, Robert L., "Cultural Adaptation," in David L. Sills (ed.), *International Encyclopedia of the Social Sciences*, New York: The Macmillan Co., and The Free Press, 1968, 3, 551-54.

1018. Carstairs, G. Morris, *This Island Now: The Surge of Social Change in the 20th Century*, New York: Basic Books, 1962.

1019. Clagett, Arthur, "Neo-behavioral Principles of Social and Cultural Change," *International Journal of Comparative Sociology*, 5(March 1964), 104-10.

1020. Concian, F., "Functional Analysis of Change," *American Sociological Review*, 25(December 1960), 818-27.

1021. Coser, Lewis, "Social Conflict and the Theory of Social Change," *British Journal of Sociology*, 8(September 1957), 197-207.

1022. Cottrell, W. F., "Death by Dieselization: A Case Study in the Reaction to Technological Change," *American Sociological Review*, 16(June 1951), 358-65.

1023. _____, *Energy and Society: The Relation Between Energy, Social Change, and Economic Development*, New York: McGraw-Hill Book Co., 1955.
    The thesis of the book is that the energy available to man limits what he can do and influences what he will do.

1024. Cressey, Donald R., "Achievement on an Unstated Organizational Goal," *Pacific Sociological Review*, 1(Fall 1958), 43-49.

1025. _____, "Contradictory Directives in Complex Organizations: The Case of the Prison," *Administrative Science Quarterly*, 4(June 1959), 1-19.

1026. Dechert, Charles (ed.), *The Social Impact of Cybernetics*, New York: Simon & Schuster, 1967.

1027. De Vries, Egbert, Man in Rapid Social Change, Garden City, N. Y.: Doubleday & Co., 1961.

1028. Diebold, John, Man and the Computer: Technology as an Agent of Social Change, New York: Frederick A. Praeger Co., 1969.

1029. Dobyns, Henry, and others, Methods for Analyzing Cultural Change, Ithaca, N. Y.: Cornell University, 1967.

1031. Drucker, Peter F., The Age of Discontinuity; Guidelines to Our Changing Society, New York: Harper & Row, 1969.
    Four major areas of 'discontinuity' are cited: the explosion of new technology that will produce major new industries; the change from an international to a world economy; a new 'society of organizations;' mass education and its implications for work and leisure. Singled out as most important is the changed position and power of knowledge, which has become America's central resource, its true basis of production.

1032. _____, "The First Technological Revolution and its Lessons," Technology and Culture, 7(Spring 1966), 143-51.

1033. Eames, E., and W. Schwab, "Urban Migration in India and Africa," Human Organization, 23(Spring 1964), 24-27.
    The article results from field studies in Rhodesia and India, and analyzes migration of rural people to urban areas in terms of demography, personal motivations and social structure. The conclusions are that Indians migrate purely for economic reasons, while the Africans do so for a variety of reasons.

1034. Eisenstadt, S. N., Analysis of Processes of Role Change, Jerusalem: Israel Universities Press, 1967.

1035. _____, Comparative Perspectives on Social Change, Boston: Little-Brown & Co., 1968.

1036. _____, Modernization: Protest and Change, Englewood Cliffs, N. J.: Prentice-Hall, 1966.

1037. _____, "Social Change, Differentiation, and Evolution," American Sociological Review, 29(June 1964), 375-85.

1037.1 _____, "Social Evolution," in David L. Sills (ed.), International Encyclopedia of the Social Sciences, New York: The Macmillan Co., and The Free Press, 1968, 5, 228-34.

1038. Epstein, T. S., Economic Development and Social Change, New York: Humanities Press, 1962.
    The effect of economic opportunities on social institutions is emphasized.

1039. Erasmus, Charles J., "Changing Folk Beliefs and the Relativity of Empirical Knowledge," Southwestern Journal of Anthropology, 9(Winter 1952), 411-28.

1040. Etzioni, Amitai and Eva (eds.), Social Change, Sources Patterns and Consequences, New York: Basic Books, 1964.

A comprehensive survey of social change. Selections cover the following aspects of change: "A Critical Evaluation of the Theory of Change," "Examples of Specific Social Changes," "Variety of Social Systems," and "Procedures and Processes by which Change is Introduced."

1041. Etzioni, Amitai, *Studies in Social Change*, New York: Holt-Rinehart & Winston, Inc., 1966.

1042. Fabun, Don, *The Dynamics of Change*, Englewood Cliffs, N. J.: Prentice-Hall, 1967.

1043. Flacks, Richard, "Protest or Conform: Some Social Psychological Perspectives on Legitimacy," *Journal of Applied Behavioral Science*, 5(2, 1969), 127-60.
    Examines the factors which determine the legitimacy of authority and concludes, "the legitimacy of established authority in the United States is reaching an historical turning point."

1044. Fontela, E., and others, "Forecasting Socio-economic Change," *Science Journal*, 1(September 1965), 81-88.

1045. Foster, George M., *Traditional Cultures and the Impact of Technological Change*, New York: Harper & Row Publishers, 1962.
    Presents the problems of culture change induced by sudden technological developments against a broad background of anthropological theory.

1046. Frey, F. W., "Surveying Peasant Attitudes in Turkey," *Public Opinion Quarterly*, 27(Fall 1963), 335-55.

1047. Ginzberg, Eli (ed.), *Technology and Social Change*, New York: Columbia University Press, 1964.
    A product of seminar held at Columbia University on "Technology and Social Change." The participants included economists, political scientists, sociologists, engineers, historians, philosophers, government administrators and businessmen. Charles R. De Carlo, Director of Education, I.B.M., in his paper, "Perspective on Technology," points out that people are generally frightened of large organizations and specialization, but in reality an individual employee in such organizations is provided a freedom which was not previously available to him. Professor Daniel Bell in his "The Post-Industrial Society," states that the post-industrial society will be dominated by intellectuals rather than by businessmen.

1048. Gittell, Marilyn, "A Typology of Power for Measuring Social Change," *The American Behavioral Scientist*, 9(April 1966), 23-28.
    Provides an operational model for analysis of social change as it relates to the distribution of power within a society.

1049. Gough, Kathleen, "Social Change in South India," *Economic Development and Cultural Change*, 13(April 1965), 358-62.

1049.1 Gross, Bertram M., *The State of the Nation, Social System Accounting*, London: Tavistock Publications, 1966.

1049.2 Gurin, Gerald, Joseph Veroff, and Sheila Feld, *Americans View Their Mental Health: A Nationwide Interview Survey*, New York: Basic Books, 1960.

1050. Hagen, Everett E., *On the Theory of Social Change: How Economic Growth Begins*, Homewood, Ill.: Dorsey Press, 1962.
    The author is concerned about those factors of personality that transform a stagnant traditional society into one that experiences continuing technological progress. He thinks that a powerful force is needed to disturb the equilibrium of a traditional society. The process begins when some group within the society finds that it no longer is accorded the respect that it had come to expect. Hagen argues that the anxiety which this loss of "status respect" causes in adults will alter the home environment in predictable ways, which, accumulating over several generations, may lead members of this group to embrace roles of creative leadership. The latter half of the book attempts to test, by means of case studies, the hypothesis that entrepreneurs arise in the early stage of growth from groups that had formerly lost status. Studies on England, Japan, Colombia, and Indonesia are included in the book. Stagnation through traditionalism is explained through the examples of Burma and the Sioux living on the Black Dakota reservations.

1051. Halpern, Joel J., "Culture Change in Laos and Serbia: Possible Tendencies Toward Universal Organizational Patterns," *Human Organization*, 20(Spring 1961), 11-14.

1052. Halpern, Manfred, *The Politics of Social Change in the Middle East and North Africa*, Princeton, N. J.: Princeton University Press, 1969.

1053. Hardyck, Jane, "Consistency, Relevance, and Resistance to Change," *Journal of Experimental Social Psychology*, 2(January 1966), 27-41.

1054. Hauser, P. M., "Cultural and Personal Obstacles to Economic Development in the Less Developed Areas," *Human Organization*, 18(Summer 1959), 78-84.

1055. Heilbroner, Robert, "Do Machines Make History?" *Technology and Culture*, 8 (July 1967), 335-45.

1056. Heirich, Max, "The Use of Time in the Study of Social Change," *American Sociological Review*, 29(June 1964), 286-97.

1057. Herskovits, Melville J., *The Human Factor in Changing Africa*, New York: Alfred A. Knopf, 1962.

1058. Hertzler, Joyce Oramel, *Social Progress: A Theoretical Survey and Analysis*, New York: Cooper Square, 1928.

1059. Hoffer, Eric, *The Ordeal of Change*, New York: Harper & Row, 1963.
    A general treatise on human problems in times of change.

1060. Hollis, Peter (ed.), *Comparative Theories of Social Change*, Ann Arbor, Mich.: University of Michigan Press, 1966.

1061. Holmberg, Allan R., "Participant Intervention in the Field," *Human Organization*, 14(Spring, 1955), 23-26.
    The author introduces the idea of cultural change from the standpoint of the intervening participant, i.e., both as designer and activator of a sociocultural process. This approach was utilized in planning changes for the hacienda Vicos, Peru. The basic concept is personal involvement

of the social investigator or worker in the milieu. The author feels that as change rates are speeded up, the hypothesis and experiment are more readily and comprehensively tested.

1062. _____, "The Research and Development Approach to Change: Participant Intervention in the Field," in R. N. Adams and J. J. Press (eds.), Human Organization Research, Homewood, Ill.: Dorsey Press, 1950, 1960, 76-89.
    Discusses the topic largely within empirical terms and notes several outstanding cases of planned change.

1063. Holmberg, Richard, and others, Social Change in Latin America, New York: Harper & Row, 1960.

1064. Hoselitz, Berthold Frank, Sociological Aspects of Economic Growth, Glencoe, Ill.: The Free Press, 1960.

1065. Howard, Alan, "Plasticity, Achievement and Adaptation in Developing Economics," Human Organization, 25(Winter 1966), 265-72.

1066. Hsu, Francis L. K., Clan, Caste, and Club, Princeton, N. J.: D. Van Nostrand, 1963.

1067. Huntington, Samuel P. (ed.), Changing Patterns of Military Politics, New York: The Free Press, 1962.

1068. Hussain, A. F. A., Human and Social Impact of Technological Change in Pakistan, Volumes 1 and 2, London: Oxford University Press, 1956.

1069. Ilchman, Warren F., and Norman Uphoff, The Political Economy of Change, Berkeley and Los Angeles: University of California Press, 1969.
    Adapting various concepts and tools of economic analysis, the authors explore the functions and characteristics of political resources, political exchange, and political productivity with a view to improving the choices made by statesmen and non-statesmen alike. This perspective opens up possibilities for comparing the efficiency of various public policies and estimating their costs. This work is particularly useful for social scientists or policy-makers who are looking for a scheme that can be applied to any regime that can adapt a time horizon relevant to real problems.

1070. Inkeles, Alex, "The Modernization of Man," in Myron Weiner (ed.), Modernization, New York: Basic Books, 1966.

1071. Jacobson, H. B., and J. B. Roncek, (eds.), Automation and Society, New York: Philosophical Library, 1959.

1072. Johnson, Chalmers, Revolutionary Change, Boston: Little-Brown & Co., 1965.

1073. Johnston, Edgar (ed.), Preserving Human Values in an Age of Technology, Detroit: Wayne State University Press, 1961.

1074. Krishna, Daya, Considerations Towards a Theory of Social Change, Bombay: Manaktalas, 1965.

1075. Kuhn, Thomas S., *The Structure of Scientific Revolutions*, Chicago: Chicago University Press, 1962.

1076. Kunkel, John, "Individuals, Behavior, and Social Change," *Pacific Sociological Review*, 9(Spring 1966), 48-56.

1077. Lambert, Richard, *Workers, Factories and Social Change in India*, Princeton, N. J.: Princeton University Press, 1963.

1078. Lane, W. Clayton, and R. A. Ellis, "Social Mobility and Anticipatory Socialization," *Pacific Sociological Review*, 11(Spring 1968), 5-15.

1079. LaPiere, Richard T., *Social Change*, New York: McGraw-Hill, 1965.
   An analysis of the processes of social change, the conditions under which changes will be generated, and the functional consequences of such changes. The author breaks with 19th Century evolutionism, including the Marxian version, and introduces a general theory of change derived from historical and contemporary evidence which can in turn be critically tested. This concept holds that there is nothing inevitable about change and that it does not come about in accordance with fixed stages or some other immutable law of social history. Change is a product of deviant individual members of the society functioning in various capacities as innovators, advocates, or adopters. The author examines the specific kinds of social circumstances that permit the emergence of such individuals and how these circumstances may come into being.

1080. Lasswell, Harold, "The Changing Image of Human Nature: The Socio-Cultural Aspect (Future-Oriented Man)," *American Journal of Psychoanalysis*, 26(2, 1966), 157-68.

1081. Lave, Lester B., *Technological Change: Its Conception and Measurement*, Englewood, N. J.: Prentice-Hall, 1966.

1082. Leighton, Alexander H., and Robert J. Smith, "A Comparative Study of Social and Cultural Change," *Proceedings of the American Philosophical Society*, 99(January 1955), 799-88.

1083. Lerner, Daniel, *The Passing of Traditional Society: Modernizing the Middle East*, New York: The Free Press, 1958.

1084. Levine, Solomon B., "Union-Management Relations and Technical Change: A Case Study," *Current Economic Comment*, 13(November 1951), 24-41.
   A case study indicating that it is difficult to approach the human problems of technical change solely at the plant level. The evolution of institutional relationships is rooted in the whole social and political complex of modern industrial society, and not merely in a plant.

1085. Lewin, Kurt, "Group Decision and Social Change," in Theodore M. Newcomb and other (eds.), *Readings in Social Psychology*, New York: Henry Holt & Co., 1959, 330-44.

1086. Lifton, Robert Jay, "Individual Patterns in Historical Change: Imagery of Japanese Youth," *The Journal of Social Forces*, 20(October 1964), 96-111.
   In spite of the inherent contradictions of the relationship between

individual lives and historical forces, "there are common patterns--shared images and styles of imagery--which men call forth in their efforts to deal with the threat and promise of a changing outer and inner world." Under radical changes that engulfed Japanese youth in the post-World War II era, there was a sense of "historical dislocation" and a "break in the sense of connection." But lingering influences of the past have a way of making themselves felt persistently within the individual character structure, creating a series of psychological conflicts which in turn add both pain and zest to their life. The article describes three modes or patterns of time imagery which promote historical changes.

1087. Lindstrom, David E., _Rural Social Change_, Champaign, Ill.: Stipes Publishing Co., 1961.

1088. Lipset, S. M., _Revolution and Counter-Revolution_, New York: Basic Books, 1968.

1089. Liska, George, "Continuity and Change in International System," _World Politics_, 16(October 1963), 118-36.

1090. Little, K. L., _West African Urbanization: A Study of Voluntary Association in Social Change_, New York: Cambridge University Press, 1965.

1091. Loomis, Charles P., and Allen J. Beagle, _Rural Sociology: The Strategy of Change_, Englewood Cliffs, N. J.: Prentice-Hall, Inc., 1957.
A summary of their earlier book, _Rural Social Systems_ (1950), less technical, covering almost the same area, i.e., rural society and rural social strata.

1092. Loomis, Charles P., _Systematic Sociology: Essays in the Persistence and Change of Social Systems_, Princeton, N. J.: Van Nostrand Co., 1960.
A solid treatment of the leading ideas on change until 1960.

1093. Malinowski, Bronislaw, _The Dynamics of Culture Change_, New Haven: Yale University Press, 1945.

1094. Marcom, S., "Social Change and Social Structure in Transitional Societies," _International Journal of Comparative Society_, 2(September 1961), 248-53.

1095. Martindale, Don, _Social Life and Cultural Change_, Princeton, N. J.: Van Nostrand Co., 1962.
Advances a general theory on social change with heavy emphasis upon Max Weber's concepts, particularly the role of religion in the determination of social stability and change.

1096. Mau, James, _Social Change and Images of the Future_, Cambridge, Mass.: Schenkman, 1967.

1097. Mead, Margaret, _Continuities in Cultural Evolution_, New Haven: Yale University Press, 1964.

1098. _____ (ed.), _Cultural Patterns and Technical Change_, New York: Mentor Books, 1955.
This book analyzes the problems of technical change in cross-cultural situations from an anthropological point of view. It constitutes a

manual for change agents whose frame of reference is the introduction of technical change within the context of the existing cultural pattern, and hence the preservation of the human values of the culture.

1099. _____, "The Future as the Basis for Establishing a Shared Culture," *Daedalus*, 94(Winter 1965), 135-55.

1100. _____, *New Lives for Old: Cultural Transformation*, New York: Morrow, 1953, 1956.
Good statement on the use of massive change strategy.

1101. Meadows, Paul, "Motivation for Change and Development Administration," in Irving Swerdlow (ed.), *Development Administration Concepts and Problems*, Syracuse, New York: Syracuse University Press, 1964, 85-102.
A short treatise on the important social elements frequently found in emerging societies that may be motivated to perform critical roles in the development process.

1102. Messinger, Sheldon L., "Organizational Transformation: A Case Study of Declining Social Movement," *American Sociological Review*, 20(February 1955), 3-10.

1103. Mesthene, Emmanuel, "On Understanding Change," *Technology and Culture*, 6 (Spring 1965), 222-35.

1104. _____ (ed.), *Technology and Social Change*, New York: Bobbs-Merrill, 1967.

1105. Montgomery, John D., "The Challenge of Change," *International Development Review*, 9(March 1967), 2-8.

1106. Moore, Wilbert E., and Arnold S. Feldman (eds.), *Labour Commitment and Social Change in Developing Areas*, New York: Social Science Research Council, 1960.
A symposium of fifteen essays with four introductory chapters by the editors. The introduction provides a framework in which factors and forces encourage or discourage laborers of developing areas in their commitment to social and economic changes. The rest of the essays are either case studies or general discussions on problems of labor and change.

1107. _____, and Robert Cook (eds.), *Readings on Social Change*, Englewood Cliffs, N. J.: Prentice-Hall, 1967.

1108. Moore, Wilbert E., "A Reconsideration of Theories of Social Change," *American Sociological Review*, 25(December 1960), 810-18.

1109. _____, *Social Change*, Englewood Cliffs, N. J.: Prentice-Hall, Inc., 1963.

1109.1 _____, "Social Change," in David L. Sills (ed.), *International Encyclopedia of the Social Sciences*, New York: The Macmillan Co., and The Free Press, 1968, 14, 365-70.

1110. Nair, Kusum, *Blossoms in the Dust: The Human Factor in Indian Development*, New York: Frederick A. Praeger Co., 1962.

(C2)

1111. Nash, Manning, *Machine Age Maya: The Industrialization of a Guatemalan Community*, New York: The Free Press, 1962.

1112. Neal, Maric, *Values and Interests in Social Change*, Englewood Cliffs, N. J.: Prentice-Hall, 1965.

1113. Niehoff, Arthur H., *A Case Book of Social Change*, Chicago: Aldine Publishing Co., 1966.

1114. _____, *Introducing Social Change*, Chicago: Aldine Publishing Co., 1964.

1115. Nisbet, Robert, *Social Change and History*, Oxford University Press.

1116. Nordskog, John E. (ed.), *Social Change*, New York: McGraw-Hill Book Co., 1960.

1117. Ogburn, William F., *Social Change*, New York: B. W. Huebsch, Inc., 1922.

1118. Oto, Sulc, "Forecasting the Interactions between Technical and Social Changes," in *Technological Forecasting*, Edinburgh: Edinburgh University Press, 1969.

1119. Pi-Sunyer, O., and T. De Georgi, "Culture Resistence to Technological Change," *Technology and Culture*, 5(Spring 1964), 247-53.
    The article rejects Peter Drucker's position that ideas are parochial while tools are universal. The authors insist that tools and ideas have to be borrowed simultaneously and any hope of importing tools without ideas shows ignorance of both culture and technology.

1120. Redfield, Robert, *A Village That Chose Progress: Chan Kom Revisited*, Chicago: University of Chicago Press, 1960.
    Robert Redfield observes the changes the village of Chan Kom underwent during his 17 years absence; the effects of economic and political modernization, the factors responsible for Chan Kom's success, and the dangers which it has yet to face.

1121. Reissman, Leonard, "Readiness to Succeed: Mobility Aspirations and Modernism among the Poor," *Urban Affairs Quarterly*, 4(March 1969), 379-95.

1122. Richards, Audrey I., *Economic Development and Tribal-Change*, London: W. Heffer & Sons, Ltd., n.d.

1123. Riegel, H. W., *Management, Labor and Technological Change*, Ann Arbor, Mich.: University of Michigan Press, 1942.

1124. Rogers, Everett M., *Social Change in Rural Society*, New York: Appleton-Century-Crofts, Inc., 1960.

1125. Rosenblith, Walter, "On Some Social Consequences of Scientific and Technological Change," *Daedalus*, 90(Summer 1961), 498-513.

1126. Rowe, William, "Contours of Culture Change in South India," Special Issue, *Human Organization*, 22(Spring 1963), 1-104.

1126.1 Runciman, W. G., <u>Relative Depravation and Social Justice: A Study of Attitudes to Social Inequality in Twentieth-Century England</u>, Berkeley: University of California Press, 1966.

1127. Ryan, Bryce, "The Recussitation of Social Change," <u>Social Forces</u>, 44(September 1965), 1-7.

1128. Schneider, Kenneth R., <u>Destiny of Change: How Relevant is Man in the Age of Development?</u> New York: Holt, Rinehart & Winston, 1968.

1129. Schuman, Howard, <u>Economic Development and Individual Change</u>, Cambridge, Mass.: Harvard University Press, 1967.

1129.1 Service, Elman R., "Cultural Evolution," in David L. Sills (ed.), <u>International Encyclopedia of the Social Sciences</u>, New York: The Macmillan Co., and The Free Press, 1968, 5, 221-28.

1130. Sheldon, Eleanor B., and Wilbert E. Moore (eds.), <u>Indicators of Social Change; Concepts and Measurements</u>, New York: Russell Sage Foundation, 1968.
Partial contents: "Population: trends and characteristics" by Conrad Taeuber; "The measurement of knowledge and technology" by Daniel Bell; "Consumption: a report on contemporary issues" by Milton Moss; and "Welfare and measurement" by Ida C. Merriam.

1131. Sherrill, Kenneth S., "The Attitudes of Modernity," <u>Comparative Politics</u>, 1(January 1969), 184-210.

1133. Siegel, Bernard J., "Some Recent Developments in Studies of Social and Cultural Change," <u>The Annals of the American Academy of Political and Social Science</u>, 363(January 1966), 137-53.

1134. Singh, S. D., K. Singh, and V. K. Singh, "A Study of Aspirations and Frustrations of the People of a Village in U.P.," <u>Indian Journal of Psychology</u>, 36(1961), 47-52.

1135. Slotkin, James Sydney, <u>From Field to Factory: New Industrial Employees</u>, Glencoe, Ill.: The Free Press, 1960.
Presents a systematic body of theory concerning the adjustment of workers with non-industrial backgrounds to industrial work situations.

1136. Smelser, Neil J., <u>Social Change in the Industrial Revolution</u>, Chicago: University of Chicago Press, 1959.

1137. Soemardjan, Selo, "Some Social and Cultural Implications Indonesia's Planned and Unplanned Development," <u>Review of Politics</u>, 25(January 1963), 64-90.
This article concentrates on the socio-cultural changes through which Indonesia has been passing in recent years, especially those which arose in the wake of the eight year development plan for 1961 to 1969.

1138. Spicer, Edward H. (ed.), <u>Human Problems in Technological Change</u>, New York: Russell Sage Foundation, 1952.

(C2)

1139. Spity, David (ed.), <u>Political Theory and Social Change</u>, New York: Atherton Press, 1967.

1140. Steward, Julian Hayes (ed.), <u>Contemporary Change in Traditional Societies</u>, Vol. I, <u>Introduction and African Tribes</u>, Urbana, Ill.: University of Illinois Press, 1967.

1141. _____, and Demitri Shimkin, "Some Mechanisms of Sociocultural Evolution," <u>Daedalus</u>, 90(Summer 1961), 477-97.

1142. Steward, Julian Hayes, <u>The Theory of Culture Change: The Methodology of Multilinear Evolution</u>, Urbana, Ill.: University of Illinois Press, 1955.
   An attempt to discover regularities in the processes of cultural change without falling into the errors of nineteenth century evolutionism.

1143. Strumpel, Burkhard, "Preparedness for Change in a Peasant Society," <u>Economic Development and Cultural Change</u>, 13(January 1956), 203-16.

1144. Tannous, A. I., "Social Change in an Arab Village," <u>American Sociological Review</u>, 6(October 1941), 650-62.

1145. Theodorson, G. A., "Acceptance of Industrialization and its Attendant Consequences for the Social Patterns of the Non-Western Societies," <u>American Sociological Review</u>, 18(October 1953), 477-84.

1146. Tilly, Charles, "Reflections on Revolutions of Paris: An Essay on Recent Historical Writing," <u>Social Problems</u>, 12(Summer 1964), 22-121.

1147. Tuma, E. H., "Agrarian Reform in Historical Perspective: A Comparative Study," <u>Comparative Studies in Society and History</u>, 6(October 1963), 47-75.
   The comparison of eleven cases of agrarian reform selected according to two criteria: (1) adaptable to comparative method of analysis and (2) representative of the history of reform.

1147.1 United States, Department of Health, Education and Welfare, <u>Toward a Social Report</u>, Washington, D. C.: U. S. Government Printing Office, annual since 1959.

1147.2 _____, Health, Education and Welfare Trends, Washington, D. C.: U. S. Government Printing Office, annual since 1959.

1148. United States, Department of Labor, <u>Impact of Automation</u>, Bulletin No. 1287, Washington, D. C.: Government Printing Office, 1960.

1148.1 United States, President, Research Committee on Social Trends in the United States, <u>Recent Social Trends in the United States</u>, New York: McGraw-Hill Book Co., 1933.

1148.2 Vogt, Evon Z., "Culture Change," in David L. Sills (ed.), <u>International Encyclopedia of the Social Sciences</u>, New York: The Macmillan Co., and The Free Press, 1968, 3, 554-58.

1149. Wallerstein, Immanuel (ed.), <u>Social Change: The Colonial Situation</u>, New York: John Wiley and Sons, 1966.

1150. Washburne, Norman, <u>Interpreting Social Change in America</u>, Random House, 1954.

1151. Watson, J., "Some Social and Psychological Situations Related to Change in Attitude," <u>Human Relations</u>, 3(February 1950), 15-56.

1152. Weaver, Thomas, and Alvin Magid, <u>Poverty: New Interdisciplinary Perspectives</u>, San Francisco: Chandler Publishing Co., 1969.

1153. Weinstein, Fred, and Gerald M. Platt, <u>The Wish to Be Free: Society, Psyche, and Value Change</u>, Berkeley, Cal.: University of California Press, 1969.
    This volume deals in psycho-social terms with the problems of radical social change, ideology, and in particular, with the effects of modernization on personality.

1154. White, Lynn, <u>Medieval Technology and Social Change</u>, New York: Oxford, 1962.

1155. Zollschan, G., and Walter Hirsch (eds.), <u>Explorations in Social Change</u>, Boston: Houghton-Mifflin Co., 1964.

1156. Zollschan, G., and R. Perrucci, "Social Stability and Social Process: An Initial Presentation of Relevant Categories," in G. Zollschan (ed.), <u>Explorations in Social Change</u>, Boston: Houghton-Mifflin, 1964.

3. PLANNED CHANGE

a. General

1157. Alder, John H., <u>Absorptive Capacity: The Concept and Its Determinants</u>, Washington, D. C.: The Brookings Institution, 1965.

1157.1 Appleby, Paul, "The Significance of the Hoover Commission Report," <u>The Yale Law Review</u>, 39(September 1949), 2-22.

1157.2 Argyris, Chris, "Effectiveness and Planning of Change," in David L. Sills (ed.), <u>International Encyclopedia of the Social Sciences</u>, New York: The Macmillan Co., and The Free Press, 1968, 11, 311-19.

1158. Barnes, Louis B., "Organizational Change and Field Experiment Methods," in Victor H. Vroom (ed.), <u>Methods of Organizational Research</u>, Pittsburgh: University of Pittsburgh, 1967, 57-113.
   A treatise on problems of organizational change including survey of literature, change models, and possibilities of change experimentation.

1159. Bauer, Raymond A. (ed.), <u>Second Order Consequences: A Methodological Essay on Impact of Technology</u>, Cambridge, Mass.: The M.I.T. Press, 1969.

1160. Bavelas, A., "Some Problems of Organizational Change," <u>Journal of Social Issues</u>, 4(Summer 1948), 48-52.
   A pioneer work on the subject of planned change.

1161. Bennis, Warren G., "Change Organizations," <u>The Technological Review</u>, 68 (April 1966).

1162. _____, <u>Changing Organizations: Essays on the Development and Evolution of Human Organization</u>, New York: McGraw-Hill Book Co., 1966.

1163. _____, "A New Role for the Behavioral Sciences: Effecting Organizational Change," <u>Administrative Science Quarterly</u>, 8(September 1963), 125-65.
   Identifies a new role for behavioral scientists and discusses some traditional strategies of change, followed by analysis of new change programs associated with National Training Laboratories, Tavistock Institute, R. R. Blake, C. Argyris, and others.

1164. _____, Kenneth D. Benne, and Robert Chin (eds.), <u>The Planning of Change</u>, New York: Holt, Rinehart and Winston, 1961, 1969.

1165. Bennis, Warren G., "Theory and Method in Applying Behavior Science to Planned Organizational Change," <u>The Journal of Applied Behavioral Science</u>, 1(October-December 1965), 337-60.

1166. Benveniste, Guy, and Warren F. Ilchman, *Agents of Change: Professionals in Developing Countries*, New York: Frederick A. Praeger Co., 1969.

1167. Biderman, Albert D., "Information ≠ Intelligence ≠ Enlightened Public Policy," Paper presented at the Sixty-fifth Annual Meeting of the American Political Science Association, New York: September 1969.

1168. Booth, D. A., and C. R. Adrian, "Power Structure and Community Change, A Replication Study of Community," *Midwest Journal of Political Science*, 6(August 1962), 277-96.

1169. Bose, Santi P., "Peasant Values and Innovations in India," *American Journal of Sociology*, 67(March 1962), 552-60.

1170. Brown, Murray, *On the Theory and Measurement of Technological Change*, London: Cambridge University Press, 1966.

1170.1 Bryson, Lyman, "Notes on Theory of Advice," *Political Science Quarterly*, 66 (September 1951), 321-39.

1171. Burns, Tom, "The Comparative Study of Organizations," in Victor H. Vroom (ed.), *Methods of Organizational Research*, Pittsburgh: University of Pittsburgh, 1967, 113-70.
    Outlines a suggested taxonomic scheme for organizations which has many features of the Human Relations Area files classification. It also contains an excellent section planned change.

1171.1 Butani, K. N., "Implementing Administrative Innovations and Reforms," *Indian Journal of Public Administration*, 12(3, 1966), 673-685.

1172. _____, "Micropolitics: Mechanisms of Institutional Change," *Administrative Science Quarterly*, 11(December 1961), 257-82.

1173. Caiden, Gerald E., *Administrative Reform*, Chicago: Aldine Publishing Co., 1969.
    Caiden has developed a number of specific suggestions and themes for administrative reform and has analyzed various approaches and obstacles to administrative reform and their relations to social change and modernization.

1174. _____, "Administrative Reform," *International Review of Administrative Science*, Brussels, Belgium: International Institute of Administrative Sciences, 34(1968), 347-54.

1175. Carlson, Richard O., *Executive Succession and Organizational Change*, Chicago: University of Chicago, Midwest Administration Center, 1961.
    An analysis of the consequences of appointing senior executives from inside and outside a school system with possible applications to other administrative systems. Successors from inside are found to have less influence on organizational change than outsiders.

1176. Cartwright, Dorwin, "Achieving Changes in People," *Human Relations*, 4(4, 1951), 381-92.

1177. Chapple, Eliot D., "Anthropological Engineering: Its Use to Administrators," *Applied Anthropology*, 2(January-March 1943), 23-32.

(C3a)

1178. _____, "Applied Anthropology in Industry," in A. L. Kroeber (ed.), <u>Anthropology Today</u>, Chicago: University of Chicago Press, 1953, 819-31.

1179. _____, and Leonard R. Sayles, <u>The Measurement of Management: Designing Organizations for Human Effectiveness</u>, New York: The Macmillan Co., 1961.
   A practical approach to the handling of human problems is presented. The book is divided into three sections: building the organization and measuring its performance; the individual, his personality and his job; and managing instability and change.

1180. Chetkow, B. Harold, "The Planning of Social-Service Changes," <u>Public Administration Review</u>, 28(May/June 1968), 256-63.

1181. Chowdhary, Amitabha, "The Reluctant Revolution," <u>International Development Review</u>, 10(December 1968), 24-25.

1181.1 Clark, D. H., <u>Administrative Therapy</u>, London: Tavistock Institute, 1964.

1182. Clark, Peter B., and James Q. Wilson, "Incentive Systems: A Theory of Organizations," <u>Administrative Science Quarterly</u>, 6(September 1961), 129-66.
   Aspects of organizational behavior and change are explained by exploring the consequences of different incentive systems.

1182.1 Cohen, Wilbur J., "Social Indicators: Statistics for Public Policy," <u>American Statistician</u>, 22(October 1968), 14-16.

1183. Coleman, James S., and others, <u>Equality of Educational Opportunity</u>, Washington, D. C.: U. S. Department of Health, Education and Welfare Office of Education, 1966.

1183.1 _____, <u>Models of Change</u>, New York: Prentice-Hall, Inc., 1964.

1184. Cooper, Joseph D., "Organization: Is the Change Necessary," <u>Management Review</u>, 51(December 1962), 4-10.

1185. Costello, Timothy W., and Sheldon S. Zalkind, <u>Psychology in Administration: A Research Orientation</u>, Englewood Cliffs, N. J.: Prentice-Hall, Inc., 1963.
   Several sections deal with planned organizational change in an excellent manner.

1186. David, Paul T., "Analytical Approaches to the Study of Change," <u>Public Administration Review</u>, 26(September 1966), 160-68.

1186.1 Davis, James A., <u>Panel Analysis: Techniques and Concepts in the Interpretation of Repeated Measurements</u>, Chicago: National Opinion Research Center, University of Chicago, 1963.

1187. Dobyns, Henry, and others, <u>Strategic Intervention in the Cultural Change Process</u>, Ithaca, N. Y.: Cornell University, 1967.

1187.1 Dorfman, Robert (ed.), <u>Measuring Benefits of Government Investments</u>, Washington, D. C.: Brookings Institution, 1965.

(C3a)

This volume contains the following articles: "Government Research and Development Programs" by Frederic Scherer; "Outdoor Recreation" by Ruth Mack and Sumner Myers; "Preventing High School Dropouts" by Burton Weisbrod; "Civil Aviation Expenditures" by Gary Fromm; "Urban Highway Investments" by Herbert Mohring; "Urban Renewal Programs" by Jerome Rothenberg; and "Syphilis Control Programs" by Herbert Klarman.

1187.2 Downs, Robert B., Books that Changed America, New York: The Macmillan Co., 1970.

1187.3 _____, Books that Changed the World, Chicago: American Library Association, 1956.

1188. Dunlap, John T. (ed.), Automation and Technological Change, Englewood Cliffs, N. J.: Prentice-Hall, Inc., 1962.
A book designed to sharpen some of the leading issues pertaining to automation. The article by Floyed C. Mann, "Psychological and Organizational Impacts," is particularly useful in providing guidelines for planned organizational change.

1189. Dunn, S. D. and E., "Directed Culture Change in the Soviet Union: Some Soviet Studies," American Anthropologist, 64(April 1962), 328-39.
A review of Soviet studies of culture change. Distinguishes between cultural change and cultural expansion and asserts that much of what has recently taken place falls into the second category.

1189.1 Educational Policy Research Center, Stanford Research Institute, "Toward Master Social Indicators," Menlo Park, Cal.: February 1969.

1190. Etzioni, Amitai, "European Unification: A Strategy of Change," World Politics, 16(October 1963), 1-163.
The author attempts to evolve a strategy of change for European unification. He begins by the comment that the success to date of European economic community was not solely due to similarities of background and interest among these countries, but it was partly due to the strategies employed. Instead of trying to create homogeneity in the beginning, the union should leave the heterogeneous elements and start with homogeneous countries bringing in others later. He traces the development of different efforts toward unification and the strategies employed.

1191. _____, "Guiding Social Change," in Philip Ehrensaft and Amitai Etzioni (eds.), Anatomies of America, Sociological Perspectives, New York: The Macmillan Co., 1969, 406-12.

1192. _____ (ed.), "Guiding Societal Change," American Behavioral Scientist, 12(November-December 1968), 1-64.
Partial contents: "A quantified description of community conflict" by Herbert Danzger; "Stable unrepresentation in American society" by William Gamson; "The nature of political beliefs and the relationship of the individual to government" by Lester W. Milbrath; "Coalition building and mobilization against poverty" by Carolyn O. Atkinson; and "Authentic planning of Afro-American Appalachia," by Philip Ehrensaft.

1193. _____, "'Shortcuts' to Social Change?" Public Interest, 12 (Summer 1968), 40-51.

1194. Finan, William F., and Alan L. Dean, <u>Procedures for the Preparation and Implementation of Administrative Reform</u>, Madrid: 10th International Confress of Administrative Sciences, 1956.
    The authors, members of the U. S. Bureau of the Budget, spell out the U. S. doctrine of administrative reform prevalent in the early 1950s.

1195. Forehand, G. A., and B. Gilmer, "Environmental Variations in Studies of Organizational Behavior," <u>Psychological Bulletin</u>, 62(December 1964), 361-81.

1196. Franklin, Richard, <u>Toward the Style of the Community Educator</u>, Washington D. C.: National Institute of Applied Behavioral Science, National Education Association, 1969.

1197. Fraser, Thomas M., Jr., "Sociocultural Parameters in Directed Change," <u>Human Organization</u>, 22(Spring 1963), 90-94.
    This article, one of a series on change in India, discusses what is involved in directed social change.

1198. French, J., and A. Marrow, "Changing Stereotype in Industry," <u>Journal of Social Issues</u>, 1(August 1945), 33-37.

1199. French, J. R. P., Jr., J. Israel, and D. As, "An Experiment on Participation in a Norwegian Factory," <u>Human Relations</u>, 13(1, 1960), 3-19.
    A significant study which illustrates that planned change objectives can differ with each culture.

1200. Friedl, Ernestine, "Hospital Care in Provincial Greece," <u>Human Organization</u>, 16(Winter 1958), 24-27.

1200.1 Friedrich, C. J., <u>The Public Interest</u>, New York: Atherton Press, 1952.
    Excellent comments on the problem of evaluating reform within the criteria of the public interest.

1201. Gallaher, Art, Jr. (ed.), <u>Perspectives in Developmental Change</u>, Lexington, Ky.: University of Kentucky Press, 1968.

1201.1 Gilb, Corinne, "Can We Measure Beauty?" Paper presented at the Sixty-fifth Annual Meeting of the American Political Science Association, New York, September 1969.

1202. Ginsberg, Eli, and Erwing W. Reilley, <u>Effective Change in Large Organizations</u>, New York: Columbia University Press, 1957.
    A leading work on the subject of planned organization change in industrial organization, with emphasis on the United States.

1203. Goffman, I. W., "Status, Consistency and Preference for Change in Power Distribution," <u>American Sociological Review</u>, 22(June 1957), 275-81.

1204. Golembiewski, Robert T., "The Laboratory Approach to Organizational Change: Scheme of a Method," <u>Public Administration Review</u>, 27(September 1967), 211-21.

1204.1 Gollin, Albert E., <u>Evaluating Programs and Personnel Overseas</u>, New York: Bureau of Applied Social Research, Columbia University, 1963.

(C3a)

1205. Goodsell, Charles T., *Administration of Revolution: Executive Reform in Puerto Rico Under Governor Tugwell, 1941-46*, Cambridge, Mass.: Harvard University Press, 1965.

1206. Greer, Scott A., *Metropolitics: A Study of Political Culture*, New York: John Wiley and Sons, 1963.
Description of campaigns in St. Louis, Miami, and Cleveland to establish metropolitan government. The efforts of reformers to bring about change are seen as "Morality Plays of American Civic Life."

1206.1 Greiner, Larry E., R. R. Black, J. S. Monton, and L. B. Barnes, "Breakthrough in Organization Development," *Harvard Business Review*, 42(November-December 1964), 22-43.

1206.2 Greiner, Larry E., "Antecedents of Planned Organizational Change," *Journal of Applied Behavioral Sciences*, 45(March, 1967), 51-85.

1206.3 _____, "Patterns of Organization Change," *Harvard Business Review*, 45(May-June 1967), 42-68.

1206.4 Gross, Bertram, "Let's Have a Real State of the Union Message," *Challenge*, 14(May-June 1966), 8-10.

1206.5 _____, and Michael Springer (eds.), "Political Intelligence for America's Future," *The Annals of the American Academy of Political and Social Sciences*, 388(March 1970).
This is the third issue of *The Annals* devoted to the discussion of social indicators and social reports. The first two volumes were published in May and September 1967 under the title "Social Goals and Indicators for American Society." The series was used in the preparation of the Johnson administration's study, *Toward a Social Report* (1969).
This issue contains such articles as: "On Social Guidance," "The uses of Social Knowledge," and "On Social Accounts."

1206.6 Gross, Bertram F. (ed.), "Social Goals and Indicators for American Society," *The Annals of the American Academy of Political and Social Science*, 371 and 373 (May and September 1967).

1206.7 _____ (ed.), *Social Intelligence for America's Future: Explorations in Societal Problems*, Boston: Allyn and Bacon, 1969.
This last of these works, a revision of materials published in *The Annals* of May 1967 and September 1967, contains the following articles: "Developing Social Intelligence" by Bertram M. Gross and Michael Springer; "Some Dangers in 'Valid' Social Measurement" by Amitai Etzioni and Edward Lehman; "Societal Feedback" by Raymond Bauer; "Electoral Participation" by Richard C. Scammon; "Civil Liberties" by Milton Konvitz; "Democratic Participation" by Sidney Verba; "Individual and Group Values" by Robin Williams, Jr.; "Education and Learning" by Wilbur Cohen; "Science, Technology, and Change" by John McHale; "The Mass Media--A Need for Greatness" by Andre Fontaine; "The Art of Measuring the Arts" by Alvin Toffler; "Poverty, Inequality, and Conflict" by S. M. Miller et al.; "Employment Goals and the 'New Economics'" by Leon Keyserling; "Discrimination Against Negroes" by Otis Dudley Duncan; "Social Breakdown" by Nathan Goldman; "Crime and Delinquency" by Daniel Glaser; "Health and Well-Being" by Philip Lee; "The Natural Environment" by

Joseph Fisher; "The Urban Environment--New York City" by Barry Gottehrer; and "The Urban Environment--General" by Daniel Moynihan.

1206.8 _____, "The Social State of the Union," *Trans-Action*, 3(November-December 1965), 5-11.

1206.9 _____, *The State of the Nation: Social Systems Accounting*, London: Tavistock Institute, 1966.

1207. Groves, Roderick T., "Administrative Reform and the Politics of Reform" *Public Administration Review*, 27(December 1967), 436-45.
 A case study of an institutional reform effort that failed; particularly valuable as a descriptive study against which to build normative theory of innovative planning.

1207.1 Grusky, O., "Review of Guest's Organizational Change," *Journal of Sociology*, 68(1962), 361-62.

1208. Guest, Robert H., *Organizational Change: The Effect of Successful Leadership*, Homewood, Ill.: Dorsey Press, 1962.
 A pioneer work on planned organizational change within empirical terms.

1208.1 Gurr, Ted, "A Causal Model of Civil Strife: A Comparative Analysis Using New Indices," *American Political Science Review*, 62(December 1968), 1104-24.

1209. Hage, Jerald, and Michael Aiken, "Program Changes and Organizational Properties: A Comparative Analysis," *American Journal of Sociology*, 72 (March 1967), 503-19.

1210. Hall, Edward T., *The Hidden Dimension*, Garden City, N. Y.: Anchor Books, 1969.
 People like to maintain certain distances between themselves and other people and things. This invisible bubble of space that constitutes each man's 'territory' is one of the key dimensions of modern society. Manipulation of this dimension is a way by which planned organizational change can be facilitated.

1211. Hardin, Einar, "Computer Automation, Work Environment, and Employee Satisfaction: A Case Study," *Industrial and Labor Relations Review*, 13(July 1960), 559-67.
 While the introduction of data-processing equipment may be technologically revolutionary, the change it introduces in work environment and work satisfaction may be very similar to that which comes about normally. This general finding is the outcome of comparisons with respect to perceived computer impact on job satisfaction, net change in the job, and feelings about perceived job change between departments which were affected or unaffected by the installation of a 650 IBM machine in a medium-sized insurance company.

1212. Harris, Chester W. (ed.), *Problems in Measuring Change*, Madison, Wis.: University of Wisconsin Press, 1963.
 Contains the proceedings of conference of participants from the areas of psychometrics and educational measurement. An integrated set of twelve papers is presented, which analyze the problem of assessing

change and deal with various models that may be employed in attacking this problem. Donald Campbell, Raymond Cattell, Wayne Holtyman, Paul Horst, Henry Kaiser, and Ledyard Tucker are among the contributors.

1212.1 Hayes, Samuel P., Jr., <u>Evaluating Development Projects</u>, Paris: UNESCO, 1959.

1212.2 _____, <u>Measuring the Results of Development Projects</u>, Paris: UNESCO, 1959.

1213. Heckman, I. L., Jr., and S. G. Huneryager, <u>Human Relations in Management</u>, Chicago: South-Western Publishing Co., 1960.
Contains several sections on planned organizational change.

1213.1 Herzog, Elizabeth, <u>Some Guidelines for Evaluative Research</u>, Washington, D. C.: Children's Bureau, Department of Health, Education, and Welfare, 1959.

1213.2 Heyel, Carl, <u>Appraising Executive Performance</u>, New York: American Management Association, 1959.
Provides a description of principles and techniques of appraising executive potentialities, taking into account factors of structure and environment.

1214. Hirschman, Albert O., <u>Development Projects Observed</u>, Washington, D. C.: Brookings Institution, 1967.

1214.1 Holden, Matthew, Jr., "Indicators of Social Stress and Social Peace," Paper presented at the Sixty-fifth Annual Meeting of the American Political Science Association, New York: September 1969.

1215. Holdord, Sir William, <u>The Built Environment</u>, London: Tavistock Pamphlet, 1965.

1216. Holmes, William F., "The Manager as Change Agent," in Harold M. F. Rush (ed.), <u>Managing Change</u>, New York: National Industrial Conference Board, 1967.
To be successful, the change effort must have behind it a total, integrated, well-planned strategy for accomplishment. Any piecemeal, one-sided, segmented or compartmentalized effort toward change is destined to be transient and limited in impact. Change to be successful must have: impetus of top management; the incorporation of structural, technical and behavior changes; the manager as change agent; and must become part of the organizational system.

1217. Hoos, Ida Russakoff, <u>Automation in the Office</u>, Washington, D. C.: Public Affairs Press, 1961.
As an account of the impact of automation upon the individual, the group, and the organization, this work is especially useful concerning readjustments necessary in organizational structure.

1218. _____, "Impact of Automation on Office Workers," <u>International Labor Review</u>, 82(October 1960), 363-88.

1219. Hovne, Avner, "Some Social Implications of Automation," <u>Impact of Science on Society</u>, 15(1, 1965), 5-26.

1220. Hyman, Herbert H., Charles R. Wright, and Terence K. Hopkins, <u>Application of Methods of Evaluation</u>, Berkeley and Los Angeles: University of California Press, 1962.
An excellent treatment on the application of systematic research techniques in the evaluation of action programs.

1220.1 Hyman, Herbert H., and Charles Wright, "Evaluating Social Action Programs," in Paul Lazarsfled, William Sewell, and Harold Wilensky (eds.), <u>Uses of Sociology</u>, New York: Basic Books, 1967.

1220.2 Hyman, Herbert H., G. N. Levine, and C. R. Wright, <u>Inducing Social Change in Developing Communities: An International Survey of Expert Advice</u>, United Nations Research Institute for Social Development, April 1967.

1220.3 Jacobs, Norman, <u>The Sociology of Development, Iran as an Asian Case Study</u>, New York: Frederick A. Praeger Co., 1966.

1221. Jaques, Eliott, <u>Equitable Payment</u>, London: Heinernann, 1961.

1221.1 John, W. A., and H. W. Singer, <u>The Role of the Economist as Official Advisor</u>, London: Allen and Unwin, 1954.

1222. Johns, R., <u>Confronted Organizational Change</u>, New York: Associated Press, 1963.
Focuses attention on social welfare organizations. Takes into account research on change and theoretical formulations. It emphasizes application of knowledge to the understanding, planning, instituting, and guiding of change in such organizations.

1223. Jones, Garth N., "Change Behavior in the Planned Organizational Change Process: Application of Socioeconomic Exchange Theory," <u>Philippine Journal of Public Administration</u>, forthcoming.

1223.1 _____, "Change Catalyst in Managed Organizational Change," <u>Indian Journal of Public Administration</u>, 22(October/December 1966), 717-42.

1224. _____, "Failure of Technical Assistance in Public Administration Abroad: A Personal Note," <u>The Journal of Comparative Administration</u>, forthcoming.

1225. _____, "Managing Changes in Organizations," <u>NIPA Journal</u>, Karachi: National Institute of Public Administration, 5(June 1966), 111-31.

1226. _____, "Pacemaker in Managed Organizational Change," <u>NIPA Reporter</u>, Karachi: National Institute of Public Administration 5(March 1966), 23-27.

1227. _____, "Planned Organizational Change: A Case from the Indonesia Malaria Eradication Program," <u>NIPA Reporter</u>, Karachi: National Institute of Public Administration, (March 1955), 57-72.
A case written within the dimensions of planned organizational change, illustrating the problems of change in a transitional-type society.

1228. _____, *Planned Organizational Change: A Set of Working Documents*, Los Angeles: Center for Research in Public Organization, School of Public Administration, University of Southern California, 1964.
   A comprehensive design by which to analyze the totality of planned organizational change. In addition, 190 cases on change have been analyzed against this design.

1229. _____, *Planned Organizational Change: A Study in Change Dynamics*, New York: Frederick A. Praeger Co., and London: Rutledge and Kegan Paul, 1969.

1230. _____, *Planned Organizational Change: Operational Focus for the Administrator*, Special Bulletin, Djakarta: Lembaga Administratrol Negara, 1963.

1231. _____, "Preventive Medicine at Work: A Hypothetical Case on Planned Organizational Change," *Philippine Journal of Public Administration*, 9(July 1965), 241-55.
   A hypothetical case illustrating the important elements involved in managed organizational change.

1232. _____, and Aslam Niaz, "Strategies and Tactics of Planned Organizational Change: A Scheme of Working Concepts," *Philippine Journal of Public Administration*, 7(October 1963), 275-85.
   By the technique of content analysis, this article identifies and classifies fourteen strategies which have been derived from case studies on planned organizational change. In addition, eight types of tactics were noted. The strategies have been classified according to their essential characteristics into three categories: normative, coercive, and utilitarian.

1233. Jones, Garth N., "Strategies and Tactics of Planned Organizational Change: Case Examples in Modernization Process of Traditional Societies," *Human Organization*, 24(Fall 1965), 192-200.
   Advances a design of strategies and tactics and gives case illustrations to show how these have been used in bringing about change in traditional societies.

1234. _____, and Shaukat Ali, "Triology on the Case Approach: The Case Study Method, A Case Study, and A Research Application," *Public Administration Review*, NIPA/Lahore, (July-September 1965), 41-108.

1235. *Journal of Social Issues*, "Consulting with Groups and Organization," 15(2, 1959), entire issue.

1236. Juran, J. M., "Improving the Relations Between Line and Staff," in I. L. Heckman, Jr. and S. G. Huneryager (eds.), *Human Relations in Management*, Chicago: South-Western Publishing Co., 1960.
   A revealing article on some of the major differences between staff and line officers in change situations.

1237. _____, *Managerial Breakthrough*, New York: McGraw-Hill Book Co., 1964.
   Chapter nine entitled, "Resistance to Change: Cultural Patterns."

(C3a)

1237.1   Kahn, Herman, and Anthony J. Wiener, <u>The Year 2000: A Framework for Speculation on the Next Thirty-Three Years</u>, New York: The Macmillan Co., 1967.

1238.   Karl, Barry Dean, <u>Executive Reorganization and Reform in the New Deal: The Genesis of Administrative Management, 1900-1939</u>, Cambridge, Mass.: Harvard University Press, 1963.
         A detailed account of the steps and considerations leading to the executive reorganization of 1939, which established the Executive Office of the President. The places of Charles E. Merriam, Louis Brownlow, and Luther H. Gullick in this process of planned organizational change receive considerable attention. In the final chapter, the old and new approaches to administrative management as they existed in the 1930's are contrasted.

1239.   Katz, Daniel, and Robert L. Kahn, "Six Approaches to Organizational Change: A Comparison of Theories and an Attempt at Integration," A Paper delivered at the International Congress of Psychology, 1963 (Processed).
         The paper advances six approaches to expedite organizational change: (1) information and persuasion, (2) individual counselling and therapy, (3) influence of the peer group, (4) sensitivity training, (5) organizational feedback, and (6) direct systematic change.

1240.   Kelley, Harold H., "Salience of Membership and Resistance to Change of Group Anchored Attitudes," <u>Human Relations</u>, 8(3, 1955), 275-89.

1240.1   King, John A., Jr., <u>Economic Development Projects and Their Appraisal: Cases and Principles from the Experience of the World Bank</u>, Baltimore: The Johns Hopkins University Press, 1967.

1240.2   Klineberg, Otto, "The Problem of Evaluation," <u>International Social Science Bulletin</u>, 7(3, 1955), 339-48.
         A social survey on the complexities of evaluating foreign training programs.

1240.3   _____, "Research in the Field of International Exchanges in Education, Science, and Culture," <u>Social Science Information</u>, 4(December 1965), 97-138.
         Contains a number of leading issues in the area of project evaluation.

1240.4   Krieger, Martin H., "The Life Cycle as a Basis for Social Policy and Social Indicators," Berkeley: University of California, Center for Planning and Development Research, October 16, 1969.

1240.5   _____, "Social Indicators for the Quality of Individual Life," Berkeley: University of California Center for Planning and Development Research, October 16, 1969.

1240.6   Landsberg, Hans H., Leonard L. Fischman, and Joseph L. Fisher, <u>Resources in America's Future: Patterns of Requirements and Availabilities, 1960-2000</u>, Baltimore: Johns Hopkins Press, 1963. Condensed version by H. H. Landsberg, <u>National Resources for U. S. Growth</u>, Baltimore: Johns Hopkins Press, 1964.

1240.7 Lawrence, J. R., *Operations Research and the Social Sciences*, London: Tavistock Institute, 1966.
Excellent comments on the problem of evaluating reform within the concept of social efficiency.

1241. Lawrence, Paul R., "How to Deal with Resistance to Change," *Harvard Business Review*, 32(May-June 1954), 49-57.
Resistance to change can be overcome by getting the people involved in the change to participate in making it. Change has both technical and social aspects. The technical aspect is the making of a measurable modification in the physical routines of a job. The social aspect refers to the way those affected by it think it will alter their established relationships in the organization. It is neglect of the social aspect which frequently results in failure to bring about change.

1242. Leavitt, Harold J., "Applied Organizational Change in Industry: Structural, Technical and Human Approaches," in William W. Cooper and others, *New Perspectives on Organizational Research*, New York: John Wiley and Sons, 1964.
A treatment on change within the human relations approach.

1242.1 Lecht, Leonard A., *Goals, Priorities, and Dollars: The Next Decade*, New York: The Free Press, 1966.

1243. Lewis, William H., "Rural Administration in Morocco," *The Middle East Journal*, 14(Winter 1960), 45-60.

1244. Liebenow, J. Gus, "Responses to Planned Political Change in a Taganyikan Tribal Group," *American Political Science Review*, 50(June 1956), 442-46.

1245. Lippit, Donald, Jeanne Watson, and Bruce Westley, *The Dynamics of Planned Change*, New York: Harcourt, Brace & Co., 1958.

1245.1 Lippitt, Gordon, *Organizational Renewal*, New York: Appleton-Century-Crofts, 1969.
This work provides a conceptual and practical frame of reference for organizational response to changing social and economic responsibilities.

1246. Litterer, Joseph A., *The Analysis of Organizations*, New York: John Wiley and Sons, 1965.
A textbook treatment of the subject of organizational analysis. Part four deals with the problems of organizational change and adaptation.

1246.1 McClelland, David C., and David G. Winter, *Motivating Economic Achievement*, New York: The Free Press, 1969.
Builds upon his earlier book on economic development, *The Achieving Society* (1961). Centers primarily on the external events that affect the motivational level of the family.

1246.2 McHale, John, *The Future of the Future*, New York: Braziller, 1969.

1247. McMurray, Robert N., "The Problem of Resistance to Change in Industry," in I. L. Heckmann, Jr. and S. G. Huneryager (eds.), *Human Relations in Management*, Chicago: South-Western Publishing Co., 1960, 427-32.

1248. McNulty, J. E., "Organizational Change in Growing Enterprises," *Administrative Science Quarterly*, 7(June 1962), 1-21.
    A study of administrative adaptations to growth in thirty California companies. Adaptation was no better in companies which explicitly introduced changes than in companies which did not.

1249. Mann, Floyd C., and L. R. Hoffman, *Automation and the Worker: A Study of Social Change in Power Plants*, New York: Henry Holt, 1960.

1250. Mann, Floyd C., *Managing Change: The Worker in the Industrial Environment*, Ann Arbor, Mich.: Foundation for Research on Human Behavior, 1962 (lithograph).

1251. _____, and Franklin W. Neff, *Managing Major Change in Organizations*, Ann Arbor, Mich.: The Foundation for Research on Human Behavior, 1961.
    A treatise for action-oriented administrators concerned with the management of planned change.

1252. Mann, Floyd C., and L. K. Williams, "Organizational Impact of White Collar Automation," *Industrial Relations Research Association Annual Proceedings*, 1958 (Publication No. 22).

1253. _____, "Some Effects of the Changing Work Environment in the Office," *Journal of Social Issues*, 18(July 1962), 99-101.

1254. Mann, Floyd C., "Studying at Creating Change: A Means to Understanding Social Organization," in Conard Arensberg and others (eds.), *Research in Industrial Human Relations*, New York: Harper & Row, 1957, 146-67.
    A survey of controlled programs to effect organizational change. Develops seven key considerations which must be taken into account when attempting to change the attitudes and behavior of individuals or groups in organizational settings.

1255. Mayne, Alvin, *Designing and Administering A Regional Economic Development Plan with Special Reference to Puerto Rico*, Paris: Organization of Economic Corporation and Development, 1961.

1256. Michael, Donald, "Social Engineering and the Future Environment," *American Psychologist*, 22(November 1967), 288-92.

1257. Miles, Matthew B., "Planned Changes and Organizational Health," in R. O. Carlson and others, *Change Processes in Public Schools*, Eugene, Ore.: Center for the Advanced Studies of Educational Administration, 1965, 11-34.

1258. Mir, Lucy P., *Studies in Applied Anthropology*, London: University of London, 1957.
    From a socio-anthropological approach, a series of essays are presented delineating the methodology for expediting change in the underdeveloped nations.

1259. Moe, Edward O., "Consulting with a Community System: A Case Study," *Journal of Social Issues*, 15(2, 1959), 28-35.

(C3a)

1260. _____, "Utah Community Development Program," Community Development Review, 8(June 1963), 61-71.
A good description of an action-oriented program within a planned change construct.

1260.1 Mondale, Walter F., "New Tools for Social Progress," Progressive, 31(September 1967), 28-31. Reprinted in Congressional Record, 90th Cong., 1st sess., September 11, 1967.

1260.2 Moore, Wilbert E., and Eleanor B. Sheldon, "Monitoring Social Change: A Conceptual and Programmatic Statement," Proceedings of the Social Statistics Section, 1965, Washington, D. C.: American Statistical Association, 1966, 144-149.

1260.3 Moore, Wilbert E., "Problems in Timing, Balance, and Priorities in Development Measures," Economic Development and Cultural Change, 2(January 1954), 239-48.

1261. Morehouse, Thomas A., "The 1962 Highway Act: A Study in Artful Interpretation," American Institute of Planners Journal, 35(May 1969), 160-68.
Shows how the Bureau of Public Roads absorbed the 1962 requirement for cooperative planning into the ongoing highway program in such a way as to leave the existing program structure and modes of operation intact.

1262. Morison, Elting E., Men, Machines and Modern Times, Cambridge, Mass.: The M.I.T. Press, 1966.

1263. Morse, Chandler, and others, Modernization by Design: Social Change in the 20th Century, Ithaca, N. Y.: Cornell University, 1969.

1264. Morse, Nancy, and E. Reimer, "The Experimental Change of a Major Organizational Variable," Journal of Abnormal and Social Psychology, 52(January 1956), 120-29.

1265. Morton, Robert B., Paul Rathaus, and Philip G. Hanson, "An Experiment in Performance Appraisal and Review," Training Directors, 15(May 1961), 19-27.

1265.1 Moses, Stanley, "The Learning Force: An Approach to the Politics of Education," Paper presented at the Sixty-fifth Annual Meeting of the American Political Science Association, New York, September 1969.

1266. Mosher, Frederick C., "Factors and Considerations in the Reorganization Process: A Research Program based on Case Studies," a paper delivered at the 1962 Annual Meeting of the American Political Science Association in Washington, D. C., September 5-18, 1962.

1267. _____ (ed.), Government Reorganizations: Cases and Commentary, Indianapolis, Ind.: Bobbs-Merrill Co., 1967.
Mosher has collected twelve case studies of organizational change in U. S. public agencies. At the end of the volume, an analytical essay on administrative reform is included which evaluates the successes and failures in the examples studies. It also includes an estimate of the cost and effectiveness of reorganizations.

(C3a)

1268. _____, "Some Notes on Reorganization in Public Agencies," in Roscoe Martin (ed.), <u>Public Administration and Democracy: Essays in Honor of Paul H. Appleby</u>, Syracuse, N. Y.: Syracuse University Press, 1965, 129-50.
    The author provides an excellent change model ranging on a continuum from incremental change to episodic change. He also examines the reasons for reorganization of public agencies.

1269. Niaz, Aslam, "Concept of Planned Change," <u>NIPA Reporter</u>, National Institute of Public Administration, Karachi, 4(March 1965), 53-56.
    A short article on the leading concepts of planned change and their applicability to Pakistan.

1270. _____, "Strategies of Planned Organizational Change," unpublished doctoral dissertation, Los Angeles: University of Southern California, School of Public Administration, 1963.
    An empirical study of 100 cases of change concerning the kinds of strategies employed, which gives some indications as to their usefulness in implementing planned organizational change.

1271. Ogden, Jean and Jess, <u>These Things We Tried: A Five Year Experiment in Community Development Initiated and Carried Out by the Extension Division of the University of Virginia</u>, Charlottsvill, Va.: University of Virginia, 1947.
    An early work on how to engineer change in community settings.

1272. Olson, Mancur, Jr., "An Agenda for the Development of Measures of the Progress of a Racial or Ethnic Group," Washington, D. C.: U. S. Department of Health, Education and Welfare, 1968.

1272.1 _____, "The Plan and Purpose of a Social Report," <u>Public Interest</u>, 15(Spring 1969), 85-97.

1272.2 "Social Welfare Indicators as Predictors of Racial Disorders in Black Ghettos," Paper presented at the Sixty-fifth Annual Meeting of the American Political Science Association, New York, September 1969.

1273. Pareek, Udai, "Motivational Patterns and Planned Social Change," <u>International Social Science Journal</u>, 20(3, 1968), 464-73.

1274. Penniman, Clara, "Reorganization and the Internal Revenue Service," <u>Public Administration Review</u>, 21(September 1961), 21-30.

1274.1 Perle, Eugene, and others, <u>Toward Regular Public Reporting on the Quality of Life</u>, Detroit: Wayne State University Center for Urban Studies, January 1970.

1274.2 Peter, Hollis W., and Edwin R. Henry, "Measuring Successful Performance Overseas," <u>International Development Review</u>, 3(October 1961), 8-12.

1275. Pfiffner, John M., "The Background of Change," Miscellaneous Papers No. 6, Los Angeles: University of Southern California, August, 1960.
    Primary focus is on the importance of the administrator as a change agent.

(C3a)

1276. _____, "An Operational Focus on Organizational Change," Miscellaneous Papers No. 10, Los Angeles: University of Southern California, Summer, 1961 (Ditto).
Proposes twelve "strategies" for accomplishing planned organizational change. The paper originated from the process of operationalizing some of the key concepts in planned organizational change that are implicit in the literature.

1277. Pieris, Ralph, Studies in the Sociology of Development, Rotterdam, Netherlands: Rotterdam University Press, 1969.

1277.1 Porter, David O., "The Who and What of Future Forecasting in Politics," Paper presented at the Sixty-fifth Annual Meeting of the American Political Science Association, New York, September 1969. To be published in Albert Somit (ed.), Political Science and the Study of the Future. New York: Holt, Rinehart, 1971.

1278. Qadir, S. A., "Adoption of Technological Change in the Philippines: An Analysis of Compositional Effects," unpublished Ph.D. dissertation, Ithaca, N. Y.: Cornell University, 1966.

1279. Rice, A. K., The Enterprise and Its Environment, London: Tavistock, 1963.

1280. _____, Productivity and Social Organization: The Ahmedabad Experiment, London: Tavistock, 1958.
A case study on facilitating change in a factory in India.

1281. Richardson, F. L. W., Jr., Talk, Work and Action: Human Relations to Organizational Change, Ithaca, N. Y.: Society for Applied Anthropology, 1961.

1281.1 Ripman, Hugh B., "Project Appraisal," Finance and Development, 1(December 1964), 178-83.

1282. Roberts, Edward B., The Dynamics of Research and Development, New York: Harper & Row, 1964.
This book is primarily meant for government or industry co-ordinators in research and development organizations. The first part is devoted to the general theory of research and the second with problems of management in research organizations.

1282.1 Robson, W. A., Nationalized Industry and Public Ownership, London: Allen and Unwin, 1960.
Comes to grips with the basic issues of evaluating change programs.

1283. Rourke, Francis E., "The Politics of Administration Organization: A Case History," Journal of Politics, 19(August 1957), 461-78.

1284. Rush, Harold M. F., Managing Change, Papers presented by the National Conference Board's Management Conference, 1967, New York: National Industrial Conference Board, 1967.

1284.1 Russett, Bruce M., and others, World Handbook of Political and Social Indicators, New Haven, Conn.: Yale University Press, 1964.

(C3a)

1285. Sayles, Leonard R., "A Case Study of Union Participation and Technological Change," Human Organization, 11(Spring 1952), 5-15.

1286. _____, "The Change Process in Organizations: An Applied Anthropology Analysis," Human Organization, 21(Summer 1962), 62-67.

1287. _____, Managerial Behavior, New York: McGraw-Hill Book Co., 1964.
Note especially chapter 11: "Introduction of Short Term and Long Term Change."

1288. Schein, Edgar H., and Waren G. Bennis, Personal and Organizational Change Through Group Methods, New York: John Wiley and Sons, 1965.

1288.1 Schubert, G., The Public Interest, Glencoe, Ill.: The Free Press, 1960.
Excellent comments on the problem of evaluating reform with the public interest in mind.

1289. Scott, W. H., "Office Automation: Administrative and Human Problems," Paris: Organization for Economic Cooperation and Development, 1965.

1290. Seashore, Stanley E., and D. G. Bowers, Changing the Structure and Functioning of an Organization: Report of a Field Experiment, Ann Arbor, Mich.: University of Michigan, 1963.

1290.1 Sheldon, Eleanor B., and Wilbert E. Moore (eds.), Indicators of Social Change: Concepts and Measurements, New York: Russell Sage Foundation, 1968.
The articles included in this volume are: Eleanor Sheldon and Wilbert Moore, "Monitoring Social Change in American Society;" Conrad Taeuber, "Population: Trends and Characteristics;" A. W. Sametz, "Production of Goods and Services: The Measurement of Economic Growth;" Stanley Legergott, "Labor Force and Employment Trends;" Daniel Bell, "The Measurement of Knowledge and Technology;" Joyce M. Mitchell and William C. Mitchell, "The Changing Politics of American Life;" William J. Goode, "The Theory of Measurement of Family Change;" N. J. Demerath III, "Trends and Anti-Trends in Religious Change;" Milton Moss, "Consumption: A Report on Contemporary Issues;" Philip Ennis, "The Definition and Measurement of Leisure;" Iwao M. Moriyama, "Problems in the Measurement of Health Status;" Beverly Duncan, "Trends in Output and Distribution of Schooling;" Otis Dudley Duncan, "Social Stratification and Mobility: Problems in the Measurement of Trend;" Ida C. Merriam, "Welfare and its Measurement."

1290.2 _____, "Toward the Measurement of Social Change: Implications for Progress," in Leonard Goodman (ed.), Economic Progress and Social Welfare, New York: Columbia University Press, 1966, 185-212.

1291. Shipman, George A., "Fresh Approaches to Organization Building," Public Administration Review, 29(March/April 1969), 209-10.

1291.1 Sibley, Willis E., "Social Structures and Planned Change: A Case Study From the Philippines," Human Organization, 19(Winter 1960-61), 209-11.

(C3a)

A Case study of failure in planned change. The conclusion is that the failure was probably due to miscalculations and lack of knowledge about the internal social and cultural framework of the village.

1292. Silberman, Bernard S., Ministers of Modernization, Tucson, Ariz.: University of Arizona Press, 1965.

1293. Sills, David L., "Voluntary Associations: Instruments and Objects of Change," Human Organization, 18(Spring 1959), 15-21.

1294. _____, The Volunteers, New York: The Free Press, 1967.

1295. Smelser, N. J., "Mechanisms of Change and Adjustment to Change," in B. F. Hoselitz and W. E. Moore (eds.), Industrialization and Society, UNESCO-Moulton, 1963, 32-33.

1296. Smith, Robert J. (ed.), "Major Issues in Modern Society," Special Issue, Human Organization, 21(Summer 1962), 61-167.
    The entire issue is concerned with problems of planned change.

1297. Sofer, Cyril, "The Assessment of Organizational Change," The Journal of Management Studies, 1(September 1964), 128-42.
    Advances several criteria by which to assess managed organizational change. One of the few articles about this subject.

1298. _____, The Organization From Within, Chicago: Quardrangle Books, Inc., 1962.
    Deals with attempts within organizations to change behavior and to overcome difficulties which are reducing the organizations capacity to achieve its objectives. The book provides useful insights in the areas of the role of the change agent, resistance to change, and clientele system.

1299. _____, "Reactions to Administrative Change: A Study of Staff Relations in Three British Hospitals," Human Relations, 8(3, 1955), 291-316.

1300. Spencer, Paul, and Cyril Sofer, "Organizational Change and its Management," Journal of Management Studies, 1(March 1964), 26-47.
    Presents leading concepts of organizational change in industrial settings.

1300.1 Starr, Chauncey, "Social Benefit versus Technological Risk," Science, 19 (September 1969), 12-32.
    Offers an approach for quantitatively measuring benefits relative to costs.

1301. Steelworkers and Technical Progress: A Comparative Report on Six National Studies, Paris: Organization for Economic Cooperation and Development, 1965.

1302. Stein, Herman D., George M. Hougham, and Serapio R. Zalba, "Assessing Social Agency Effectiveness, A Goal Model," Welfare in Review, 6(March/April 1968), 13-18.

(C3a)

This is a product of an organizational effectiveness research project at Case Western Reserve University. It has an excellent discussion on goals. For a summary see George A. Shipman, "Developments in Public Administration--Measurement of Agency Effectiveness," Public Administration Review, 24(March/April 1969), 206-7.

1302.1 Stouffer, Samuel A., Measurement and Prediction, Princeton, N. J.: Princeton University Press, 1949.

1302.2 Suchman, Edward A., Evaluative Research: Principles and Practice in Public Services and Social Action Programs, New York: Russell Sage Foundation, 1967.

1303. Tannenbaum, Robert, The Introduction of Change in Industrial Organizations: Improving Managerial Performance, Series 186, New York: American Management Association, 1957.

1303.1 Tatham, L., The Efficiency Experts: An Impartial Survey of Management Consultancy, London: Business Publications, 1964.
Comes to grips with the basic issues of evaluating change.

1303.2 Taylor, F. W., Scientific Management, New York: Harper Bros., 1947.
Contains a number of sections which deal with the fundamental problems of project evaluation.

1304. Tax, Sol, "The Fox Project," Human Organization, 17(Spring 1958), 17-19.

1305. Thomas, William, and others, Man's Role in Changing the Face of the Earth, Chicago: University of Chicago Press, 1956.

1306. Touraine, Alain and others, Acceptance and Resistance, Paris: Organization for Economic Cooperation and Development, 1965.
A short treatise on the basic problems pertaining to the implication of social, technological and organization changes.

1307. Tsonderos, John E., "Organizational Change in Terms of a Series of Selected Variables," American Sociological Review, 20(April, 1955), 206-10.

1307.1 Udall, Stewart L., 1976: Agenda for Tomorrow, New York: Harcourt, Brace, and World, 1968.

1308. United Nations Technical Assistance Program, Administrative Problems of Rapid Urban Growth in the Arab States, New York: United Nations, 1964.

1308.1 United Nations, The Evaluation of Technical Assistance, Paris: Organization for Economic Co-operation and Development, 1969.

1309. United States, Bureau of Labor Statistics, Studies of Automation Technology: A Case Study of Large Mechanized Bakery, Washington, D. C.: Department of Commerce, 1958.

1310. _____, Studies of Automation Technology: A Case Study of Modernized Petroleum Refinery, Washington, D. C.: Department of Commerce, 1958.

1311. _____, Studies of Automation Technology: The Introduction of an Electronic Computer in a Large Insurance Company, Washington, D. C.: Department of Commerce, 1955.

1311.1 United States Bureau of the Budget, Measuring Productivities of Federal Government Organizations, Washington, D. C.: Government Printing Office, 1964.

1311.2 United States, Department of Health, Education, and Welfare, Education in Mental Health, Public Health Service No. 413, Washington, D. C.: Government Printing Office, 1955.

1311.3 _____, Toward a Social Report, Washington, D. C.: Government Printing Office, 1969.

1311.4 United States, President, Commission on National Goals, Goals for Americans: Programs for Action in the Sixties, Englewood Cliffs, N. J.: Prentice-Hall, Inc., 1960.

1311.5 United States, President, Office of the White House Press Secretary, "Statement by the President on the Establishment of a National Goals Research Staff," July 13, 1969.

1311.6 United States, Senate, Committee on Government Operations, Subcommittee on Government Research, 90th Cong., 1st sess., Hearings on the Full Opportunity and Social Accounting Act (S.843). Parts I, II, III, 1967.

1311.7 University of Connecticut, Second Annual Conference on the Role of Management Analysis in Government, The Possibilities and Potentialities of Measuring the Health of Government Organizations, Storrs, Conn.: 1965.

1312. Utoila, Jaako, "Improving Public Administration in Finland," International Review of Administrative Sciences, 27(1961), 65-70.
Discusses problems of administrative reorganization which are being encountered in Finland, and numberates reforms which have been introduced since the conclusion of the World War II.

1313. Waldo, Dwight, "Public Administration and Change: Terra Paene Incognita," Journal of Comparative Administration, 1(May 1969), 94-113.

1314. Walker, Charles R., Stedtown: An Industrial Case; History of Conflict Between Progress and Security, New York: Harper Bros., 1950.

1315. _____, Technology, Industry and Man: The Age of Acceleration, New Haven, Conn.: Yale University Press, 1968.

1316. Walton, Richard E., Two Strategies of Social Change and Their Dilemmas, Paper No. 95, Institute for Research on the Behavioral, Economic and Management Sciences, Purdue University, 1964. Also The Journal of Applied Behavioral Science, 1(April-June 1965), 167-79.

1316.1 Wasserman, P., Measurement and Evaluation of Organizational Reforms, Ithaca, N. Y.: Cornell University Press, 1959.

1317. Weidner, Edward W., *The World Role of Universities*, New York: McGraw-Hill Book Co., 1962.

1318. Weinberg, Alvin M., "Can Technology Replace Social Engineering?" *American Behavioral Scientist*, 10(May 1967), 7-10.

1319. Weinberg, E., "Experiences with the Introduction of Office Automation," *Monthly Labor Review*, 83(April 1960), 376-80.

1320. Weingrod, Alex, "Administered Communities: Some Characteristics of New Immigrant Villages in Israel," *Economic Development and Cultural Change*, 11(October 1962), 69-84.

1321. Whyte, William Foote, "Models for Building and Changing Organization," *Human Organization*, 26(Spring/Summer 1967), 22-31.
    Excellent on problem of traditional pyramid scheme. For a commentary see George A. Shipman, "Developments in Public Administration--Approaches to Organizational Building," *Public Administration Review*, 24(March/April 1969), 209-10.

1321.1 Wilensky, Harold L., *Organizational Intelligence*, New York: Basic Books, 1967.

1321.2 Wilson, John O., "Inequality of Racial Opportunity--An Excursion into the New Frontier of Socioeconomic Indicators," New Haven, Conn.: Yale University Department of Economics, June 1968.

1321.3 _____, "Quality of Life in the United States: An Excursion into the New Frontier of Socio-Economic Indicators," Kansas City: Midwest Research Institute, 1969.

1321.4 _____, "Regional Differences in Social Welfare," Paper presented at the Inter-University Consortium for Political Research," Ann Arbor, Mich., July 1968.

1322. Wooden, Howard E., *Family-Center Maternity Care Hospital Progress*, Evansville, Ind.: U. S. Public Health Service Research Project GN-7721, August, 1960.

1323. Zaleznik, Abraham, and David Moment, *Casebook on Interpersonal Behavior in Organizations*, New York: John Wiley and Sons, 1964.
    A companion volume to Zaleznik's *The Dynamics of Interpersonal Behavior*.

1324. Zaleznik, Abraham, *The Dynamics of Inter-personal Behavior*, New York: John Wiley and Sons, 1964.
    The part on leadership and change is a particularly useful treatise on planned change. The book is based upon the conclusion that technical, social and organizational environments are products of what man experiences internally.

1325. _____, *Foreman Training in a Growing Enterprise*, Cambridge, Mass.: Harvard Graduate School of Business Administration, 1951.

1326. Zamora, Mario D., "Tradition, Social Control, and Village Administration: An Indian Case," <u>Thai Journal of Public Administration</u>, 6(October 1965), 303-13.

1327. Zander, Alvin, "Resistance to Social Change--Its Analysis and Prevention," in I. L. Heckman, Jr., and S. G. Huneryager (eds.), <u>Human Relations in Management</u>, Chicago: South-western Publishing Co., 1960, 433-39.

b. Institution Building and Development

1328. Adams, Robert M., "The Development of Political Institutions," <u>Economic Development and Cultural Change</u>, 13(January 1965), 245-48.

1329. Agency for International Development, <u>Building Institutions to Serve Agriculture: A Summary Report of the CIC-AID Rural Development Research Project</u>, La Fayette, Ind.: Purdue University, Committee on Institutional Cooperation, 1968.

1330. Birkhead, Guthrie, <u>Institutionalization at a Modest Level: Public Administration Institute for Turkey and the Middle East</u>, Pittsburgh: Inter-University Research Program in Institution Building, March, 1967.

1331. Braibanti, Ralph, <u>Note on Institutional Change</u>, Cambridge, Mass.: MIT Title IX Conference, June, 1968, 52-61.

1332. Eisenstadt, S. N., <u>Essays on Comparative Institutions</u>, New York: John Wiley and Sons, 1965.

1333. _____ (ed.), <u>Max Weber on Charisma and Institution Building</u>, Chicago: The University of Chicago Press, 1968.

1334. Ellsworth, David F., <u>Maximizing Individual and Project Performance in Technical Assistance--Institution Building Projects</u>, Purdue University, (One draft portion of the CIC-AID Rural Development Research Project), February, 1968.

1335. Esman, Milton J., <u>The Institution Building Concepts--An Interim Appraisal</u>, Pittsburgh: Inter-University Research Program in Institution Building, March, 1967.

1336. _____, and Fred C. Bruhns, "Institution Building in National Development, An Approach to Induced Social Change in Transitional Societies," in Hollis W. Peter (ed.), <u>Comparative Theories on Social Change</u>, Ann Arbor, Mich.: Foundation for Research on Human Behavior, 1966, 318-42.

1337. Esman, Milton J., "Institution Building in National Development: A Research Note," <u>Institutional Development Review</u>, 4(December 1963), 27-30.

1338. _____, and Hans C. Blaise, "Institution Building Research: The Guiding Concepts," <u>NIPA Reporter</u>, Karachi: National Institute of Public Administration, 5(June 1966), 88-98.

1339. Esman, Milton J., and Fred Bruhns, <u>Institution Building Research: The Guiding Concepts</u>, Pittsburgh: Inter-University Program in Institution Building, February, 1966.

1340. Esman, Milton J., "The Politics of Development Administration," in John D. Montgomery and William J. Siffin (eds.), <u>Approaches to Development</u>, Politics, Administration and Change, New York: McGraw-Hill Book Co., 1966, 59-112.

1341. Hamilton, William B. (ed.), <u>The Transfer of Institutions</u>, Durham, N. C.: Duke University Press, 1964.

1342. Hubbell, Robert L., "Institution Building," Washington, D. C.: Agency for International Development, Circular XA-4247, August 31, 1968 (PE#7)
Includes Inter-University Program in Institution Building excerpts and Thomas Thorsen, USAID/Turkey, "Institutional Development Profile."

1343. Kaplan, Berton H. (ed.), "Organizations and Social Development," <u>Administrative Science Quarterly</u>, 9(December 1968), entire issue.

1344. Lin, Nan, D. J. Leu, Everett M. Rogers, and Donald F. Schwartz, <u>The Diffusion of an Innovation in Three Michigan High Schools: Institution Building through Political Change</u>, (Research Report No. 1), Institute for International Studies in Education, Michigan State University, December, 1966.

1345. Perlmutter, Howard V., <u>Towards a Theory and Practice of Social Architecture, The Building of Indispensable Institutions</u>, London: Tavistock Publications, 1965.

1346. Phillips, Hiram S., <u>Guide for Development: Institution Building and Reform</u>, New York: Frederick A. Praeger, 1969.
The author considers the social, political, and administrative contexts of the institutions through which development programs are carried out. Emphasis is given to the fields of education, training, and administration, and the purpose is to make such institutions more effective.

1347. _____, Handbook for Development: Changing Environments and Institutions, Washington, D. C.: Frederick A. Praeger, 1968.

1348. Roskelley, R. W., and J. A. Rigney, <u>Measuring Institutional Maturity in the Development of Indigenous Agricultural Universities</u>, (One portion of the Final Report of the CIC-AID Rural Development Research Project), 1968.

1349. Siegel, Gilbert B., "The Strategy of Public Administration Reform: The Case of Brazil," <u>Public Administration Review</u>, 26(March 1966), 45-55.
The author cites the government of Brazil as an example of the use of one central agency as the primary locus of reform over the last 30 years. This agency, the Administrative Department of the Public Service (DASP), has emphasized personnel administration, budget management and organizational analysis. The author points out that DASP has failed and that administrative reform has been unsuccessful. The beginning, operation, and decline of DASP are studied.

(C3c)

1350. Siffin, William J., The Thai Bureaucracy: Institutional Change and Development, Honolulu: East-West Center Press, 1966.

1351. _____, The Thai Institute of Public Administration: A Case Study in Institution Building, Pittsburgh: Inter-University Program in Institution Building, March, 1967.

1352. Sufrin, Sidney C., "Administration as Institution Building," Punjab Economic Review, 2(Fall 1960), 67-76.

1353. Taylor, Donald A., Institution Building in Business Administration: The Brazilian Experience, East Lansing, Mich.: Michigan State University, Graduate School of Business Administration, 1968.

c. Technical Assistance/Cooperation

1354. Adams, Walter (ed.), The Brain Drain, New York: The Macmillan Co., 1968.

1354.1 Adelman, Irma, and Hollis Chenery, "Foreign Aid and Economic Development," Review of Economics and Statistics, 48(February 1966), 1-19.

1355. Ahmad, Jaleel, The Expert and the Administrator, Pittsburgh: University of Pittsburgh Press, 1959.

1356. Albertson, Maurice L., and Wesley L. Orr, Engineering in Economic Development, New York: Frederick A. Praeger Co., 1970.
   The role of the engineer in economic development, including discussion of outside experts as a means of introducing and implementing internal change and developing physical and human resources; research and methodology essential to programme planning and evaluation; the need for systems.

1357. Alexander, Yonah, International Technical Assistance Experts: A Case Study of U. N. Experience, New York: Frederick A. Praeger Co., 1966.

1358. Allen, Harold B., Rural Reconstruction in Action: Experience in the Near and Middle East, Ithaca, N. Y.: Cornell University Press, 1953.

1359. Amuzegar, Jahangir, Technical Assistance in Theory and Practice: The Case of Iran, New York: Frederick A. Praeger Co., 1965.

1360. Arensberg, Conard M., and Arthur H. Niehoff, Technical Co-operation and Cultural Reality, Washington, D. C.: Department of State, Agency for International Development 1963.

1361. Arnold, H. J. P., Aid for Developing Countries: A Comparative Study, London: The Bodley Head, 1962.

1362. Asher, Robert E., "How to Succeed in Foreign Aid Without Really Trying," Public Policy, Cambridge, Mass.: Harvard Graduate School of Public Administration, 13(1964), 109-32.

(C3c)

1363. Attir, Aryeh, "Administration and Development," *International Review of Administrative Sciences*, 30(1964), 335-44.

1364. Baldwin, David Allen, *Foreign Aid and American Foreign Policy, A Documentary Analysis*, New York: Frederick A. Praeger Co., 1966.

1364.1 _____, "Foreign Aid, Intervention, and Influence," *World Politics*, 21(April 1969), 376-402.

1365. Balogh, T., "The Strategy and Tactics of Technical Asistance," *Public Administration*, 37(Winter 1959), 327-42.

1366. Banfield, Edward, "American Foreign Aid Doctrines," *Public Policy*, Vol. 10, Cambridge, Mass.: Harvard Graduate School of Public Administration, 1961, 44-94.

1366.1 _____, *American Foreign Aid Doctrines*, Washington, D. C.: American Enterprise Institute for Public Policy Research, 1963.

1367. Benveniste, Guy, and Warren F. Ilchman (eds.), *Agents of Change: Professionals in Developing Countries*, New York: Frederick A. Praeger Co., 1969
    Discusses the American-trained professional as an agent of social, economic, and political change in developing countries. Focuses on such issues as the shortcomings of past programs, the lack of adequate theories of social change, and the futility of perpetuating technological modernization for its own sake. Emphasizes responsibility of the university in generating new knowledge and disseminating it to the developing countries. Contributors include Adam Curle, John Friedmann, Brian Holmes, Vernon Ruttan, and Harold L. Wilensky.

1368. Black, Eugene, *The Diplomacy of Development*, Cambridge, Mass.: Harvard University Press, 1960.

1368.1 _____, "Policy for a New Era," *Foreign Service Journal*, 46 (October 1969), 14-19, 51-52.
    An insightful piece stressing the need for a major change in U. S. Development assistance policies and practices. Makes a case for multi-assistance economic support and low American profile.

1369. Black, Lloyed D., *The Strategy of Foreign Aid*, Princeton, N. J.: Van Nostrand, 1968.

1370. Bock, Edwin A., *Fifty Years of Technical Assistance*, Chicago: Public Administration Clearing House, 1954.
    A comprehensive study of United States technical assistance, including both governmental and private programs.

1371. Braibanti, Ralph, "External Inducement of Political-Administrative Development: A Design for Strategy," in Ralph Braibanti (ed.), *Politics and Administrative Development*, Durham, N. C.: Duke University Press, 1969, 3-106.

1372. _____, "Transitional Inducement of Administrative Reform: A Survey of Scope and Critique of Issues," in John D. Montgomery and

William D. Siffin (eds.), *Approaches to Development: Politics, Administration and Change*, New York: McGraw-Hill Book Co., 1966, 133-84.
   Compares the activities of the U. N., Ford Foundation, and AID in administrative reform activities, with particular reference to India and Pakistan. Questions are raised concerning the relationship of cultural aspects to the possibilities and requirements for change.

1373. Briggs, Ellis, *Anatomy of Diplomacy, The Origin and Execution of American Foreign Policy*, New York: David McKay Co., 1968.

1374. Brzezinski, Zbigniew, "The Politics of Underdevelopment," *World Politics*, 9(October 1956), 55-75.

1375. Byrnes, Francis C., *Americans in Technical Assistance*, New York: Frederick A. Praeger Co., 1965.

1375.1 _____, "Role-Shock: An Occupational Hazard of American Technical Assistants Abroad," *Annals of the American Academy of Political and Social Science*, 368(November 1966), 95-108.

1376. Caldwell, Lynton K., "The Role of the Technical Expert," *The Annals of the American Academy of Political and Social Science*, 322(March 1959), 91-96.

1377. Cardozo, Michael H., *Diplomats in International Co-operation: Stepchildren of the Foreign Service*, New York: Cornell University Press, 1962.
   Pertains to the problems of overseas Americans who influence international relations but are not part of the diplomatic processes.

1378. Cerych, Ladislav, *Problems of Aid to Education in Developing Countries*, New York: Frederick A. Praeger Col, 1965.

1379. Chandrasekhar, Sripati, *American Aid and India's Development*, New York: Frederick A. Praeger Co., 1965.

1380. Charlick, Robert B., "U. S. and French Aid Rationales," in John D. Montgomery and Arthur Smithies (eds.), *Public Policy*, Cambridge, Mass.: Harvard Graduate School of Public Administration, 14(1965), 117-40.

1381. Chenery, Hollis B., and Alan M. Strout, "Foreign Assistance and Economic Development," *American Economic Review*, 56(September 1966), 679-733.

1382. Cleveland, Harlan, Gerald J. Mangone, and John C. Adams, *The Overseas Americans*, New York: The Macmillan Co., 1960.

1383. Danhof, Clarence H., *Government Contracting and Technological Change*, Washington, D. C.: The Brookings Institution, 1968.
   Focuses on the Government's ability to manage the system it has created and the ability of private institutions to serve the Government's objectives while maintaining their private character and discharging adequately their other functions.

1384. Development Assistance Committee, 1967, *Review of Development Assistance Efforts and Policies*, Paris: Organization for Economic Cooperation and Development, 1967.

1385. Dey, Suchil K., "The Role of Foreign Aid in Development," *Political Quarterly*, 30(July-September 1959), 283-92.

1386. Domergue, Maurice, *Technical Assistance, Definition and Aims, Ways and Means, Conditions and Limits*, Paris: Organization for Economic Cooperation and Development, 1961.

1386.1 _____, *Technical Assistance: Theory, Practice, and Policies*, New York: Frederick A. Praeger Co., 1968.
   Short and long-term objectives and policy problems of technical assistance are discussed from several points of view--donor and recipient, multilateral and bilateral, public and private, minister to small farmer.

1387. Duncan, Richard L., and William S. Pooler, "Technical Assistance and Institution Building," Syracuse, N. Y.: Maxwell School of Citizenship and Public Affairs, Syracuse University, 1967 (dittoed).

1388. Erasmus, Charles J., "An Anthropologist Views Technical Assistance," in Lyle Shannon (ed.), *Underdeveloped Areas. A Book of Readings and Research*, New York: Harper Bros., 1957, 295-308.

1389. _____, *Man Takes Control: Cultural Development and American Aid*, Minneapolis, Minn.: University of Minnesota Press, 1961.

1390. Esman, Milton J., and D. S. Cheever, *The Common Aid Effort*, Columbus: Ohio State University Press, 1967.

1391. Feder, E., "When Is Land Reform a Land Reform? The Columbian Case," *The American Journal of Economics and Sociology*, 24(April 1965), 113-34.
   The writer is of the opinion that for continued technical and financial assistance, it is essential to evolve and implement satisfactorily plans for economic development and social reforms. In feudalistic and traditional societies land reforms are of fundamental significance. The article makes a general survey of this problem in Latin America, and then gives Columbia as a case study to support his contentions.

1392. Feis, Herbert, *Foreign Aid and Foreign Policy*, New York: St. Martin's, 1964.
   The author advances the notion that the application of technical cooperation seems to be governed by a "law of unintended consequences."

1393. Fenley, John M., *The Role and Problems of Wives of American Technicians Overseas in Rural Development*, Ithaca, N. Y.: Cornell University Press, 1961.

1393.1 Ferkiss, Victor C., *Foreign Aid, Moral and Political Aspects*, New York: Council on Religion and International Affairs, 1965.

1394. Foster, Ellery, "Planning for Community Development Through Its People," *Human Organization*, 12(Summer 1953), 5-9.
   Illustrates the concept of the social catalyst.

1395. Glick, Philip M., *The Administration of Technical Assistance: Growth in the Americas*, Chicago: University of Chicago Press, 1957.
   A classical work on the administrative problems of programming United States technical assistance in South America.

(C3c)

1397. Goldwin, Robert A., _Why Foreign AID?_ Chicago: Rand McNally, 1963.

1398. Gollin, Albert E., _Education for National Development. Effects of U. S. Technical Training Programs_, New York: Frederick A. Praeger Co., 1970.
   Six thousand people, primarily from underdeveloped nations, arrive in the United States every year for technical training; thousands more are trained in their own countries or elsewhere outside the United States. In this study, Dr. Gollin examines the implications of developing these human resources through participant training, basing his analysis on data collected in 23 countries by the International Cooperation Administration and its successor, the Agency for International Development. Using the tools of sociological analysis, Dr. Gollin deals with such topics as the consequences of assistance for technological change, the limits of training as a viable strategy for human resources development, and the preconditions under which the program can be most effective.

1399. Goodenough, Ward Hunt, _An Anthropological Approach to Community Development_, New York: Russell Sage Foundation, 1963.
   A synthesis of the concepts and issues of agent-client and co-operation in the processes of change. In his opinion community development is a profession, which requires application of the knowledge of behavioral sciences in cross-cultural change.

1400. _____, _Cooperation in Change_, New York: John Wiley and Sons, 1966.

1401. Gouldner, Alvin W., and R. A. Peterson, _Notes on Technology and the Moral Order_, New York: Bobbs-Merrill, 1962.

1402. Guthrie, George M., and Richard E. Spencer, _American Professions and Overseas Technical Assistance_, University Park, Pa.: Pennsylvania State University, 1965.

1402.1 Hapgood, David, and Meridan Bennett, _Agents of Change: A Close Look at the Peace Corps_, Boston: Little, Brown and Co., 1968.

1402.2 Hayter, Teresa, _Effective Aid_, London: Overseas Development Institute, 1967.
   The report and papers of a conference in 1966 on improving the effectiveness of aid for development. The participants were mostly senior officials directly concerned with administering aid from the United States, France, Britain, Germany, and from international institutions.

1403. Higgins, Benjamin and Jean, _Indonesia: The Crisis of the Millstones_, New York: Van Nostrand, 1963.

1404. Hirschman, Albert O., and Richard M. Bird, _Foreign Aid: A Critique and a Proposal_, Princeton, N. J.: Princeton University Press, 1968.

1404.1 Hoselitz, Bert F., and Ann R. Willner, "Economic Development, Political Strategies, and American Aid," in Morton A. Kaplan (ed.), _The Revolution in World Politics_, New York: John Wiley and Sons, 1962, 355-80.

1405. Jackson, Robert, _The Case for an International Development Authority_, Syracuse, N. Y.: Syracuse University Press, 1959.
   The case for such an authority rests on failure of the West to assess

accurately the problem of economic assistance and to recognize its full political significance; short time available in which to act; lack of proportion between Western defense efforts and its aid efforts; desperate need for imagination, initiative and leadership comparable to that of the Marshall Plan; underestimation of USSR's economic strength; need for West and East to develop multinational approach in providing economic assistance; necessity for West to better understand dominant political factors in underdeveloped countries; need for all governments concerned to make a new effort to explain to the people of the West the need for economic assistance to less developed areas.

1405.1 Jacoby, Neil H., U. S. AID to Taiwan, A Study of Foreign Aid, Self Help and Development, New York: Frederick A. Praeger Co., 1966.

1406. Jones, Garth N., Technical Assistance in Public Administration for Indonesia: The 1960's--A Decade of Challenge, Jogjakarta, Indonesia: University of Gadjah Mada, 1960.
   The author holds that one of the basic requirements of modern government and society is an effective system of public administration, but that in many countries this is difficult to obtain. He discusses three essential elements which are always involved in the initial stages of any technical assistance program: (1) establishing rapport and mutual understanding between the parties concerned, (2) determining the role public administration is supposed to perform in the overall program of social and economic development and (3) developing cooperative arrangements by which specific objectives are to be achieved. The final section reviews four approaches used in three years of the U. S. technical assistance program in public administration: in-service training, institutions of higher learning, applied management research, and short-term training including training abroad.

1407. Kaplan, Jacob J., The Challenge of Foreign Aid, New York: Frederick A. Praeger Co., 1967.

1408. Kazemian, Gholam H., Impact of U. S. Technical Aid in the Rural Development of Iran, Brooklyn, N. Y.: Theo-Gaus & Sons, 1968.
   A penetrating study treating in rather comprehensive terms the impact of U. S. technical aid in rural development in Iran.

1409. King, Clarence, Working with People in Small Communities, New York: Harper Bros., 1958.

1410. Kingdom, Thomas Doyle, Improvement of Organization and Management in Public Administration: A Comparative Study, Brussells: International Institute of Administrative Sciences, 1960.
   Treats the nature of organization, management, selection procedures, budgetary processes, extra-governmental influences, and other problems which are commonly experienced by government departments.

1411. Krassowski, Andryej, The Aid Relationship, London: The Overseas Development Institute, 1968.
   A study concerned with the contribution donors can make to maximise the effectiveness of the aid they provide. First, three pre-conditions for a good bilateral aid programme are put forward: a clear and consistent donor policy; close donor/recipient co-operation; and co-ordination of various donors' efforts. Second, the problem of planning and

implementing country aid programs is examined in detail by means of a case study. Special attention is paid to the role of permanent aid missions and the considerations which should guide donors in selecting projects and aid forms, techniques, and terms appropriate to the development needs of recipients.

1412. Lionberger, H. F., <u>Adoption of New Ideas and Practices: A Summary of the Research Dealing with the Implications for Action in Facilitating Such Change</u>, Ames, Iowa: Iowa State University Press, 1960.

1413. Liska, George, <u>The New Statecraft: Foreign Aid in American Policy</u>, Chicago: The University of Chicago Press, 1960.

1414. Livingstone, A. S., "Training in Public Administration for Overseas Government Servants," <u>Journal of African Administration</u>, 13(April 1961), 105-7.
A review of the program conducted by the University of Manchester for imparting administrative knowledge to foreign civil servants.

1415. Loomis, Ralph A., "Why Overseas Technical Assistance is Ineffective," <u>American Journal of Agricultural Economics</u>, 50(December 1968), 1329-44.
"Unless we are willing to become more serious about the job of goal definition, critical problem identification, and alternative ways of contributing to the modernization processes, we may be well advised to withdraw completely from assistance efforts."

1416. Maddison, Angus, <u>Foreign Skills and Technical Assistance in Economic Development</u>, Paris: Development Centre of the Organization for Economic Co-operation and Development, 1965.

1417. Malek, T. Abdel, "Some Problems of Technical Assistance Administration in Developing Countries," <u>International Review of Administrative Science</u>, 34(1968), 315-23.

1418. Martin, Roscoe E., "Technical Assistance: The Problem of Implementation," <u>Public Administration Review</u>, 12(Autumn 1952), 258-66.

1419. Mason, Edward S., "On the Appropriate Size of a Development Program," Occasional Papers in International Affairs, 8(August 1964), Cambridge, Mass.: Harvard University Center for International Affairs.

1419.1 Mihaly, Eugene B., <u>Foreign Aid and Politics in Nepal</u>, London: Oxford University Press, 1965.

1420. Montgomery, John D., "Field Organization, Administrative Relationships and Foreign Aid Policies," <u>Public Policy</u>, Cambridge, Mass.: Harvard Graduate School of Public Administration, 10(1960), 297-331.

1421. _____, <u>Foreign Aid in International Politics</u>, Englewood Cliffs, N. J.: Prentice-Hall, Inc., 1967.

1422. _____, "Gilded Missiles: Reflections on the Politics of Foreign Aid," <u>Far Eastern Survey</u>, 28(June 1959), 81-89.

1423. _____, <u>The Politics of Foreign Aid, American Experience in Southeast Asia</u>, New York: Frederick A. Praeger Co., 1962.

(C3c)

A solid treatise on the problems of administering U. S. technical assistance in countries experiencing political instability, particularly in South Vietnam.

1424. Mosher, Arthur T., Getting Agriculture Moving: Essentials for Development and Modernization, New York: Frederick A. Praeger Co., for the Agricultural Development Council, 1966.

1425. _____, Technical Cooperation in Latin American Agriculture, Chicago: University of Chicago Press, 1957.

1425.1 Myers, Robert G., "'Brain Drains' and 'Brain Gains,'" International Development Review, 10(December 1967), 4-9.

1426. Nairn, Roland C., International Aid to Thailand: The New Colonialism, New Haven, Conn.: Yale University Press, 1965.

1427. National Planning Association Special Policy Committee in Technical Cooperation, Technical Cooperation in Latin America--Recommendations for the Future, Washington, D. C.: National Planning Association, 1956.

1428. Nelson, Joan, Aid, Influence and Foreign Policy, New York: The Macmillan Co., 1968.

1429. Northrop, F. S. C., and H. M. Lingonston, Cross-cultural Understanding, New York: Harper & Row, 1964.

1430. O'Leary, Michael Kent, The Politics of American Foreign Aid, New York: Atherton Press, 1967.

1430.1 Overseas Development Institute, Effective Aid, London: The Overseas Development Institute Ltd., 1967.

1431. Pearson, Lester B. (Chairman), Partners in Development: Report of the Commission on International Development, New York: Frederick A. Praeger Co., 1969.

1432. _____, The World Bank's Commission on International Development, Washington, D. C.: International Bank for Reconstruction and Development, 1969.

1432.1 Perkins, James A., "Foreign Aid and the Brain Drain," Foreign Affairs, 44 (July 1966), 608-19.

1433. Peter, Hollis W., and Edwin R. Henry, "Measuring Successful Performance Overseas," International Development Review, 3(October 1961), 8-12.

1434. Pye, Lucian W., "Soviet and American Styles in Foreign Aid," Orbis, 4(Summer 1960), 159-73.

1435. Rigney, J. A., and J. K. McDermott, Role of Technical Personnel in the Technical Assistance Institution Building Process. (One portion of the Final Report of the CIC-AID Rural Development Research Project), June, 1968.

(C3c)

1436. Rogers, Everett M. and George H., "The Importance of Personal Influence in the Adoption of Technical Change," Social Forces, 36(May 1958), 329-40.

1437. Rostow, W. W., The U. S. in the World Arena, New York: Harper & Row, 1960.

1439. Rubin, Seymour, The Conscience of the Rich Nations: The Development Assistance Committee and the Common Aid Effort, New York: Harper & Row, 1966.

1440. Sander, Irwin T., Interprofessional Training Goals in Technical Assistance Personnel Abroad, New York: Council of Social Work Education, 1959.

1441. Schlesinger, Arthur, Jr., A Thousand Days, John F. Kennedy in the White House, Boston: Houghton Mifflin Co., 1965.

1442. Scott, Andrew M., The Revolution in Statecraft, New York: Random House, 1967.

1443. Sharp, Walter, International Technical Assistance, Chicago: Public Administration Service, 1952.

1444.1 Smith, Hadley E. (ed.), Problems of Foreign AID, New York: Oxford University Press, 1964.

1445. Spencer, Daniel L., and Alexander Woronook (eds.), The Transfer of Technology to Developing Countries, New York: Frederick A. Praeger Co., 1967.

1446. Storm, William B., and Jason L. Finkle, American Professionals in Technical Assistance, Los Angeles: School of Public Administration, University of Southern California, 1965.

1447. Sufrin, Sidney C., Technical Assistance--Theory and Guidelines, Syracuse, N. Y.: Syracuse University Press, 1966.

1447.1 Sutton, Francis, "Technical Assistance," in David L. Sills (ed.), International Encyclopedia of the Social Sciences, New York: The Macmillan Co., and The Free Press, 1968, 15, 565-76.

1448. Svennilson, Ingvar, "Technical Assistance: The Transfer of Industrialized Know-How to Non-Industrialized Countries," in Kenneth Berrill (ed.), Economic Development with Special Reference to East Asia, New York: St. Martin's, 1966, 405-28.

1449. Tickner, Fred, Technical Cooperation, New York: Frederick A. Praeger Co., 1966.
Discusses lessons of the U. N. experience and the contribution that technical cooperation can make to the future development.

1450. Tinker, High, "The Human Factor in Foreign Aid," Pacific Affairs, 32(September 1959), 288-97.

1451. Trail, Thomas F., Education of Development Technicians: A Guide to Training and Programs, New York: Frederick A. Praeger Co., 1968.

1452. United Kingdom, Technical Assistance from the United Kingdom for Overseas Development, London: Her Majesty's Stationery Office, 1961.

1453. United Nations, *Science and Technology for Development. Report on the United Nations Conference on the Application of Science and Technology for the Benefit of Less Developed Areas*, (8 volumes), New York: United Nations, 1963.

    These volumes are devoted to the following subjects: (1) world of opportunity (general survey of the needs and prospects of less developed areas), (2) natural resources, (3) agriculture, (4) industry, (5) people and living, (6) education and training, (7) science and planning, (8) plenary proceedings and list of papers and index.

1453.1 Van der Veen, G., *Aiding Underdeveloped Countries through International Economic Cooperation*, Delft, Netherlands: Naamloze Vennootschap W. D. Meinema, 1970.

1454. Vrancken, Fernand, *Technical Assistance in Public Administration: Lessons of Experience and Possible Improvements*, Brussels: International Institute of Administrative Sciences, 1963.

1455. Waltman, Howard L., "Cross-Cultural Training in Public Administration," *Public Administration Review*, 21(Summer 1961), 141-47.

1456. Weidner, Edward W., *Technical Assistance in Public Administration Overseas: The Case for Development Administration*, Chicago: Public Administration Service, 1964.

1457. Westwood, Andrew F., *Foreign Aid in a Foreign Policy Framework*, Washington, D. C.: The Brookings Institution, April 1966.

1457.1 White, John, *Pledged to Development*, London: Overseas Development Institute, 1967.

    A study of the way in which the notion of a consortium, and then of a consultative group, evolved. A general history is given, with case studies of the consortia for Pakistan and Turkey. The scope for these mechanisms is analysed and their long-term significance as a framework for relations between aid-receiving countries. The study also touches on multilateral aid and discusses in some detail the proper relationship between multilateral financial institutions and the bilateral donor countries.

1458. Whiteford, Andrew H. (ed.), *A Reappraisal of Economic Development: Perspectives for Cooperative Research*, Chicago: Aldine Publishing Co., 1967.

1459. Whitman, David, *Toward Economic Co-operation in Asia*, (The United Nations Economic Commission for Asia and the Far East), New Haven, Conn.: Yale University Press, 1963.

    Gives an historical appraisal of the Economic Commission for Asia and the Far East (ECAFE).

1460. Whyte, William Foote, "The Role of the U. S. Professor in Developing Countries," *American Sociologist*, 4(February 1969), 19-28.

1461. Wolf, Charles, "Economic Aid Reconsidered," *Yale Review*, 50(Summer 1961), 518-32.

    Gives a rebuttal to Milton Friedman's, "Foreign Economic Aid: Means and Objectives."

(C3d)

1462. _____, Foreign Aid: Theory and Practice of Southern Asia, Princeton, N. J.: Princeton University Press, 1960.

1463. Wurfel, David, "The Bell Report and After: A Study of Political Problems of Social Reform Stimulated by Foreign Aid," unpublished Ph.D. Dissertation, Ithaca, N. Y.: Department of Political Science, Cornell University, 1960.

1464. _____, "Foreign Aid and Social Reform in Political Development: A Philippine Case Study," American Political Science Review, 53(June 1959), 456-82.
Attempts to establish a relationship between social reform and economic development. Social reform does not always support economic growth. The author defines social reform as directed social change involving the political-economic power structure. More narrowly, it is governmentally encouraged action. He refutes the objections to social reform in foreign countries made by some American scholars. He infers that to intervene without reform is merely to strengthen the ruling elite and support the existing pattern of inequality.

1464.1 Young, Charles, Consultancy in Overseas Development, London: Overseas Development Institute, 1968.
This study is based on the discussions of a group brought together by the Overseas Development Institute. It contains information on the range of consultancy services available to developing countries, an assessment of the advantages and problems arising from the use of consultants, and ends with conclusions by consultants themselves, and by those concerned with aid to developing countires, to increase the advantages and overcome the problems.

1465. Zack, Arnold, Labor Training in Developing Countries: A Challenge in Responsible Democracy, New York: Frederick A. Praeger Co., 1963.

d. Diffusion

1466. Blake, Robert F., and Jane S. Mouton, Increasing the Flow and Utilization of New Ideas in Organizational Problem-Solving, Austin, Texas: Scientific Methods, Inc. (stenciled paper).

1467. Copp, James H., Maurice L. Sill, and Emory J. Brown, "The Function of Information Sources in Farms Practice Adoption Process," Rural Sociology, 23(June 1958), 146-77.

1468. Deutchman, P., "The Mass Media in an Underdeveloped Village," Journalism Quarterly, 40(Winter 1963), 27-35.

1469. Erasmus, Charles J., "Agricultural Changes in Haiti: Patterns of Resistance and Acceptance," Human Organization, 2(Winter 1952), 20-26.

1470. Karpot, Kemal H., "Social Effects of Farm Mechanization in Turkish Villages," Social Research, 27(Spring 1960), 83-105.

(C3d)

Investigates twenty Turkish villages which were faced with sudden mechanization of agriculture. The initiators did not envision the social consequences of the technological change.

1471. La Porte, Todd, "Diffusion and Discontinuity in Science, Technology, and Public Affairs," *American Behavioral Scientist*, 10(May 1967), 3-9.

1472. Lerner, Daniel, and Wilbur Schram, *Communications and Change in the Developing Countries*, Honolulu: East-West Center Press, 1967.

1473. Liebermann, S., "The Effects of Change on the Attitudes of Role Occupants," *Human Relations*, 9(4, 1956), 385-402.

1474. Lippitt, Donald, "Methods for Producing and Measuring Change in Group Functioning: Theoretical Problems," *General Semantics Bulletin*, 14 and 15 (Winter-Spring 1954), 28-33.

1475. Loomis, Charles P., and others (eds.), *Turialba: Social System and the Introduction of Change*, Glencoe, Ill.: The Free Press, 1953.
Reports the results of an interdisciplinary research program on the introduction of change and the nature of social systems in the Central American Community of Turialba, Costa Rica. Special emphasis is given to an analysis of the communication process. Various systems are analyzed: demographic, educational, religious, agricultural, and political.

1475.1 Rao, Lakshmana, *Communication and Development: A Study of Two Indian Villages*, Minneapolis, Minn.: University of Minnesota Press, 1966.

1476. Rogers, Everett M., *Diffusion of Innovations*, New York: The Free Press, 1962.
Proposes an integrated theory of the diffusion of innovations. Although "diffusion" is a broader topic than "planned organizational change," many of the 500 research studies cited in the bibliography are subsumed under this concept. "The Role of the Change Agent Innovation" are examples of chapter titles.

1477. _____, *Modernization Among Peasants: Impact of Communication*, New York: Holt, Rinehart & Winston, 1969.

1478. Ryan, Bryce, "A Study in Technological Diffusion," *Rural Sociology*, 13(September 1948), 273-84.

1479. Scott, Thomas M., "The Diffusion of Urban Governmental Forms as a Case of Social Learning," *Journal of Politics*, 30(November 1968), 1091-1108.

1480. Sherif, Muzafer, Caralyn Sharif, and R. E. Nebergall, *Attitude and Attitude Change: The Social Judgment Involvement Approach*, Philadelphia: W. B. Saunders & Co., 1964.
The authors have traced psychological processes by which an individual accepts or rejects persons, groups, ideas and events. The attitudes of an individual, in his experience with other individuals, are classified into three categories: acceptance, rejection, and non-commitment.

1481. Spencer, Daniel L., and Alexander Woroniak (eds.), *The Transfer of Technology to Developing Countries*, New York: Frederick A. Praeger Co., 1967.

(C3e)

The search for an optimum method of transferring technology is the central theme. The authors--policy-oriented economists and econometricians, administrators and scientists--have been selected for differences of viewpoint and methodology. A strategy of technological transfer emerges from the discussion between those favouring concrete solutions to immediate problems.

1482. Thurber, Clarence, "Training Administrators for Developing Countries," International Development Review, 3(June 1961), 34-38.
   The article makes recommendations for training administrators of less developed countries. The crux of the discussion is that administration, like many other aspects of national growth, is culture bound and that the developing countries will have to evolve administrative procedures and practices which are in keeping with their cultural heritage.

1483. Van Mook, H. J., "Note on Training Abroad in Public Administration for Students from Under-developed Countries," International Review of Administrative Sciences, 26(1, 1960), 67-69.

e. Innovation

1484. American Economic Review, "Theory of Innovation," American Economic Review, 59(May 1969), 18-49.
   Contents: "An economic theory of technological change" by William D. Nordhus; "Classificatory notes on the production and transmission of technological knowledge" by Kenneth J. Arrow; "Technological progress and microeconomic theory" by Werner Z. Hirsch; "Discussion" by Evsey D. Domar and Joseph Stigitz.

1485. Argyris, Chris, Organization and Innovation, Homewood, Ill.: R. D. Irwin, 1965.

1486. Bennett, H. S., Innovation: The Basis of Cultural Change, New York: McGraw-Hill Book Co., 1953.

1487. Bennett, Thomas R., The Leader and the Process of Change, New York: Association Press, 1962.

1488. Blaise, Hans C., and Luis A. Rodriquez, "Introducing Innovations at Ecuadorean Universities," Pittsburgh, Pa.: Inter-University Research Program in Institution Building, 1968 (processed).

1489. Bright, James R., Research, Development and Technological Innovation, R. D. Irwin, 1964.

1490. Burns, Tom, and C. M. Stalker, The Management Innovation, London: Tavistock Publications, 1961.

1491. Carlson, Richard O., Adoption of Educational Innovations, Eugene, Ore.: Center for Advanced Study of Education Administration, University of Oregon, 1965.
   An empirical study investigating the processes and characteristics of adopters of innovative educational methods and practices.

1492. Dasgupta, Satadal, "Communication and Innovation in Indian Villages," *Social Forces*, 43(March 1965), 330-37.

    Sources of information vary with the farmer's socio-economic status and type of practice for which information is sought. When the farmers are divided into three groups--innovators, early adopters, and later adopters--according to immediacy of response to an innovation--the innovators are found to utilize institutionalized sources, while the late adopters rely more upon non-institutionalized sources. The position of early adopters is intermediate.

1493. De Simone, Daniel, "Education for Innovation," *IEEE Spectrum*, 5(January 1968), 83-89.

1494. Fairweather, George W., *Methods for Experimental Social Innovation*, New York: John Wiley and Sons, 1967.

1495. Gold, Bela, "Economic Effects of Technological Innovation," *Management Science*, 11(September 1964), 105-34.

1496. Gordon, Gerald, and Sue Marquis, "Freedom, Visibility of Consequences, and Scientific Innovation," *American Journal of Sociology*, 72(September 1966), 195-202.

1497. Jewkes, David Sawers, and Richard Stillerman, *The Sources of Invention*, New York: St. Martin's, 1958.

    This work treats the relationships between the state, its institutions, and technological innovation.

1498. Kahn, Herman, and Anthony Wiener, "Technological Innovation and the Future of Strategic Warfare," *Astronautics and Aeronautics*, 5(December 1967), 28-48.

1499. Lake, Dale G., "Concepts of Change and Innovation in 1966," *Journal of Applied Behavioral Science*, 4(January/March 1968), 2-24.

1500. Marsh, C. Paul, and A. Lee Coleman, "Group Influences and Agricultural Innovations--Some Findings and Hypotheses," *American Journal of Sociology*, 61(May 1956), 588-94.

1501. Michaelis, Michael, "Obstacles to Innovation," *International Science and Technology*, 35(November 1964), 40-46.

1502. Miles, Matthew B., "Educational Innovation: Resources, Strategies, and Unanswered Questions," *The American Behavioral Scientist*, 7(February 1964), 10-14.

    Discusses climate, rate, and causes of change; presents a typology of strategies of change, and raises many unanswered questions about the nature of innovation and its acceptance.

1503. _____ (ed.), *Innovation in Education*, New York: Bureau of Publications, Teachers College, Columbia University, 1964.

1504. Morse, Dean, and Aaron Warner (eds.), *Technological Innovation and Society*, New York: Columbia University Press, 1966.

1504.1 Mosher, Frederick, and John E. Harr, *Programming Systems and Foreign Affairs Leadership: An Attempted Innovation*, New York: Oxford University Press, 1970.

1504.2 Nelson, Richard R., "Innovation," in David L. Sills (ed.), *International Encyclopedia of the Social Sciences*, New York: The Macmillan Co., and The Free Press, 1968, 7, 339-45.

1505. Nieburg, Harold L., "Social Control of Innovation," *American Economic Review*, 58(May 1968), 666-680.

1506. Niehoff, Arthur H., and J. Charnel Anderson, "The Progress of Cross-Cultural Innovation," *International Development Review*, 6(June 1964), 5-11.

1507. Press, Charles, and Alan Arian (eds.), *Empathy and Ideology: Aspects of Administrative Innovation*, Chicago: Rand McNally, 1966.

1508. Rogers, Everett M., *Communication of Innovations: A Cross-Cultural Approach*, New York: The Free Press, 1969.

1509. Rosner, Martin, "Economic Determinants of Organizational Innovation," *Administrative Science Quarterly*, 12(March 1968), 614-25.

1510. Schon, Donald, "The Fear of Innovation," *International Science and Technology*, 59(November 1966), 70-78.

1511. _____, "Innovation by Invasion," *International Science and Technology*, 27(March 1964), 52-60.

1512. Thompson, Victor A., "Bureaucracy and Innovation," *Administrative Science Quarterly*, 10(June 1965), 1-20.

1513. _____, *Bureaucracy and Innovation*, Birmingham, Ala.: University of Alabama Press, 1969.
   Discusses the relationship between organizational structures and innovation. In the past, innovation in society took place largely through the birth of new organizations and the death of old ones. Given the capital requirements of today s technology, this method seems too wasteful. Existing organizations must learn to be more innovative to conserve scarce resources.

1514. Wilkening, E. A., "Role of Communicating Agents in Technological Change in Agriculture," *Social Forces*, 34(May 1956), 361-67.

1515. Wilson, James A., "Innovation in Organizations: Notes Toward a Theory," paper read at American Political Science Association, New York, September 1963.

D. BIBLIOGRAPHIES AND SUPPLEMENTARY ITEMS

(D1)

1. BIBLIOGRAPHIES

1516.   Ahmad, Jaleel, <u>Natural Resources in Low-Income Countries: An Analytical Survey of Socio-Economic Research</u>, Pittsburgh, Pa.: University of Pittsburgh Press, 1960.

1517.   Alexander-Frutschi, Marian Crites (ed.), <u>Human Resources and Economic Growth: An International Annotated Bibliography on the Role of Education in Economic and Social Development</u>, Palo Alto, Cal.: Stanford Research Institute, 1963.

1518.   The American Behavioral Scientist, <u>The ABS Guide to Recent Publications in the Social and Behavioral Sciences</u>, New York: Sage Publications, Inc., 1965.
    Contains over 6,500 citations published from 1957 to 1964. Each book or article is abstracted to indicate approach, methodology, and major findings. Included are topical listings and a comprehensive index. <u>The ABS Guide Supplements</u> are published yearly beginning with 1966.

1519.   The American Behavioral Scientist, <u>New Studies in the Social and Behavioral Sciences</u>, New York: Russel Sage Publications, Inc., monthly.

1520.   American Universities Field Staff, <u>A Select Bibliography: Asia, Africa, Eastern Europe, Latin America</u>, New York, 1960-64.

1521.   Balandier, G., "Social Implications of Technical Advance in Under-developed Countries: A Trend Report and Bibliography," <u>Current Sociology</u>, 6 (1954-55), 5-75.

1522.   Baranson, Jack, <u>Technology for Underdeveloped Areas: An Annotated Bibliography</u>, New York: Pergamon Press, 1967.

1523.   Baster, J., "Recent Literature on the Economic Development of Backward Areas," <u>Quarterly Journal of Economics</u>, 68(November 1954), 585-602.

1524.   Beck, Carl, and J. Thomas McKechnie, <u>Political Elites: A Selected Computerized Bibliography</u>, Cambridge, Mass.: The M.I.T. Press, 1968.

1525.   Bienen, Henry, <u>Violence and Social Change: A Review of Current Literature</u>, Chicago: University of Chicago Press, 1968.

1526.   Brode, John, <u>The Process of Modernization, An Annotated Bibliography on the Socio-cultural Aspects of Development</u>, Cambridge, Mass.: Harvard University Press, Center for International Affairs, 1969.

(D1)

1527. Carnell, Francis, <u>The Politics of the New States--A Selected Bibliography with Special Reference to the Commonwealth</u>, London: Oxford University Press, 1961.
    1599 references on various aspects of the politics of the developing countries have been divided into 21 sections. There is a separate section on administration which contains nearly 160 items. The bibliography has been compiled with a good deal of care and is a useful reference work on countries of Asia and Africa.

1528. Center for Comparative Political Analysis, <u>Bibliography on Planned Social Change</u>, Minneapolis, Minn.: Department of Political Science, University of Minnesota, 1967.

1529. Cheek, Gloria, <u>Economic and Social Implication of Automation: A Bibliographical Review</u>, East Lansing, Mich.: Labor and Industrial Center, Michigan State University, 1957.

1530. Commission for Technical Cooperation in Africa South of the Sahara, <u>Inventory of Economic Studies Concerning Africa South of the Sahara</u>, London, 1960.

1531. Eisenstadt, S. N., "Bureaucracy and Bureaucratization," <u>Current Sociology</u>, 7(2, 1958), 99-164.

1532. "Focus on Foreign Aid," <u>Intercom</u>, 54(July 1963), Entire issue.

1533. Food and Agriculture Organization, <u>Bibliography on Land Tenure</u>, Rome, 1955-59.

1534. Frey, Frederick W. (ed.), <u>Survey Research in Comparative Social Change: A Bibliography</u>, Cambridge, Mass.: The M.I.T. Press, 1969.
    Contains 1600 individual annotations as well as a good breakdown of general social science items.

1535. Gable, Richard W., <u>Development Administration and Assistance--An Annotated Bibliography</u>, Washington: Agency for International Development, 1963.

1536. Gilfillan, S. C., "Social Implications of Technical Advance," <u>Current Sociology</u>, 1(4, 1953), 191-266.

1537. Gross, Bertram M., <u>An Annotated Bibliography of National Economic Planning</u>, Syracuse, N. Y.: Syracuse University Press, 1963.

1538. Hagen, Everett E., "Bibliography," in <u>On the Theory of Social Change</u>, Homewood, Ill.: Dorsey, 1962, 524-48.

1540. Hanson, A. H., <u>Problems of Public Enterprise With Special Reference to Developing Countries</u>, Pittsburgh, Pa.: University of Pittsburgh, 1962 (mimeographed).

1541. Hardin, Einar, William B. Eddy, and Steven B. Deutsch (eds.), <u>Economic and Social Implications of Automation: An Annotated Bibliography</u>, East Lansing, Mich.: Labor and Industrial Relations Center, Michigan State University, 1958 and 1961.

(D1)

1542. Harrison, Annette, <u>Bibliography on Automation and Technological Change and Studies of the Future</u>, Santa Monica, Cal.: Rand Corporation, P-3365-3, March 1968, 34p.

1543. Hart, Donn V., and Paul Meadows, <u>An Annotated Bibliography of Directed Social Change</u>, Syracuse, N. Y.: Syracuse University, 1961.

1544. Harvard University Law School, <u>Bibliography on Taxation in Underdeveloped Countries</u>, Cambridge, Mass.: Harvard University Press, 1962.

1545. Havighurst, Robert J., and Anton J. Jansen, "Community Research," <u>Current Sociology</u>, 15(2, 1967), 1-120.

1546. Hazlewood, A., <u>The Economics of "Underdeveloped" Areas: An Annotated Reading List of Books, Articles, and Official Publications</u>, London: Oxford University Press, 1954.

1547. Heady, Ferrel, and Sybil L. Stokes, <u>Comparative Public Administration: A Selective Annotated Bibliography</u>, Ann Arbor, Mich.: Institute of Public Administration, University of Michigan, 1960.
    Selections are centered around: (1) the general area of public and comparative administration, (2) the development and major characteristics of some major modern bureaucracies, (3) administrative organization and relationships, (4) personnel management, (5) fiscal administration, and (6) administrative law, responsibility and control.

1548. <u>Implications of Automation and Other Technological Development: A Selected Annotated Bibliography</u>, Bulletin No. 1319-1, Washington, D. C.: Government Printing Office, 1963.

1548.1 Institute for Social Research, "Research Publications and Bibliographies," series from 1946 to 1965, Ann Arbor, Mich.: University of Michigan.
    An excellent source for leading research and publications in the field of organizational theory and behavior.

1549. Jones, Garth N., <u>Planned Organizational Change: A Set of Working Documents</u>, Los Angeles: Center for Research in Public Organization, School of Public Administration, University of Southern California, 1964.
    Contains 190 abstracted cases on planned change.

1551. Lackey, Alvin S., "A Working Bibliography in Community Development," <u>Community Development Review</u>, 3(June 1963), 101-4.

1552. Marsh, Robert M., "Comparative Sociology, 1950-1963," <u>Current Sociology</u>, 14(2, 1966), 5-152.

1553. Massachusetts Institute of Technology, Center for International Studies, <u>Official Serial Publications Relating to Economic Development in Africa South of the Sahara</u>, Cambridge, Mass.: 1961.

1554. Mayntz, Renate, "The Study of Organizations," <u>Current Sociology</u>, 13(3, 1964), 95-156.

1555. National Diet Library, <u>Bibliography on Planning With Special Reference to Long-term Project</u>, Tokyo: National Diet Library, 1963.

1556. Niehoff, Arthur H., and Anderson J. Charnel, A Selected Bibliography of Cross-Cultural Change Projects, Alexandria, Va.: Department of Defense, Human Resources Research Office, 1965.
   A collection of cases on planned change with emphasis on the cultural aspects.

1557. Office of Technical Cooperation and Research, "Public Administration Technicians' Reports, An Annotated Bibliography of Technicians' Reports in File Covering the Years 1959-66," Washington D. C.: Agency for International Development, 1966 (processed).

1558. ReQua, Eloise, and Jane Statham (eds.), The Developing Nations: A Guide to Information Sources Concerning their Economic, Political, Technical, and Social Problems, Detroit: Gale Research Company, 1965.

1560. "A Selected Bibliography on Technical Assistance," Technical Assistance Quarterly Bulletin, Nos. 1-4, 1956-57.

1561. Selected Rand Abstracts, Santa Monica, Cal.: Rand Corporation, 1(1963)-- quarterly

1561.1 Shannon, Lyle W., "Social Factors in Economic Growth," Current Sociology, 6(3, 1957), 173-237.

1562. Siegel, Bernard J. (ed.), Biennial Review of Anthropology, Stanford, Cal.: Stanford University Press, 1959.

1563. Simpson, Keith, Manpower Problems in Economic Development, A Selected Bibliography, Princeton, N. J.: Princeton University, Industrial Relations Section, 1958.

1564. Spitz, Allan H., and Edward W. Weidner, Development Administration: An Annotated Bibliography, Honolulu: East-West Center Press, 1963.

1565. Spitz, Allan H., Developmental Change: An Annotated Bibliography, Lexington, Ky.: University of Kentucky Press, 1969.

1566. Steiner, George A., Top Management Planning, New York: The Free Press, 1969.
   This volume includes an 875 item bibliography dealing mainly with corporate planning.

1567. Sufrin, Sidney C., A Brief Annotated Bibliography on Labor in Emerging Societies, Syracuse, N. Y.: Syracuse University Press, 1961.

1569. Trager, Frank N., "A Selected and Annotated Bibliography on Economic Development, 1952-57," Economic Development and Cultural Change, 6(July 1958), part 1.

1570. Weidlund, Jane, and others, Comparative Public Administration: A Selected Annotated Bibliography, Ann Arbor, Mich.: University of Michigan, 1963.

1571. Wolf, Charles, Jr., Rand Work on International Development: A Brief Overview, Santa Monica, Cal.: Rand Corporation, RM-6017, June 1969, 15p.

1572. Yale University, Economic Growth Center Library, List of new titles, New Haven, Conn., 1962--.

2. SUPPLEMENTARY ITEMS

This section includes useful items discovered after the bibliography had been completed. Each has been coded as to the section in which it would normally have been placed.

1573. Asher, Robert E., <u>Development Assistance in the Seventies, Alternatives for the United States</u>, Washington, D. C.: The Brookings Institution, 1970.
C3C

1573.1 Averch, H. A., F. H. Denton, and J. E. Koehler, "A Crisis of Ambiguity: Political and Economic Development in the Philippines," A Report Prepared for Agency for International Development, Santa Monica, Cal.: The Rand Corporation, 1970.
B2a

1573.2 Balogh, Thomas, <u>The Economics of Poverty</u>, London: Weidenfeld and Nicolson, 1966.
B1

1574. Barton, Allan H., "Organizations: Methods of Research," in David L. Sills (ed.), <u>International Encyclopedia of the Social Sciences</u>, N. Y.: Macmillan Co., and The Free Press, 1968, 11, 334-43.
A1

1575. Bauchet, Pierre, <u>Economic Planning; the French Experiment</u>, New York: Frederick A. Praeger Co., 1962.
ACa

1576. Bauer, Raymond A. (ed.), <u>Social Indicators</u>, Cambridge, Mass.: The M.I.T. Press, 1966.
C3a
This volume includes articles by Bertram M. Gross, "A Historical Note on Social Indicators" and "The State of the Nation: Social Systems Accounting"; Raymond A. Bauer, "Detection and Anticipation of Impact: The Nature of the Task"; Albert D. Biderman, "Social Indicators and Goals" and "Anticipatory Studies and Stand-by Research Capabilities"; and Robert A. Rosenthal and Robert S. Weiss, "Problems of Organizational Feedback Processes"

1577. Center for Urban Studies, University of Chicago, <u>Social and Economic Information for Urban Planning</u>, vol. 1: <u>Its Selection and Use</u>; vol. 2: <u>A Directory of Data Sources</u>, Chicago: Center for Urban Studies, 1969.
A2a

1578. David, Paul T., "Index Numbers of Party Strength: National, State, and Local," Paper presented at the Sixty-fifth Annual Meeting of the American Political Science Association, New York, September 1969.
B2a

1579. Drewnowski, Jan, and Scott Wolf, <u>The Level of Living Index</u>, Geneva: United Nations Research Institute for Social Development, Report No. 4, September 1966 (Supplement: <u>Programme II</u>, Nov. 27, 1968).
B1

1580. Gottehrer, Barry, "A Human Information System for the Governing of New York City," Paper presented at the Sixty-fifth Annual Meeting of the American Political Science Association, New York, September 1969.   B2a

1581. Bross, Bertram M., "The Coming General Systems Theories of Social Systems," *Human Relations*, 20(November 1967), 357-374.   A2c

1582. _____, "The New Systems Budgeting," *Public Administration Review*, 29(March-April 1969), 113-137.   A2b

1583. _____, "Urban Mapping for 1976 and 2000," *Urban Affairs Quarterly*, 5(December 1969), 121-142.   A2a

1584. Heer, David M. (ed.), *Social Statistics and the City*, Cambridge, Mass.: M.I.T.-Harvard Joint Center for Urban Studies, 1968.   A2a
    This report of a conference held in Washington, D. C. in June 1967 contains the following articles: "Completeness of Coverage of the Nonwhite Population in the 1960 Census and Current Estimates, and Some Implications," by Jacob S. Siegel; "Procedural Difficulties in Taking Past Censuses in Predominantly Negro, Puerto Rican, and Mexican Areas," by Leon Pritzker and N. D. Rothwell; "Needed Innovations in 1970 Census Data Collection Procedures," by Conrad Taeuber; "Needed Improvements in Census Data Collection Procedures With Special Reference to the Disadvantaged," by Everett S. Lee; "Vital Statistics for the Negro, Puerto Rican and Mexican Populations: Present Quality and Plans for Improvement," by Robert D. Grove; "Needed Statistics for Minority Groups in Metropolitan Areas," by Daniel O. Price; and "An Evaluation of Coverage in the 1960 Census of Population by Techniques of Demographic Analysis and by Composite Methods," by Jacob S. Siegel and Melvin Zelnick.

1585. Holleb, Doris, "Social Statistics for Social Policy," in American Society of Planning Officials (eds.), *Planning 1968*, Chicago: ASPO, 1968, 80-94.   C3a

1585.1 Mikesell, Raymond F., *The Economics of Foreign Aid*, London: Weidenfeld and Nicolson, 1968.   C3c

1586. Morgan, Theodore, "The Theory of Error in Centrally Directed Economic Systems," *Quarterly Journal of Economics*, 78(August 1964), 395-416.   A2a

1587. Mosher, Arthus, *A Progressive Rural Structure*, New York: Frederick A. Praeger Co., 1970.   A2a
    Points out that by dividing a locality into areas of immediate, future, and low potential by relatively simple and inexpensive planning techniques, resources can be conserved, and precision in promoting development attained.

1588. National Planning Association, *A New Conception of U. S. Foreign AID, A Joint Statement by the NPA Joint Subcommittee on U. S. Foreign Aid and the NPA Board of Trustees and Standing Committee*, Special Report No. 64, Washington, D. C.: National Planning Association, 1970.   C3c

(D2)

1589. _____, *U. S. Foreign Assistance in the 1970s: A New Approach Report to the President from the Task Force on International Development*, Washington, D. C.: National Planning Association, 1970.   C3c

1590. Nye, J. S., "Corruption and Political Development: A Cost Benefit Analysis," *American Political Science Review*, 61(June 1967), 417-27.   B2a

INDEX

Abegglen, J. C. -- (C1) 713
Abraham, William I. -- (A2b) 129
Ackoff, Russell -- (A1) 1*
Adams, John C. -- (C3c) 1382*
Adams, Richard N. -- (A1) 2*, (B2a) 405, (C2) 990*
Adams, Robert M. -- (C3b) 1328
Adams, Walter -- (C3c) 1354
Adelman, Irma -- (B1) 223*, (B2a) 406*, (C3c) 1354.1*
Adrian, C. R. -- (C3a) 1168*
Adu, A. L. -- (B2a) 407
Agarwala, A. N. -- (B1) 224*
Agency for International Development - (C3b) 1329
Agpalo, Remigio E. -- (B2a) 408
Agricultural Policy Institute -- (A2a) 40
Ahmad, J. M. -- (B2a) 409, (C3c) 1355, (D1) 1516
Ahmad, Munir -- (B2b) 654
Ahmad, Mushtaq -- (B2a) 410
Aiken, Michael -- (C3a) 1209 *
Aktan, Tahir -- (B2a) 538*
Albers, Henry H. -- (C1) 713.1
Albert, Ethel M. -- (C2) 991
Albertson, Maurice L. -- (C3c) 1356*
Alder, John H. -- (C3a) 1157
Alderfer, Harold F. -- (B2a) 411, 412,* 413
Alexander, Yonah -- (C3c) 1357
Alexander-Frutschi, Marian -- (D1) 1517
Alford, Robert F. -- (B2b) 654.1
Ali, Shaukat -- (C3a) 1234*
Allen, Francis R. -- (C2) 992*
Allen, Harold B. -- (C3c) 1358
Allen, Louis A. -- (C1) 714, 715
Almond, Gabriel A. -- (B2a) 414, 415,* 416*, 417, 418, 419*
American Behavioral Scientist -- (D1) 1518, 1519
American Economic Review -- (C3e) 1484

American Universities Field Staff -- (D1) 1520
Amuzegar, Jahangir -- (C3c) 1359
Anderson, Arnold C. -- (B1) 225*
Anderson, Charles W. -- (B2a) 420, 421*
Anderson, J. Charnel -- (C3e) 1506*, (D1) 1556*
Anderson, James G. -- (B2b) 654.2
Anderson, Stanford -- (A2a) 41
Andrain, Charles -- (B2a) 422*
Angus, N. C. -- (B2a) 423*
Anthony, Robert N. -- (A2c) 166
Appleby, Paul H. -- (B2a) 424, (C3a) 1157.1
Applewhite, Philip D. -- (C1) 716 *
Apter, David E. -- (A2c) 167, (B2a) 422, 425, 426, 427, 476*, (B2b) 655
Ardant, G. -- (B1) 226
Arensberg, C. M. -- (C1) 717, (C2) 993*, (C3c) 1360*
Areskoug, Kaj -- (B1) 227
Argyris, Chris -- (C1) 718, 719, 720, 721, 722, 723, 724, (C3a) 1157.1, (C3e) 1485
Arian, Alan -- (C3e) 1507*
Armand, Louis -- (C2) 994
Arnold, H. J. P. -- (C3c) 1361
Aron, Raymond -- (B1) 228
Aronson, Sidney H. -- (B2b) 656
As, D. -- (C3a) 1199*
Ashby, Eric -- (C2) 995
Asher, Robert E. -- (B1) 229*, (C3c) 1362, (D1) 1573
Ashford, Douglas E. -- (B2a) 428, 429, (B2b) 657
Astin, Alexander W. -- (C1) 725
Athos, Anthony C. -- (C1) 726*
Attir, Aryeh -- (C3c) 1363
Austin, Dennis -- (B2a) 430
Averch, H. A. -- (D2) 1573.1*
Avery, Robert S. -- (C1) 727
Ayal, E. B. -- (B1) 230

Backstrom, Charles H. -- (A1)3*
Bailey, F. G. -- (B2a)431
Balandier, G. -- (D1)1521
Baldwin, David A. -- (C3c)1364, 1364.1
Baldwin, G. B. -- (B2a)432
Bales, Robert F. -- (C1)728, 910*
Ballachery, Egerton S. -- (C1)858*
Balogh, Thomas -- (C3c)1365, (D1)1573.2
Banani, Amin -- (B1)231
Banfield, Edward C. -- (A2a)92*, (C2)996*, (C3c)1366, 1366.1
Banfield, Laura -- (C2)996*
Banks, Arthur S. -- (B2a)433*
Bantock, G. H. -- (B1)232
Baranson, Jack -- (D1)1522
Barbichon, Guy -- (C2)997
Bardis, P. D. -- (C2)998
Barnabas, A. P. -- (B2a)482*
Barnard, Chester I. -- (C1)729
Barnes, Louis B. -- (C3a)1158, 1206.1*
Barnett, A. D. -- (B2a)434
Barnett, H. G. -- (C2)999, 1000
Baron, Paul -- (B1)233
Baronson, J. -- (B1)234
Barringer, Herbert -- (C2)1001*
Barth, Frederick -- (C2)1002
Barton, Allen H. -- (C1)730, 731, (D2)1574
Basia, K. A. -- (B1)235
Bass, Bernard -- (C1)732
Baster, J. -- (D1)1523
Basu, A. K. -- (B1)236
Basu, T. K. -- (C2)1003
Bauchet, Pierre -- (D2)1575
Bauer, Peter T. -- (B1)237*
Bauer, Raymond -- (A2a)42, (C1)733, 734,*(C3a)1159, (D2)1576
Bavelas, A. -- (C3a)1160
Bayley, David H. -- (B2a)435, 436, 437
Beagle, Allen J. -- (C1)880, (C2)1091*
Beaglehole, Earnest -- (C2)1004
Beals, Alan R. -- (C2)1005, 1006*
Beck, Carl -- (D1)1524*
Becker, Gary S. -- (B1)238
Behrendt, R. F. -- (B2a)438
Belknap, D. -- (C1)735*
Bell, Daniel -- (A2a)43, (A2a)44, (C2)1007, 1007.1
Bell, Earl H. -- (C1)736
Belshaw, Cyril S. -- (C1)737, (C2)1008
Bendix, Reinhard -- (B1)239, (C1)738

Bendix, Richard -- (B2a)439
Benedict, Ruth -- (C2)1009
Benham, Frederick -- (B1)240
Benne, Kenneth D. -- (C3a)1164*
Bennett, H. S. -- (C3e)1486
Bennett, Meridan -- (C3c)1402.1*
Bennett, Thomas R. -- (C3e)1487
Bennis, Warren G. -- (B2b)658, 659, (C1)739, 740, 741, (C3a)1161, 1162, 1163, 1164*, 1165, 1288*
Bent, Frederick T. -- (B2b)660
Benveniste, Guy -- (C3a)1166*, (C3c)1367*
Bereday, George Z. F. -- (B1)241
Berger, Morroe -- (B1)242, (B2b)661
Beringer, Christoph -- (B1)243
Berrelson, Bernard -- (C1)742*
Berrien, F. Kenneth -- (A2c)168
Berrill, Kenneth -- (B1)244
Berry, Brian J. L. -- (C2)1009.1
Bertalanffy, Ludwig Von -- (A2c)168.1
Biderman, Albert D. -- (C3a)1167
Bienen, Henry -- (B2a)440, (C2)1010, (C1)1525
Bill, J. A. -- (B1)245
Binder, Leonard -- (B2a)441
Bird, Richard M. -- (C3c)1404*
Birkhead, Guthrie -- (C3b)1330
Black, Cyril Edwin -- (B2a)442
Black, Eugene -- (C3c)1368, 1368.1
Black, Guy -- (A2c)169
Black, Lloyed D. -- (C3c)1369
Black, Max -- (C1)743
Black, R. R. -- (C3a)1206.1*
Blacker, Donald L. M. -- (B1)331*
Blackman, Allan -- (A2a)45
Blaise, Hans C. -- (C3b)1338*, (C3e)1488*
Blake, Robert F. -- (C3d)1466*
Blake, Robert R. -- (A2c)170*
Blalock, Ann B. -- (A1)4*
Blalock, Hubert M., Jr. -- (A1)4*, (A1)5
Blank, Blanche Davis -- (B2b)662, 672*
Blau, Peter M. -- (B2b)663*, (C1)744, 745*, 746
Blellock, David -- (B1)246
Blick, Larry N. -- (A2b)150*
Blumer, Herbert -- (B1)247, 248, 249, 250
Bobrow, Davis B. -- (B2a)443
Bock, Edwin A. -- (C3c)1370
Bock, Kenneth E. -- (C2)1011
Boguslaw, Robert -- (C2)1012
Booth, D. A. -- (C3a)1168*

Bordis, P. D. -- (C2) 1013
Borgatta, Edgar -- (A1) 6*
Borkner, Lloyd -- (C2) 1014
Borko, Harold -- (A1) 7
Bose, Santi P. -- (C3a) 1169
Boucher, W. I. -- (A2c) 207*
Boulding, Elise -- (C1) 847*
Boulding, Kenneth -- (B1) 251, (C1) 747, 748, 749, 750
Bowen, Howard -- (B1) 252*
Bowers, David G. -- (C1) 891*, (C3a) 1290*
Bowles, Samuel -- (A2a) 46
Bowmer, Mary Jean -- (B1) 225*
Bradburn, Norman -- (C1) 750.1*
Braibanti, Ralph -- (A1) 8, (B1) 253*, 376*, (B2a) 444*, 445, 446, (B2b) 664, 665, 666, (C3b) 1331, (C3c) 1371, 1372
Branch, Melville C. -- (A2a) 47
Braum, Ludwig, Jr. -- (A2c) 203*
Brausch, Georges -- (B2a) 447
Brecher, Michael -- (B2a) 448
Bretton, Henry L. -- (B2a) 449
Brickman, William -- (C2) 1015
Briggs, Ellis -- (C3c) 1373
Briggs, G. E. -- (C1) 895*
Bright, James -- (A2a) 49, (C3e) 1489
Brockway, Fenner -- (B2a) 450
Brode, John -- (D1) 1526
Brody, Richard A. -- (A1) 9
Brown, Bernice -- (C1) 829.1*
Brown, Emery J. -- (C3d) 1467*
Brown, Murray -- (C3a) 1170
Bruce, R. D. -- (A1) 27*
Bruhns, Fred -- (C3b) 1336*, 1339*
Bruton, Henry J. -- (B1) 254
Bryson, Lyman -- (C3a) 1170.1
Brzezinski, Zbigniew -- (B2a) 451*, (C3c) 1374
Buchanan, Norman S. -- (B1) 255
Buchanan, Robert -- (B1) 256
Buckley, Walter -- (A2c) 171, 172
Buesnel, E. L. -- (A2c) 198*
Burke, Fred G. -- (B2a) 452, 453
Burke, John -- (B1) 257
Burns, Tom -- (C3a) 1171, 1172, (C3e) 1490*
Burton, Ralph -- (B2b) 667*
Butani, K. N. -- (C3a) 1171.1
Byrnes, Francis C. -- (C3c) 1375, 1375.1

Cahnmon, Werner J. -- (C2) 1016
Caiden, Gerald -- (B2a) 454, (C3a) 1173, 1174
Cairncross, A. K. -- (B1) 258
Caldwell, Lynton -- (A2a) 51, (C3c) 1376
Cantril, Hadley -- (C1) 750.2
Caplovitz, David -- (C1) 750.1*
Caplow, Theodore -- (B2a) 455*, (C1) 751, 752
Cardozo, Michael H. -- (C3c) 1377
Carlson, Richard O. -- (C3a) 1175, (C3e) 1491
Carlson, Sune -- (B2a) 456
Carneiro, Robert L. -- (C2) 1017
Carnell, Francis -- (C1) 1527
Carstairs, G. Morris -- (C2) 1018
Cartwright, Dorwin -- (C1) 753*, (C3a) 1176
Carzo, Rocco -- (C1) 754*, 755
Center for Comparative Political Analysis -- (D1) 1528
Cerych, Ladislav -- (C3c) 1378
Cetron, Marvin -- (A2a) 52
Chamberlain, Neil W. -- (C1) 756
Chance, William A. -- (A1) 10
Chandler, Alfred A., Jr. -- (C1) 757
Chandrasekhar, Sripati -- (C3c) 1379
Chapman, Brian -- (B2b) 668
Chapman, John W. -- (C1) 912*
Chapple, Eliot D. -- (C3a) 1177, 1178, 1179*
Charlesworth, James C. -- (A1) 11
Charlick, Robert B. -- (C3c) 1380
Chartrand, Robert -- (A2b) 130*
Chaudhri, Muzaffer Ahmad -- (B2b) 669
Cheek, Gloria -- (D1) 1529
Cheever, D. S. -- (C3c) 1390*
Chenery, Hollis -- (C3c) 1354.1*, 1381*
Chernoff, Herman -- (C1) 758*
Chetkow, B. Harold -- (C3a) 1180
Chin, Robert -- (C3a) 1164*
Chowdhary, Amitabha -- (C3a) 1181
Christ, Carl -- (A1) 12
Christoph, James B. -- (B2a) 457
Churchman, Charles W. -- (A2c) 173
Clagett, Arthur -- (C2) 1019
Clark, D. H. -- (C3a) 1181.1
Clark, Peter B. -- (C3a) 1182*
Cleland, David -- (A2c) 174*, 175
Cleveland, Harlan -- (C3c) 1382*
Coffey, Robert E. -- (C1) 726*
Cohen, Wilbur J. -- (C3a) 1182.1
Coleman, A. Lee -- (C3e) 1500*
Coleman, J. R. -- (C1) 826*
Coleman, James S. -- (B2a) 419*, 458, (C3a) 1183*, 1183.1

Collins, Alan Keith -- (C1) 759
Colm, Gerhard -- (A2a) 53*, (A2b) 131
Commission for Technical Cooperation in Africa South of the Sahara -- (D1) 1530
Conant, James B. -- (A1) 13
Concian, F. -- (C2) 1020
The Congress for Cultural Freedom -- (B2a) 460
Cook, Robert -- (C2) 1107*
Cooper, Joseph D. -- (C1) 760, (C3a) 1184
Cooper, William W. -- (C1) 761*
Copp, James H. -- (C3d) 1467*
Cornog, Geoffrey Y. -- (A2c) 176*
Coser, Lewis -- (C2) 1021
Costello, Timothy W. -- (C3a) 1185*
Cottam, Richard -- (B2a) 461
Cottrell, W. F. -- (C2) 1022, 1023
Cowan, C. D. -- (B1) 259
Cressey, Donald R. -- (C2) 1024, 1025
Croft, D. B. -- (C1) 824*
Crowther, Betty -- (A1) 6*
Crozier, Michel -- (C1) 762
Crutchfield, Richard S. -- (C1) 858*
Currie, Lauchlin -- (A2a) 83*
Curry, Robert L. -- (C1) 763*
Cutright, Philip -- (B2a) 462
Cutt, James -- (B1) 260
Cyert, Richard M. -- (C1) 764*

Daalder, H. -- (B2a) 463
Dahl, Robert A. -- (C1) 765*
Daland, Robert -- (A2a) 54, (B2a) 464, 465
Dale, Ernest -- (C1) 766
Dalton, Gene W. -- (C1) 767
Dang, Nghiem -- (B2a) 466
Danhardt, Robert B. -- (C1) 768
Danhof, Clarence H. -- (C3c) 1383
Dasgupta, Satadel -- (C3e) 1492
Dator, James A. -- (B1) 261
David, Paul T. -- (C3a) 1186, (D2) 1578
Davis, James A. -- (C3a) 1186.1
Davis, James W. -- (A2b) 132
Davis, Kingsley -- (C2) 1025.1
Dean, Alan L. -- (B2a) 558*, (C3a) 1194*
Dechert, Charles -- (C2) 1026
De Georgi, T. -- (C2) 1119*
De Guzman, Raul P. -- (B2a) 467
de Jouvenel, Bertrand -- (A2a) 55
Delany, William -- (B2b) 670
Denton, F. H. -- (D2) 1573.1*
Department of Economic and Social Affairs, United Nations -- (B2a) 467.1
De Schweinitz, Karlde -- (B1) 262
De Simone, Daniel -- (C3e) 1493
de Smith, S. A. -- (B2a) 468
Deutchman, P. -- (C3d) 1468
Deutsch, Karl W. -- (B2a) 469*, 470*, (C1) 769
Deutsch, Steven B. -- (D1) 1541*
Devries, Egbert -- (C2) 1027
Dey, S. K. -- (B2a) 471, (C3c) 1385
Diamant, Alfred -- (B2b) 671, 672*, (C1) 770
Diebold, John -- (C2) 1028
Dill, W. R. -- (C1) 770.1
Dimock, Marshall E. -- (B2b) 673
Dirlan, Jil B. -- (A2a) 123*
Dix, Robert H. -- (B2a) 472
Dobyns, Henry -- (C2) 1029*, (C3a) 1187*
Dobzhansky, Theodosius -- (C1) 771, 772
Domergue, Maurice -- (C3c) 1386, 1386.1
Donaldson, Loraine -- (A2b) 55.1
Dorfman, Robert -- (A2b) 133, (C3a) 1187.1
Downs, Anthony -- (B2b) 674
Downs, Robert B. -- (C3a) 1187.2, 1187.3
Doxiadis, Constantinas -- (A2a) 56*, (C1) 773
Drabek, Thomas E. -- (C1) 774*
Drewnowski, Jan -- (D2) 1579*
Dror, Yehzkel -- (A2a) 57, 58
Drucker, Peter -- (C1) 775, (C2) 1031, 1032
Dube, S. C. -- (B2b) 674.1
Duncan, Richard L. -- (C3c) 1387*
Dunlap, John T. -- (C3a) 1188
Dunn, S. D. and E. -- (C3a) 1189
du Sautoy, Peter -- (B2a) 473
Dusek, Val -- (B2a) 474
Dwarkadas, R. -- (B2a) 475

Eames, E. -- (C2) 1033*
Easton, David -- (A2c) 177, 178, 179
Eckous, Richard S. -- (A2a) 60*
Eckstein, Harry -- (C1) 776
Eckstein, J. -- (B2a) 476*
Eddison, John C. -- (B1) 263
Eddy, William B. -- (D1) 1541*
Educational Policy Research Center, Stanford Research Institute -- (C3a) 1189.1
Egger, Rowland A. -- (B2b) 675
Ehrmann, Henry W. -- (B2a) 477, 478

Eisenstadt, N. B. -- (C1) 777
Eisenstadt, S. N. -- (B1) 264, 265, 266, 267, (B2a) 479, 480, 481, (B2b) 676, 677, (C2) 1034, 1035, 1036, 1037, 1037.1, (C3b) 1332, 1333, (D1) 1531
Eldersveld, S. J. -- (B2a) 482*
Eldredge, H. Wentworth -- (A2a) 61
Ellis, R. A. -- (C2) 1078*
Ellsworth, David F. -- (C3b) 1334
Emerson, Rupert -- (B2a) 483, 483.1
Emery, F. E. -- (A2c) 180*, (C1) 778*
Emery, James C. -- (C1) 778.1
England, George W. -- (C1) 779
Enthoven, Alain -- (A2b) 134
Epstein, T. S. -- (C2) 1038
Erasmus, Charles J. -- (C2) 1039, (C3c) 1388, 1389, (C3d) 1469
Esman, Milton J. -- (A2c) 181*, (B2a) 484, (C3b) 1335, 1336*, 1337, 1338*, 1339*, 1340, (C3c) 1390*
Etzioni, Amitai -- (A1) 14, (C1) 780, 781, 782, 783, 784, 785, 788, (C2) 1040*, 1041, (C3a) 1190, 1191, 1192, 1193
Etzioni, Eva -- (C2) 1040*
Eulau, Heinz -- (C1) 789
Ewald, William, Jr. -- (A2a) 62
Ezera, Kalu -- (B2a) 485

Fabun, Don -- (C2) 1042
Fairweather, George W. -- (C3e) 1494
Fallers, L. A. -- (B2a) 486
Feder, E. -- (C3c) 1391
Fei, John C. H. -- (A2a) 63*
Feis, Herbert -- (C3c) 1392
Feith, Herbert -- (B2a) 487
Feld, Sheila -- (C2) 1049.2*
Feldman, A. S. -- (B1) 268, (C2) 1106*
Fenley, John M. -- (C3c) 1393
Ferkiss, Victor C. -- (B2a) 488, (C3c) 1393.1
Festinger, Leon -- (A1) 15*
Fickett, Lewis, Jr. -- (B1) 269
Field, Lowell G. -- (B2a) 489
Finan, William F. -- (C3a) 1194*
Finer, S. E. -- (B2a) 490
Finkle, Jason -- (B2a) 491*, (C3c) 1446*
Finsterbusch, Kurt -- (B2a) 455*
Firth, Raymond -- (B1) 270*
Fischer, J. -- (B2a) 492*
Fischman, Leonard L. -- (C3a) 1240.6*
Fisher, Joseph L. -- (C3a) 1240.6*
Fisk, E. K. -- (B1) 370*

Flacks, Richard -- (C2) 1043
Foltz, William J. -- (B2a) 470*
Fontela -- (C2) 1044*
Food and Agriculture Organization -- (D1) 1533
Forehand, G. A. -- (C3a) 1195*
Forrester, J. W. -- (C1) 790
Foster, Ellery -- (C3c) 1394
Foster, George M. -- (C2) 1045
Foundation for Research on Human Behavior -- (C1) 791
Fox, Guy H. -- (B2a) 493*
Frank, Andrew Gunder -- (C1) 792
Franklin, Richard -- (C3a) 1196
Fraser, Thomas M., Jr. -- (C3a) 1197
Freilich, Morris -- (C1) 793, 794
French, J. -- (C3a) 1198*
French, J. R. P., Jr. -- (C3a) 1199*
Frey, Frederick W. -- (C2) 1046, (D1) 1534
Frieden, Bernard -- (A2a) 64*
Friedl, Ernestine -- (C3a) 1200
Friedman, John -- (A2a) 65, 65.1, (C1) 795
Friedman, Milton -- (B1) 271
Friedrich, C. J. -- (C3a) 1200.1
Froman, Lewis A., Jr. -- (B2a) 494
Frost, Raymond -- (B1) 272
Fulton, Lord -- (B2b) 678
Furse, Sir Ralph -- (B2a) 495

Gable, Richard W. -- (B2a) 491*, (D1) 1535
Gabor, Dennis -- (A2a) 66
Galbraith, John K. -- (B1) 273, 274, 275
Galenter, E. -- (C1) 901*
Gallaher, Art, Jr. -- (C3a) 1201
Gamson, William A. -- (C1) 796
Gans, Herbert J. -- (A2a) 87.1*
Gant, George F. -- (B2a) 497
Gardner, Burleigh -- (C1) 797*
Garthrop, Louis C. -- (C1) 798
Garvey, Gerald -- (C1) 798.1
Gaus, John M. -- (B2a) 498*
Geertz, Clifford -- (B1) 276, (B2a) 499
Geiger, Theodore -- (A2a) 53*
Gellner, Ernest -- (C1) 799
Geoffrey, Sir Vickers -- (C1) 799.1
George Washington University -- (A2b) 135
Gergen, Kenneth -- (C1) 734*
Gerth, H. H. -- (C1) 800*
Gibb, J. R. -- (C1) 801*
Gibson, Frank -- (C1) 807*

Gilb, Corinne -- (C3a)1201.1
Gilfillan, S. C. -- (D1)1536
Gilmer, B. -- (C3a)1195*
Gilpin, Robert -- (C1)802*
Ginsburgh, R. N. -- (B2a)500
Ginzberg, Eli -- (C2)1047, (C3a)1202*
Gittell, Marilyn -- (C2)1048
Glass, David C. -- (C1)803
Glick, Philip M. -- (C3c)1395, 1396
Glickman, Harvey -- (B2a)501
Gluckman, Max -- (B2a)502, (C1)804, 805
Gochman, David S. -- (A2c)209.1
Goffman, I. W. -- (C3a)1203
Gold, Bela -- (C3e)1495
Goldman, A. S. -- (A2c)182*
Goldman, Thomas -- (A2b)136
Goldschmidt, Arthur -- (B1)277
Goldwin, Robert A. -- (C3c)1397
Golembiewski, Robert T. -- (A2b)136.1, (C1)806, 807*, 808, 809, (C3a)1204
Gollin, Albert E. -- (C3a)1204.1, (C3c)1398
Gonzales, Richard F. -- (A2c)199*
Goode, Harry H. -- (A2c)183*
Goodenough, Ward Hunt -- (C3c)1399, 1400
Goodnow, Henry Frank -- (B2b)679
Goodsell, Charles T. -- (C3a)1205
Goody, Jack -- (B1)278
Gordon, Gerald -- (C3e)1496*
Gordon, Theodore -- (C1)829.1*
Gore, William J. -- (C1)810, 811
Gottehrer, Barry -- (D2)1580
Gough, Kathleen -- (C2)1049
Gouldner, Alvin Ward -- (C1)812, 813, (C3c)1401*
Graham, Lawrence S. -- (B2b)680
Grasberg, Edward -- (A2a)67
Greer, Scott A. -- (C1)814, (C3a)1206
Greiner, Larry E. -- (C3a)1206.1*, 1206.2, 1206.3
Grimshaw, Austin -- (C1)815*
Gross, Bertram M. -- (A2a)68, 69, 69.1, 70, (A2c)184, 185, (C1)816, 816.1, 817, (C2)1049.1, (C3a)1206.4, 1206.5*, 1206.6, 1206.7, 1206.8, 1206.9, (D1)1537, (D2)1581, 1582, 1583
Groves, Roderick T. -- (C3a)1207
Grusky, O. -- (C3a)1207.1
Gue, Ronald L. -- (A1)16*
Guenther, H. P. -- (B2a)504
Guest, Robert H. -- (C3a)1208
Gulati, I. S. -- (A2a)71

Gulley, William H. -- (C1)951*
Gunnell, John G. -- (A1)17
Gurin, Gerald -- (C2)1049.2*
Gurr, Ted -- (C3a)1208.1
Gutheridge, William F. -- (B2a)505
Guthrie, George M. -- (C3c)1402*
Guyot, James F. -- (B2b)681

Haas, Eugene -- (C1)774*, 823*
Haas, Michael -- (A2c)186, (C1)818
Haberler, Gottfried -- (B1)279*
Hage, Jerald -- (C3a)1209*
Hagen, Everett E. -- (B1)280, 281, (C2)1050, (D1)1538
Haire, Mason -- (C1)819*, 820, 821
Hall, Arthur D. -- (A2c)187
Hall, C. P. -- (B1)282
Hall, Edward T. -- (C1)822, (C3a)1210
Hall, Richard H. -- (C1)823*
Halpern, Joel J. -- (C2)1051
Halpern, Manfred -- (B2a)506, 507, (C2)1052
Halpin, Andrew W. -- (C1)824*, 825
Hambidge, Gove -- (B1)283
Hamilton, Herbert -- (C1)851*
Hamilton, William B. -- (C3b)1341
Hancock, M. Donald -- (B2a)617*
Hansen, W. Lee -- (B1)397*
Hanson, A. H. -- (D1)1540
Hanson, Niles -- (B1)284
Hanson, Philip G. -- (C3a)1265*
Hapgood, David -- (B1)332*, (C3c)1402.1*
Harbison, Frederick -- (B1)285*, 287*, (C1)826*
Hardin, Einar -- (C3a)1211, (D1)1541*
Hardwich, Clyde T. -- (C1)827*
Hardyck, Jane -- (C2)1053
Harr, John Ensov -- (B2b)682, (C3e)1504.1*
Harris, Chester W. -- (C3a)1212
Harris, Richard L. -- (B2a)508
Harrison, Annette -- (D1)1542
Harrod, Sir Roy -- (B1)288
Hart, Donn V. -- (D1)1543*
Hartley, Harry J. -- (A2b)137
Harvard University Law School -- (D1)1544
Harvey, E. -- (C1)828
Harwitz, Mitchell -- (B1)293*
Hausser, Philip M. -- (B1)289, (C2)1054
Havens, A. Eugene -- (C1)980*
Havighurst, Robert J. -- (D1)1545*

Hawley, Willis D. -- (C1)829*
Hayes, Samuel P., Jr. -- (C3a)1212.1, 1212.2
Hayter, Teresa -- (C3c)1402.2
Hazlewood, A. -- (D1)1546
Heady, Ferrel -- (B2a)509*, 510, (D1)1547*
Heaphey, James -- (A1)18, (B2a)511*
Heckman, I. L., Jr. -- (C3a)1213*
Heckscher, Gunnar -- (B2a)512
Heer, David M. -- (D2)1584
Heilbroner, Robert -- (C2)1055
Hein, Leonard W. -- (A1)19
Heirich, Max -- (C2)1056
Helmer, Olaf -- (B1)290, (C1)829.1*
Henderson, Julia J. -- (B1)291
Henderson, Keith M. -- (B2a)513, 514
Hennessy, John W., Jr. -- (C1)815*
Henning, Dale A. -- (A2a)72*
Henry, Edwin R. -- (C3a)1274.2*, (C3c)1433*
Herbert, John D. -- (A2a)72.1*
Herschlag, Z. Y. -- (B1)292
Herskovits, Melville J. -- (B1)293*, (C1)830, (C2)1057
Hertzler, Joyce Oramel -- (C2)1058
Herzog, Elizabeth -- (C3a)1213.1
Heussler, Robert -- (B2a)515
Heverstroh, Chadwick J. -- (C1)929*
Heydebrand, Wolf V. -- (B2b)663*
Heyel, Carl -- (C3a)1213.2
Hicks, Herbert G. -- (C1)831
Hicks, Ursula K. -- (B2a)516
Hickson, D. J. -- (C1)922*
Higgins, Benjamin and Jean -- (C3c)1403*
Hinings, C. R. -- (C1)922*
Hinrichs, Harley H. -- (A2b)138*
Hirschman, Albert O. -- (A2a)73, (B1)294*, 295, 296, (C3a)1214, (C3c)1404*
Hobhouse, Leonard -- (B1)297
Hoffer, Eric -- (C2)1059
Holden, Matthew -- (C3a)1214.1
Holford, Sir William -- (C3a)1215
Hollander, Samuel -- (C1)832
Holleb, Doris -- (D2)1585
Hollis, Peter -- (C2)1060
Holmberg, Allan R. -- (C2)1061, 1062
Holmberg, Richard -- (C2)1063*
Holmes, William F. -- (C3a)1216
Holt, Robert T. -- (B1)298*
Holton, Gerald -- (B1)299
Homans, George Casper -- (C1)833, 834, 835, 836
Honey, John C. -- (B2a)517
Hong, Sung Chick -- (B1)300
Hoore, David G. -- (C1)797*
Hoos, Ida Russakoff -- (C3a)1217, 1218
Hopkins, Jack W. -- (B2b)683
Hopkins, Terence K. -- (C1)837, (C3a)1220*
Horowitz, Irving Louis -- (A2a)74, (B2a)518, (C1)838, 839
Hoselitz, Bert F. -- (B1)301*, 302, 303, 304*, (C2)1064, (C3c)1404.1*
Hoselitz, R. B. -- (B1)305
Hougham, George M. -- (C3a)1302*
Hovey, Harold A. -- (A2b)139, 140
Hovne, Avner -- (C3a)1219
Howard, Alan -- (C2)1065
Howton, F. William -- (B2b)684
Hsu, Francis L. K. -- (C2)1066
Hsueh, S. S. -- (B2a)519
Hubbell, Robert L. -- (C3b)1342
Humes, Samuel -- (B2a)520*
Huneryager, S. G. -- (C3a)1213*
Hunter, Guy -- (B2a)521, 521.1
Huntington, Samuel P. -- (B2a)451*, 522, 523, 524, (C1)840, (C2)1067
Hursh, Gerald D. -- (A1)3*
Hussain, A. F. A. -- (C2)1068
Hutchings, Edward -- (B1)306*
Hutchings, Elizabeth -- (B1)306*
Hutchinson, John G. -- (C1)841
Hyman, Herbert -- (B2a)525, (C3a)1220*, 1220.1*, 1220.2*

Iatridis, Demetrius -- (A2a)75
Ibrahim, Abdel Kadir -- (B1)287*
Ilchman, Warren F. -- (B2a)526, (C1)842*, (C2)1069*, (C3a)1166*, (C3c)1367*
Inayatullah -- (B2b)685
Inkeles, Alex -- (C2)1070
Institute for Social Research -- (D1)1548.1
<u>Intercom</u> -- (D1)1532
International Bank for Reconstruction and Development -- (B1)307
International Conference on the Problems of Modernization in Asia -- (B1)308
<u>International Social Science Bulletin</u> (D1)1568
Israel, J. -- (C3a)1199*
Ivakhnenko, A. C. -- (A2a)76*

Jackson, Robert -- (C3c)1405
Jacob, Philip E. -- (B2a)469*
Jacobs, Norman -- (C3a)1220.3
Jacobson, H. B. -- (C2)1071
Jacoby, Neil H. -- (C3c)1405.1
Jagannadham, V. -- (B2a)482*
Janda, Kenneth -- (A1)20
Janowitz, Morris -- (B2a)527
Janson, Anton J. -- (D1)1545*
Jantsch, Erich -- (A2a)77
Jacques, Eliott -- (C3a)1221
Jasinski, Frank J. -- (C1)843
Jennings, Sir Ivor -- (B2a)528
Jernberg, James -- (A2b)140.1
Jewkes, David S. -- (C3e)1497*
John, W. A. -- (C3a)1221.1*
Johns, R. -- (C3a)1222
Johnson, A. W. -- (A2b)141
Johnson, Chalmers -- (C2)1072
Johnson, Harry G. -- (B1)309
Johnson, John J. -- (B2a)529, 530, (B2b)686
Johnson, Norman J. -- (C1)823*
Johnson, Richard -- (C1)844*
Johnson, Robert L. -- (A2b)150*
Johnson, Walter -- (C1)845
Johnston, Edgar -- (C2)1073
Joiner, Charles A. -- (B2a)493*
Jones, Edward E. -- (C1)846
Jones, Garth -- (C3a)1223, 1223.1, 1224, 1225, 1226, 1227, 1228, 1229, 1230, 1231, 1232*, 1233, 1234*, (C3c)1406, (D1)1549
Journal of Social Issues -- (C3a)1235
Jowitt, Kenneth -- (B2a)531
Juran, J. M. -- (C3a)1236, 1237
Juyal, B. N. -- (B1)353*

Kahl, Joseph A. -- (B1)311
Kahn, Herman -- (C3a)1237.1*, (C3e)1498*
Kahn, Robert L. -- (C1)847*, 849*, (C3a)1239*
Kahn, Robert S. -- (C1)848*
Kaplan, Abraham -- (A1)21
Kaplan, Berton H. -- (C3b)1343
Kaplan, Jacob J. -- (C3c)1407
Kaplan, Morton -- (A2c)209.1
Kapp, W. K. -- (A2a)78
Kariel, Henry S. -- (A2c)188
Karl, Barry Dean -- (C3a)1238
Karpot, Kemal H. -- (C3d)1470
Katz, Daniel -- (A1)15*, (C1)849*, (C3a)1239*

Katz, Elihu -- (C1)850*, 851*
Katz, Fred E. -- (C1)852
Katz, Saul M. -- (A2c)189, (B2a)532
Kaufman, Herbert -- (C1)853
Kautsky, John H. -- (B2a)533
Kazemian, Gholam H. -- (C3c)1408
Kearney, Robert N. -- (B2b)687
Kebschull, Harvey G. -- (B2a)534
Kelley, Allen C. -- (B1)312*
Kelley, Harold H. -- (C1)854, 961*, (C3a)1240
Kelly, Joe -- (C1)855
Kerekes, Tibor -- (B1)313
Kerr, Clark -- (C1)856*
Keyfitz, Nathan -- (B1)314
Khan, Muhammad Ayub -- (B2a)535
Khera, S. S. -- (B2a)536
Kilson, Martin L. -- (B2a)537
King, Clarence -- (C3c)1409
King, John A., Jr. -- (C3a)1409
King, William R. -- (A2c)174*
Kingdom, Thomas Doyle -- (C3c)1410
Kingsbury, Joseph B. -- (B2a)538*
Klineberg, Otto -- (C3a)1240.2, 1240.3
Koehler, J. E. -- (D2)1573.1*
Kolaja, Jiri -- (A2c)190
Konig, Rene -- (C1)857
Kranch, Helmut -- (A2a)79
Krassowski, Awdryej -- (C3c)1411
Krause, Walter -- (A2a)80
Krech, David -- (C1)858*
Krieger, Martin H. -- (C3a)1240.4, 1240.5
Kriesberg, Martin -- (B2a)538.1, 539
Krishna, Daya -- (C2)1074
Kroll, Morton -- (B2a)540, (C1)881*
Kronenberg, Philip -- (B2a)511*
Krupp, Sherman -- (C1)859
Kudson, Harry R., Jr. -- (C1)860
Kuhn, Thomas S. -- (C1)861, (C2)1075
Kulp, Earl M. -- (A2c)191
Kunkel, John H. -- (B1)315, (C1)862, (C2)1076
Kuznets, Simon -- (B1)317

Lackey, Alvin S. -- (D1)1551
Lake, Dale G. -- (C3e)1499
Lamb, Robert K. -- (B1)318
Lambert, Richard -- (C2)1077
Landau, Martin -- (C1)978*
Landsberg, Hans H. -- (C3a)1240.6*
Landuyt, Bernard F. -- (C1)827*
Lane, Robert -- (B2a)541
Lane, W. Clayton -- (C2)1078*

Lange, Oskar -- (A2a)81
Lapa, V. C. -- (A2a)76*
LaPalombara, Joseph -- (B2a)542*, (B2b)688
LaPiere, Richard T. -- (C2)1079
LaPorte, Robert, Jr. -- (A1)22*
LaPorte, Todd -- (A2a)82, (C1)842, (C3d)1471
Larsson, Pieter de Wolff -- (A2a)83*
Lasswell, Harold D. -- (A1)23, (B1)319, (B2a)543, (C2)1080
Lave, Lester, B. -- (C2)1081
Lawler, Edward E. -- (C1)916*
Lawrence, J. R. -- (C3a)1240.7
Lawrence, Paul R. -- (C1)863*, 864*, (C3a)1241
Lazaesfeld -- (C1)850*
Leach, E. -- (B2a)544
Learned, Edmund Philipp -- (C1)865*
Leavitt, Harold J. -- (C1)761*, 866, 867, (C3a)1242
LeBreton, Preston P. -- (A2a)72*, (C1)868*, 869, 870
Lecht, Leonard A. -- (C3a)1242.1
Lee, Hahn-Been -- (B2a)545, (B2b)689
Leibenstein, Harvey - (B1)320,(C1)871
Leighton, Alexander H. -- (C1)872, (C2)1082*
Leiserson, Avery -- (B2b)690
Lekacchman, Robert -- (B1)346*
Leondes, Cornelius - (A2c)192,193,194
Lerner, Daniel -- (A2c)195, (B2a)546*, (C2)1083, (C3d)1472*
Leser, Conrad -- (A1)24
Leu, J. -- (C3b)1344*
Levin, Martin -- (C1)851*
Levine, G. N. -- (C3a)1220.2*
Levine, Soloman B. -- (C1)873*, (C2)1084
Levy, Marion J., Jr. -- (B1)321, (B2a)547, (C1)874, 875
Lewin, Kurt -- (A1)25, (C2)1085
Lewis, W. Arthur -- (A2a)83.1, 84
Lewis, William H. -- (C3a)1243
Liebenow, J. Gus -- (C3a)1244
Liebermann, S. -- (C3d)1473
Lieuwen, Edwin -- (B2a)548
Lifton, Robert Jay -- (C2)1086
Likert, Rensis -- (C1)876, 877
Lin, Nan -- (C3b)1344*
Lindblom, Charles E. -- (B1)294*, (C1)765*, 878
Lindstrom, David E. -- (C2)1087
Lingonston, H. M. -- (C3c)1429*

Linowes, David F. -- (A2b)142
Lionberger, H. F. -- (C3c)1412
Lippit, Donald -- (C3a)1245*, (C3d)1474
Lippitt, Gordon -- (C3a)1245.1
Lipset, S. M. -- (C2)1088
Lish, Monty -- (A2b)150*
Liska, George -- (C2)1089, (C3c)1413
Litterer, Joseph -- (C1)879, (C3a)1246
Little, K. L. -- (C2)1090
Livingstone, A. S. -- (C3c)1414
Loebs, C. David -- (A2a)85
Loomis, Charles P. -- (C1)880*, (C2)1091*, 1092, (C3d)1475*
Loomis, Ralph A. -- (C3c)1415
Lorsch, Jay W. -- (C1)863*
Lovell, John P. -- (A1)26
Lyden, Fremont J. -- (A2b)143*, (A2c)196, (C1)881*
Lynch, Charles J.-- (C1)882

Maass, Arthur -- (A2b)144
McClelland, David -- (B2a)549, (C3a)1246.1*
McConkey, William C. -- (A2b)145*
McDermott, J. K. -- (C3c)1435*
Macesich, George -- (A2a)86
McEwen, William J. -- (C1)964*
McGregor, Douglas -- (C1)883, 884
McHale, John -- (C3a)1246.2
Machol, Robert E. -- (A2c)183*
McKean, Roland N. -- (A2c)197
McKechnie, J. Thomas -- (D1)1524*
MacKenzie, W. J. M. -- (C1)885
McKinney, John C. -- (A2a)87
Mackintosh, J. P. -- (B2a)550
McLaren, K. G. -- (A2c)198*
McLoughlin, P. F. M..-- (B1)322
MacMillan, Claude -- (A2c)199*
McMurray, Robert N. -- (C3a)1247
McNulty, J. E. -- (C3a)1248
Macridis, Roy C. -- (B2a)551, 639*
Madan, B. K. -- (B1)323
Maddison, Angus -- (C3c)1416
Madge, Charles -- (A2a)87.1*
Magid, Alvin -- (C2)1152*
Mahalonobis, P. C. -- (A2a)88
Mahbub-ul-Haq -- (A2a)89
Maier, Norman R. F. -- (C1)886
Mailick, Sidney -- (C1)887*
Mair, Lucy P. -- (B2a)552
Malcolm, Donald S. -- (A2c)200*
Malek, T. Abdel -- (C3c)1417
Malenbaum, Wlfred -- (B1)324, (B2a)553

Malinowski, Bronislaw -- (C2)1093
Manane, Joseph H. -- (A2c)201
Mangone, Gerald J. -- (C3c)1382*
Mangum, Garth -- (B1)252*
Maniha, John -- (C1)888*
Mann, Floyd C. -- (C3a)1249, 1250, 1251*, 1252*, 1253*, 1254
Mansfield, Edwin -- (B1)325
Mansur, Fatima -- (B2a)554
March, James G. -- (C1)764*, 889, 890*
Marcom, S. -- (C2)1094
Markham, Emerson -- (A2b)145*
Marquis, Sue -- (C3e)1496*
Marrows, Alfred J. -- (C1)891*
Mars, David -- (B2b)691
Marsh, C. Paul -- (C3e)1500*
Marsh, Robert M. -- (C1)892, (D1)1552
Martin, Eilean H. -- (B2a)520*
Martin, Roscoe E. -- (C3c)1418
Martindale, Don -- (C2)1095
Marx, Fritz Morstein -- (B2b)692
Mason, Edward -- (A2a)90, (C3c)1419
Massachusetts Institute of Technology (D1)1553
Massarik, Fred -- (A1)28*
Mau, James -- (C2)1096
Mayne, Alvin -- (C3a)1255
Mayntz, Renate -- (D1)1554
Mead, Margaret -- (C2)1097, 1098, 1099, 1100
Meadows, Paul -- (A1)29, (C2)1101, (D1)1543*
Meier, Gerald M. -- (B1)326, 327
Meier, Richard G. -- (C1)893
Meier, Richard L. -- (A2a)87.1*, 91, (B1)328, (C1)89
Meister, David -- (A2c)202*
Melton, A. W. -- (C1)895*
Merton, R. K. -- (C1)896
Meshkin, Eli -- (A2c)203*
Messinger, Sheldon L. -- (C2)1102
Mesthene, Emmanuel -- (B2a)555, (C2)1103, 1104
Meyer, Marshall -- (B2b)693
Meyerson, Martin -- (A2a)92
Meynaud, Jean -- (B1)329
Micaud, Charles A. -- (B2a)556*
Michael, Donald -- (A2a)93, (B1)330, (C1)897, (C3a)1256
Michaels, Michael -- (C3e)1501
Michioglu, Cemal -- (B2a)557
Mihaly, Eugene B. -- (C3c)1419.1
Mikesell, Raymond F. -- (D2)1585.1

Miles, Arnold -- (B2a)558*
Miles, Matthew B. -- (C3a)1257, (C3e)1502, 1503
Millen, Bruce H. -- (B2a)559
Miller, David -- (C1)898*
Miller, Eric -- (C1)899*, 900
Miller, Ernest G. -- (A2b)143*
Miller, G. A. -- (C1)901*
Miller, Lorraine F. -- (C1)801*
Miller, R. B. -- (A2c)204*
Millett, John D. -- (C1)902
Millikan, Max F. -- (B1)331*, 332*, (B2a)560
Mills, C. Wright -- (C1)800*
Milne, R. S. -- (B2a)561
Mincer, Jacob -- (B1)333
Mir, Lucy P. -- (C3a)1258
Mitchell, Joan -- (A2a)94
Mitchell, William C. -- (A2c)209.1
Mockler, Robert J. -- (A2c)205
Moe, Edward O. -- (C3a)1259, 1260
Moment, David -- (C3a)1323*
Mondale, Walter F. -- (C3a)1260.1
Montgomery, John D. -- (A2c)181*, (B2a)562*, 563, 564, (C2)1105, (C3c)1420, 1421, 1422, 1423
Monton, J. S. -- (C3a)1206.1*
Moore, Wilbert E. -- (B1)268*, 301*, 334, (C1)903, (C2)1106*, 1107*, 1108, 1109, 1109.1, 1130*, (C3a)1260.2*, 1260.3, 1290.1*, 1290.2*
Morehouse, Thomas A. -- (C3a)1261
Morgan, Theodore -- (D2)1586
Morison, Elting E. -- (C3a)1262
Morris, Cynthia T. -- (B1)223*, (B2a)406*
Morris, G. M. -- (B2a)565
Morrow, A. -- (C3a)1198*
Morse, Chandler -- (C3a)1263*
Morse, Dean -- (C3e)1504*
Morse, Nancy -- (C3a)1264*
Morse, Philip M. -- (A1)30, (A2c)206
Morse, Richard -- (B1)378*
Morton, Robert B. -- (C3a)1265*
Moses, Lincoln -- (C1)758*
Moses, Stanley -- (C3a)1265.1
Mosher, Arthur T. -- (C3c)1424, 1425, (D2)1587
Mosher, Frederick C. -- (A2b)146, (B2a)566, (C3a)1266, 1267, 1268, (C3e)1504.1*
Mountjoy, Allan B. -- (B1)335
Moussa, Pierre -- (B1)336
Mouton, Jane S. -- (C3d)1466*

Mouzelis, Necos P. -- (B2b) 694
Mudd, Stuart -- (B1) 337
Mukerji, B. -- (B1) 338
Mumford, Enid -- (A2a) 95*
Muscat, Robert J. -- (B1) 339
Myers, Charles A. -- (B1) 285*
Myers, Robert G. -- (C3c) 1425.1
Myint, H. -- (B1) 340
Myrdal, Gunnar -- (A2a) 96, (B1) 341, 342

Nagel, Ernest -- (A1) 31
Nair, Kusum -- (C2) 1110
Nairn, Roland C. -- (C3c) 1426
Narayan, Shirman -- (A2a) 97
Nash, Manning -- (B1) 343, 344, (C2) 1111
National Association of State Budget Officers (NASBO) -- (A2b) 147
National Council of Applied Economic Research -- (B1) 345
National Diet Library -- (D1) 1555
National Institute of Public Administration -- (B2a) 567, 568, (B2b) 695, 708
National Planning Association -- (A2a) 97.1, (C3c) 1427, (D2) 1588, 1589
National Research Council -- (C1) 903.1
Neal, Marie -- (C2) 1112
Neff, F. W. -- (C3a) 1251*
Nelson, Joan -- (C3c) 1428
Nelson, Richard R. -- (C3c) 1504.2
Nettle, J. P. -- (B2a) 569
Newman, A. -- (C1) 904
Niaz, Aslam -- (C3a) 1232*, 1234, 1269, 1270
Nieburg, Harold L. -- (C3e) 1505
Niehoff, Arthur H. -- (C2) 993*, 1113, 1114, (C3c) 1360*, (C3e) 1506*, (D1) 1556*
Nisbet, Robert -- (C2) 1115
Noralau, P. -- (B2b) 701*
Nordskog, John E. -- (C2) 1116
North, R. C. -- (A1) 33*
Northrop, F. S. C. -- (C3c) 1429*
Novick, D. -- (A2b) 149, (B1) 346*
Noville, Pierre -- (C1) 905
Nsarkoh, J. K. -- (B2a) 570
Nurske, Ragnar -- (B1) 347
Nye, J. J. -- (D2) 1590

Oching, Adonijah -- (B2b) 696
O'Dea, Thomas F. -- (C1) 974*
Office of Technical Cooperation and Research -- (C1) 1557
Ogburn, William F. -- (C2) 1117
Ogden, Jean and Jess -- (C3a) 1271*
Okun, Bernard -- (B1) 348*
O'Leary, Michael Kent -- (C3c) 1430
Olmsted, Donald W. -- (C1) 906
Olsen, Marvin E. -- (C1) 907
Olson, Mancur, Jr. -- (B1) 349, (C3a) 1272, 1272.1
Organization for Economic Cooperation and Development -- (C3a) 1301, (C3c) 1384
Organski, A. F. K. -- (B2a) 571
Orr, Wesley L. -- (C3c) 1356*
Oto, Sulc -- (C2) 1118
Overseas Development Institute -- (C3c) 1430.1

Packenham, Robert A. -- (B2a) 573
Palley, Marion and Howard -- (C3a) 1272.2
Palmier, Leslie H. -- (B1) 350
Papanek, Gustav F. -- (A2a) 98, (B1) 350.1
Pareek, Udai -- (C3a) 1273
Parikh, K. S. -- (A2a) 60*
Parsons, Talcott -- (A2c) 209.1*, (C1) 908, 909*, 910*
Paul, Benjamin D. -- (B1) 351
Peabody, Robert L. -- (B2b) 697*, (C1) 911
Pearson, Lester -- (C3c) 1431, 1432
Penniman, Clara -- (C3a) 1274
Pennock, J. Roland -- (B2a) 574, 575, (C1) 912*
Pentony, Devere E. -- (B1) 352
Perkins, James A. -- (C3c) 1432.1
Perle, Eugene -- (C3a) 1274.1*
Perlmutter, Amos -- (B2b) 698
Perlmutter, Howard V. -- (C3b) 1345
Perrow, Charles -- (C1) 888*, 913, 914
Perrucci, R. -- (C2) 1156
Peter, Hollis W. -- (C3a) 1274.2*, (C3c) 1433*
Peterson, R. A. -- (C3c) 1401*
Petras, James F. -- (A1) 22*
Pfiffner, John M. -- (C1) 915*, (C3a) 1275, 1276
Phillips, Hiram S. -- (C3b) 1346, 1347
Pieris, Ralph -- (C3a) 1277
Pincus, John A. -- (B1) 401*
Pi-Sunyer, O. -- (C2) 1119*
Platt, Gerald M. -- (C2) 1153*
Platts, Grace N. -- (C1) 801*

175

Pooler, William S. -- (C3c)1387*
Porter, David O. -- (C3a)1277.1
Porter, Lyman W. -- (C1)916*
Potter, David C. -- (B2a)576
Powell, S. Bingham, Jr. -- (B2a)416*
Prasad, N. -- (B1)353*
Prehoda, Robert -- (A2a)99
Preiss, Jack J. -- (A1)2*
Press, Charles -- (C3e)1507*
Presthus, Robert V. -- (B2b)699, (C1) 917, 918, 919
Pribram, K. H. -- (C1)901*
Price, James -- (C1)920
Pugh, D. S. -- (C1)921, 922*
Pye, Lucian W. -- (B2a)577, 578, 579, 580, 581, 582*, 583, (C3c)1434*

Qadir, S. A. -- (C3a)1278
Quade, E. S. -- (A2c)207*

Rabideau, Gerald F. -- (A2c)202*
Rahman, Habibur -- (A2a)100
Rahman, M. Anisur -- (A2a)101
Raiffa, Howard -- (C1)923
Rakowski, Mieczyslaw -- (B1)353.1
Ramo, Simon -- (A2c)208
Ramsoy, Odd -- (C1)924
Ramzani, R. -- (B1)354
Rand Corporation -- (D1)1561
Ranis, Gustav -- (A2a)63*
Rao, Lakshmana -- (B2b)699.1, (C3d) 1475.1
Rapaport, Anatol -- (A2c)209, 209.1*, (C1)925
Raphaeli, Nimrod -- (B2a)584
Rathaus, Paul -- (C3a)1265*
Ratoosh, Philburn -- (A1)28
Raymond, Vernon -- (B1)355
Redfield, Robert -- (C2)1120
Rehman, A. T. R. -- (B2a)585
Reilley, Erwing W. -- (C3a)1202*
Reimer, E. -- (C3a)1264*
Reina, Ruben -- (B1)356
Reissman, Leonard -- (C2)1121
Rejai, Mostafa -- (A1)34
Requa, Eloise -- (D1)1558*
Retzlaff, Ralph H. -- (B2a)586
Rice, A. K. -- (C1)899*, (C3a)1279, 1280
Richards, Audrey I. -- (C2)1122
Richardson, F. L. W., Jr. -- (C3a)1281
Richardson, Richard -- (B1)348*
Riegel, H. W. -- (C2)1123
Riesman, David -- (A2a)102

Riggs, Fred W. -- (B2a)587, 588, 589, 590, 591, 592, 593, 594, 595, 596, 597, 598, (B2b)700
Rigney, J. A. -- (C3b)1348*, (C3c) 1435*
Rima, Ingrid H. -- (A2c)210
Ripman, Hugh B. -- (C3a)1281.1
Rivkin, Arnold -- (B2a)599
Rivkin, Malcolm G. -- (A2a)103
Roberts, Edward B. -- (C3a)1282
Roberts, James S. -- (B2a)600
Robinson, Richard D. -- (B1)357, (B2a) 546*
Robock, Stefan H. -- (A2a)104
Robson, W. A. -- (C3a)1282.1
Rodriquez, Louis A. -- (C3e)1488*
Rogers, Carl -- (C1)926*
Rogers, Everett M. -- (C2)1124, (C3b) 1344*, (C3c)1436*, (C3d)1476, 1477, (C3e)1508
Rogers, George H. -- (C3c)1436*
Rokkan, Stein -- (A1)34.1, (B2a)601*
Rome, Beatrice -- (A2a)105*
Rome, Sydney -- (A2a)105*
Roncek, J. B. -- (C2)1071*
Roos, Leslie L. -- (B2b)701*
Rosenblith, Walter -- (C2)1125
Rosenhead, J. V. -- (A2c)211
Rosenstein-Rodan, P. N. -- (B1)358, 359
Roskelley, R. W. -- (C3b)1348*
Rosner, Martin -- (C3e)1509
Ross, Murray G. -- (C1)921
Rostow, Walt W. -- (B1)360, 361, (C3c) 1437
Roth, J. A. -- (C1)928
Rothenberg, Jerome -- (A2a)105.1
Rourke, Francis E. -- (B2b)697*, 702, (C3a)1283
Rowe, William -- (C2)1126
Royal Institute of Public Administration -- (C3c)1438
Rubenstein, Albert H. -- (C1)929*
Rubin, Seymour -- (C3c)1439
Rubin, Vera -- (B1)362
Ruitenbeck, Hendrick M. -- (C1)930
Rush, Harold M. F. -- (C3a)1284
Russett, Bruce M. -- (C3a)1284.1*
Rustov, Dankwart A. -- (B1)394*
Ryan, Bryce -- (C2)1127, (C3d)1478

Sackman, Harold -- (A2c)212
Salazar, Rodolpho C. -- (A2b)153*
Sametz, A. W. -- (B1)363

Samuel, Viscount -- (B2a) 602
Sander, Irwin T. -- (C3c) 1440
Sanders, Ralph -- (A2c) 213
Sayeed, Khalid Bin -- (B2a) 603
Sayles, Leonard R. -- (C3a) 1179*, 1285, 1286, 1287
Scarrow, Howard A. -- (B2a) 604
Schaafhausen, Irma -- (B1) 365
Schacter, Ruth -- (B2a) 605
Schapera, I. -- (B2a) 606
Schatz, Sayre P. -- (A2a) 106
Schein, Edgar H. -- (C1) 931, (C3a) 1288*
Schelling, Thomas C. -- (C1) 932
Schick, Allen -- (A2b) 154
Schickele, Rainer -- (B1) 366
Schlaifer, Robert -- (A1) 35
Schlesinger, Arthur, Jr. -- (C3c) 1441
Schneider, Kenneth R. -- (C2) 1128
Schon, Donald -- (C3e) 1510, 1511
Schramm, Wilbur -- (B1) 367, (C1) 933, (C3d) 1472*
Schubert, G. -- (C3a) 1288.1
Schultze, Charles L. -- (A2b) 155
Schuman, Howard -- (C2) 1129
Schutz, Theodore W. -- (B1) 368
Schwab, W. -- (C2) 1033*
Schwartz, Donald F. -- (C3b) 1344*
Scott, Andrew M. -- (A2c) 214, (C3c) 1442
Scott, Richard -- (C1) 745*
Scott, Thomas M. -- (C3d) 1479
Scott, W. H. -- (C3a) 1289
Scott, William G. -- (C1) 868*, 934
Seashore, Stanley E. -- (C1) 891*, 935, (C3a) 1290*
Seiler, John A. -- (C1) 936
Seiler, Karl -- (A2c) 215
Seligman, L. G. -- (B2a) 607
Sells, O. R. -- (A2c) 216
Selznick, Philip -- (C1) 937, 938, 939
Sen, Subrath K. -- (A2b) 153*
Service, Elman R. -- (C2) 1129.1
Shannon, Lyle W. -- (B1) 369, (D1) 1561.1
Sharp, Walter -- (C3c) 1443
Sheldon, Eleanor B. -- (C2) 1130*, (C3a) 1260.2*, 1290.1*, 1290.2*
Shelly, Maynard W., II -- (C1) 761*
Sherif, Muzafer -- (C1) 940, (C3d) 1480
Sherrill, Kenneth S. -- (C2) 1131
Sherwood, Frank P. -- (C1) 915*, 941
Shils, Edward -- (B2a) 608, 609, 610, (C1) 909*, 910*
Shimkin, Demitri -- (C2) 1141*

Shipman, George A. -- (C1) 881*, 942, 943, (C3a) 1291
Shubik, Martin -- (A2c) 217
Sibley, Willis E. -- (C3a) 1291.1
Siegel, Bernard J. -- (C2) 1133, (D1) 1562
Siegel, Gilbert B. -- (C3b) 1349
Siffin, William J. -- (B2a) 562*, 611, 612, (C3b) 1350, 1351
Sigmund, Paul E. -- (B2a) 613
Silberman, Bernard S. -- (C3a) 1292
Silcock, T. H. -- (B1) 370*
Silj, Alessandro -- (B1) 371
Sill, Maurice -- (C3d) 1467*
Sills, David L. -- (C3a) 1293, 1294
Silvert, K. H. -- (B2a) 614, 615
Simmons, John L. -- (A2a) 107
Simon, Herbert A. -- (C1) 890*, 944, 945, 946, 947, 948, 949*, 950
Simpkins, Edgar -- (B2a) 651*
Simpson, Keith -- (D1) 1563
Simpson, Richard L. -- (C1) 951*
Sinai, I. R. -- (B1) 372
Singer, H. W. -- (C3a) 1221.1*
Singer, M. R. -- (B2a) 616
Singh, K. N. -- (B2b) 703, (C2) 1134*
Singh, S. D. -- (C2) 1134*
Singh, S. P. -- (B1) 224
Singh, V. K. -- (C2) 1134*
Sisger, H. W. -- (B1) 373
Sisson, Richard -- (B2b) 704
Sjoberg, Gideon -- (B2a) 617*, 952
Skinner, B. F. -- (C1) 926*, 953, 954
Sklar, Richard L. -- (B2a) 618
Slattery, T. B. -- (A2c) 182*
Slotkin, James Sydney -- (C2) 1135
Smelser, Neil J. -- (C2) 1136, (C3a) 1295
Smith, Hadley E. -- (C3c) 1444
Smith, Robert J. -- (C2) 1082*, (C3a) 1296
Smith, Rufus D. -- (B2a) 632*
Smith, T. E. -- (B2a) 619
Smithburg, Donald W. -- (C1) 949*
Smithies, Arthur -- (A2b) 156, 156.1
Society of International Development - (B1) 374
Soemardjan, Selo -- (C2) 1137
Sofer, Cyril -- (C3a) 1297, 1298, 1299, 1300*
Solomon, Morris J. -- (A2a) 108
Spencer, Daniel L. -- (C3c) 1445*, (C3d) 1481*
Spencer, Paul -- (C3a) 1300*
Spencer, Richard E. -- (C3c) 1402*

Spengler, Joseph J. -- (B1)253*, 375, 376*, (B2a)444*, (B2b)705
Spicer, Edward H. -- (C2)1138
Spindler, Arthur -- (A2b)157
Spiro, Herbert J. -- (B2a)620, 620.1
Spity, David -- (C2)1139
Spitz, Allan H. -- (D1)1564*, 1565
Springer, Michael -- (C3a)1206.5*
Sproat, Audrey T. -- (C1)865*
Srygley, Jane -- (A2c)170*
Staley, Eugene -- (B1)377, 378
Stalker, C. M. -- (C3e)1490*
Starr, Chauncey -- (C3a)1300.1
Starr, Martin K. -- (C1)898*
Statham, Jane -- (D1)1558*
Stauffer, Robert B. -- (B2a)621, 622, 623, (B2b)663*
Stedman, Murray, Jr. -- (B2a)624
Stein, Harold -- (B2a)625
Stein, Herman D. -- (C3a)1302*
Stein, Robert M. -- (B1)279
Steiner, Gary A. -- (C1)742*, 956
Steiner, George A. -- (A2a)110, (D1)1566
Steinle, J. G. -- (C1)735*
Steward, Julian Hayes -- (C2)1140, 1141*, 1142
Stewart, Charles, F. -- (B1)379
Stillerman, Richard -- (C3e)1497*
Stokes, Sybil L. -- (B2a)509*, (D1)1547*
Stone, Donald C. -- (B2a)626
Storm, William B. -- (C3c)1446*
Stouffer, Samuel A. -- (C3a)1302.1
Stover, Carl F. -- (C1)957
Strait, Edward B. -- (B2b)667*
Strassman, Paul W. -- (B1)380
Strout, Alan M. -- (C3c)1381*
Strumpel, Burkhard -- (C2)1143
Suchman, Edward A. -- (C3a)1302.2
Sufrin, Sidney C. -- (B1)402*, (C3b)1352, (C3c)1447, (D1)1567
Sugel, Bernard J. -- (C2)1006*
Sutermeister, Robert A. -- (C1)958
Sutton, Francis -- (C3c)1447.1
Svennilson, Ingvar -- (C3c)1448
Swee, Goh Keng -- (A2a)111
Sweetman, L. T. -- (A2a)112
Swerdlow, Irving -- (B2a)627

Tachau, Frank -- (B2a)633*
Takezawa, Shinichi -- (C1)984*
Tannenbaum, Arnold S. -- (C1)959, 959.1
Tannenbaum, Robert -- (C1)960*, (C3a)1303
Tannous, A. I. -- (C2)1144
Tatham, L. -- (C3a)1303.1
Tausky, Curt -- (C1)960.1
Tax, Sol -- (C3a)1304
Taylor, Donald A. -- (C3b)1353
Taylor, F. W. -- (C3a)1303.2
Taylor, Graeme M. -- (A2b)138*
Taylor, J. Clagett -- (B2a)628
<u>Technical Assistance Quarterly Bulletin</u> (D1)1560
Teitz, Michael B. -- (A2c)218
Teune, Henry -- (B2a)469*
Texter, Robert B. A. -- (B2a)433*
Theobold, Robert -- (B2a)629
Theodorson, G. A. -- (C2)1145
Thibaut, John W. -- (C1)961*
Thomas, Michael E. -- (A1)16
Thomas, William -- (C3a)1305*
Thompson, James D. -- (C1)962, 963*, 964*, 965
Thompson, Victor A. -- (C1)949*, 966, (C3e)1512, 1513
Thurber, Clarence -- (C3d)1482
Tickner, Fred -- (C3c)1449
Tilly, Charles -- (C2)1146
Tilman, Robert O. -- (B2b)706, 707
Tinbergen, Jan -- (A2a)113, 114, 115, (B1)381
Tinker, Hugh -- (B2a)630, (C3c)1450
Toch, Hans -- (A2a)116
Tonnies, Ferdinand -- (C1)967
Torgerson, Paul E. -- (C1)968
Toscano, James V. -- (B2a)469*
Tottenham Report -- (B2b)708
Touraine, Alain -- (C3a)1306*
Trager, Frank N. -- (D1)1569
Trail, Thomas F. -- (C3c)1451
Trist, E. L. -- (A2c)180*, (C1)778*, 968.1*
Tsantis, Andreas C. -- (B1)382
Tsonderos, John E. -- (C3a)1307
Tucker, Robert C. -- (B2a)631
Tullock, Gordon -- (B2b)709
Tuma, E. H. -- (C2)1147
Turner, John E. -- (B1)298*
Turner, Roy -- (B1)383

Udall, Stewart L. -- (C3a)1307.1
Udy, Stanley H., Jr. -- (C1)969, 970
Udyanin, Kasem -- (B2a)632*
Ulman, A. Haluk -- (B2a)633*
United Kingdom -- (C3c)1452
United Nations -- (B1)384, 385, (B2a)

467.1, (B2b) 710, (C3a) 1308, 1308.1, (C3c) 1453
United States Government --
  Bureau of the Budget -- (C3a) 1311.1
  Congress -- (A2b) 158, 159, 160, (C3a) 1311.6
  Dept. of Commerce -- (C3a) 1309, 1310, 1311
  Dept. of Health, Education and Welfare -- (C2) 1147.1, 1147.2, (C3a) 1311.2, 1311.3
  Dept. of Labor -- (C2) 1148
  Dept. of State -- (A2a) 118, (D1) 1557
  President -- (C2) 1148.1, (C3a) 1311.4, 1311.5
University of Connecticut -- (C3a) 1311.7
Uphoff, Norman Thomas -- (C2) 1069*
Utoila, Jaako -- (C3a) 1312

Van Der Veen -- (C3c) 1453.1
Vanek, Jaroslav -- (B1) 386, 387
Van Huyck, Alfred P. -- (A2a) 72.1*
Van Mook, H. J. -- (C3d) 1483
Van Ness, Edward H. -- (C1) 887*, 971
Vatikiotis, P. J. -- (B2a) 634
Verba, Sidney -- (B2a) 415*, 582*, (C1) 972
Vernon, Raymond -- (B1) 388, 389
Veroff, Joseph -- (C2) 1049.2*
Vickers, Geoffrey -- (A1) 36, (C1) 973
Vogt, Evon Z. -- (C1) 974*, (C2) 1148.2
Von der Mehden, Fred R. -- (B2a) 421*, 635
Von Vorys, Karl -- (B1) 390, (B2a) 636
Vrancken, Fernand -- (C3c) 1454
Vroom, Victor H. -- (C1) 975

Wade, L. L. -- (C1) 763*
Wadia, Maneck S. -- (C1) 975.1
Waldo, Dwight -- (B2a) 637, (C1) 976, 977, 978*, (C3a) 1313
Walinsky, Louis J. -- (A2a) 120, (B1) 391
Walker, Charles R. -- (C3a) 1314, 1315
Wallace, Edward L. -- (A2c) 219
Wallerstein, Immanuel -- (C2) 1149
Walterhouse, Harry F. -- (B1) 392
Waltman, Howard L. -- (C3c) 1455
Walton, Richard E. -- (C3a) 1316
Ward, Barbara -- (B1) 393
Ward, James A. -- (B2a) 638
Ward, Robert E. -- (A1) 37*, (B1) 394*, (B2a) 639*
Ward, T. B. -- (A2a) 95

Warner, Aaron W. -- (C1) 979, 980*, (C3e) 1504*
Warner, W. Keith -- (C1) 980*
Washburne, Norman -- (C2) 1151
Wasserman, P. -- (C3a) 1316.1
Waterston, Albert -- (A2a) 121, 122
Watson, Andrew -- (A2a) 123*
Watson, Jeanne -- (C2) 1151, (C3a) 1245*
Weaver, Thomas -- (C2) 1152*
Weidenbaum, Murray L. -- (A2b) 161
Weidlund, Jane -- (D1) 1570*
Weidner, Edward W. -- (C3a) 1317, (C3c) 1456, (D1) 1564*
Weinberg, E. -- (C3a) 1319
Weinberg, Ian -- (B1) 395
Weinberg, Stanley L. -- (A2c) 220
Weiner, Myron -- (B1) 396, (B2a) 542*, 640, 641, 642
Weingrod, Alex -- (C3a) 1320
Weinstein, Fred -- (C2) 1153*
Weisbrod, Burton A. -- (B1) 397*
Weiss, Robert S. -- (C1) 981
Welch, Claude E. -- (B2a) 643
Wellisz, Stanislaw -- (B1) 398
Wertheim, W. F. -- (C1) 982
Westcott, John H. -- (C1) 983
Westley, Bruce -- (C3a) 1245*
Westwood, Andrew F. -- (B2a) 644, (C3c) 1457
Wheaton, William L. C. -- (B2a) 469*
White, John -- (C3c) 1457.1
White, Lynn -- (C2) 1154
White, Orion, Jr. -- (B2a) 617*
White, Paul E. -- (C1) 873*
Whiteford, Andrew H. -- (C3c) 1458
Whitehill, Arthur M., Jr. -- (C1) 984*
Whitman, David -- (C3c) 1459
Whitten, Norman E., Jr. -- (B2a) 645
Whyte, William F. -- (B1) 399*, (C1) 985, (C3a) 1321, (C3c) 1460
Wickesberg, Albert K. -- (C1) 986
Wickwar, W. Hardy -- (B1) 400, (B2a) 646
Wiener, Anthony -- (C3a) 1237.1*, (C3e) 1498*
Wiener, Norbert -- (C1) 987
Wilcox, Wayne -- (B2a) 647, 648
Wildavsky, Aaron -- (A2b) 162, 163, 164, 165
Wilensky, Harold L. -- (C1) 987.1, 987.2, (C3a) 1321.1
Wilkening, E. A. -- (C3e) 1514
Wilkinson, Rupert -- (B2a) 649
Williams, L. -- (B1) 399*, (C3a) 1252*, 1253*

Williams, V. -- (B2b)711
Willner, Ann Ruth -- (B2a)650*, (C3c)1404.1*
Willner, Dorothy -- (B2a)650*
Wilson, A. G. -- (A2a)125
Wilson, James -- (C3a)1182*, (C3e)1515
Wilson, John O. -- (C3a)1321.2, 1321.3, 1321.4
Winsemius, Albert -- (B1)401*
Winter, David G. -- (C3a)1246.1*
Winthrop, Henry -- (A2a)126
Wirt, Frederick M. -- (C1)829*
Wiseman, Herbert V. -- (A2c)221
Wittfogel, Karl -- (B2b)712
Wold, Herman -- (A1)38
Wolf, Charles -- (B1)402*, (C3c)1461, 1462, (D1)1571
Wolf, Scott -- (D2)1579*
Wooden, Howard E. -- (C3a)1322
Woroniak, Alexander -- (C3c)1445, (C3d)1481*
Wraith, Ronald -- (B2a)651*
Wriggins, W. Howard -- (B2a)652
Wright, Charles -- (C3a)1220*, 1220.1*, 1220.2*
Wright, Christopher -- (C1)802*
Wurfel, David -- (C3c)1463, 1464

Yale University Economic Growth Center (D1)1572
Yamey, Basil S. -- (B1)237*, 270*
Yanouzas, John N. -- (C1)754*
Young, Charles -- (C3c)1464.1
Young, Crawford -- (B2a)421*
Young, Kenneth -- (B1)403
Young, Michael -- (A2a)127
Young, Oran R. -- (A2c)222
Young, Pauline -- (A1)39
Young, Stanley -- (C1)988

Zack, Arnold -- (C3c)1465
Zalba, Serapio R. -- (C3a)1302*
Zaleznik, Abraham -- (C3a)1323*, 1324, 1325
Zalkind, Sheldon S. -- (C3a)1185*
Zamora, Mario D. -- (C3a)1326
Zander, Alvin -- (C1)753*, (C3a)1327
Zebot, Cyril A. -- (B1)404
Zetterberg, Hans -- (C1)989
Zielinski, Janusz G. -- (A2a)128
Zinkin, Maurice -- (B2a)653
Zollschan, G. -- (C2)1155, 1156*